CMMI® Distilled
Second Edition

*A Practical Introduction
to Integrated
Process Improvement*

**Dennis M. Ahern
Aaron Clouse
Richard Turner**

✦Addison-Wesley

Boston • San Francisco • New York • Toronto • Montreal
London • Munich • Paris • Madrid
Capetown • Sydney • Tokyo • Singapore • Mexico City

Carnegie Mellon
Software Engineering Institute

The SEI Series in Software Engineering

Many of the designations used by manufacturers and sellers to distinguish their products are claimed as trademarks. Where those designations appear in this book, and Addison-Wesley was aware of a trademark claim, the designations have been printed with initial capital letters or in all capitals.

CMM, CMMI, Capability Maturity Model, Capability Maturity Modeling, Carnegie Mellon, CERT, and CERT Coordination Center are registered in the U.S. Patent and Trademark Office by Carnegie Mellon University.

ATAM; Architecture Tradeoff Analysis Method; CMM Integration; COTS Usage-Risk Evaluation; CURE; EPIC; Evolutionary Process for Integrating COTS Based Systems; Framework for Software Product Line Practice; IDEAL; Interim Profile; OAR; OCTAVE; Operationally Critical Threat, Asset, and Vulnerability Evaluation; Options Analysis for Reengineering; Personal Software Process; PLTP; Product Line Technical Probe; PSP; SCAMPI; SCAMPI Lead Appraiser; SCAMPI Lead Assessor; SCE; SEI; SEPG; Team Software Process; and TSP are service marks of Carnegie Mellon University.

The authors and publisher have taken care in the preparation of this book, but make no expressed or implied warranty of any kind and assume no responsibility for errors or omissions. No liability is assumed for incidental or consequential damages in connection with or arising out of the use of the information or programs contained herein.

The publisher offers discounts on this book when ordered in quantity bulk purchases and special sales. For more information, please contact:

U.S. Corporate and Government Sales
(800) 382-3419
corpsales@pearsontechgroup.com

For sales outside of the U.S., please contact:

International Sales
(317) 581-3793
international@pearsontechgroup.com

Visit Addison-Wesley on the Web: www.awprofessional.com

Library of Congress Cataloging-in-Publication Data

Ahern, Dennis M.
    CMMI distilled : a practical introduction to integrated process improvement /
Dennis M. Ahern, Aaron Clouse and Richard Turner.
        p. cm.
    ISBN 0-321-18613-3 (alk. paper)
    1. Capability maturity model (Computer software)   I. Clouse, Aaron.   II. Turner,
Richard, 1954–   III. Title.

QA76.758.A397 2003
005.1'068'5—dc21   2003012672

For information on obtaining permission for use of material from this work, please submit a written request to:

Pearson Education, Inc.
Rights and Contracts Department
75 Arlington Street, Suite 300
Boston, MA 02116
Fax: (617) 848-7047

ISBN: 0-321-18613-3

Text printed on recycled and acid-free paper.

ISBN 0321186133

4 5 6 7 8 9   CRS   07 06 05

4th   Printing   February 2005

Contents

Figure List

Preface to the Second Edition

Since the first edition of *CMMI*^{SM} *Distilled* was published, there have been significant changes in the CMMI world. As promised, CMMI-SE/SW/IPPD/SS version 1.1 was released in 2002. Later that year, CMMI-SW was released. In just three years we have seen amazing worldwide adoption rates of the CMMI Product Suite, with implementation evenly divided between government suppliers and commercial sector organizations. The suite has become recognized as the cutting edge of process-improvement technology.

There has been considerable activity in the availability of CMMI-based material, as well. In February 2003, the SEI published its hardbound reference version of the complete model with practitioner information and guidance. The number of technical notes and other guidance published continues to increase. CMMI Transition Partners (licensed by SEI, and currently numbering over 100) have developed their own supplementary materials.

Given this explosion of material, along with the continuing ability to download from the Web the models and other components of the Product Suite, we felt a real need to bring out a second edition of *CMMI*^{SM} *Distilled*. Here are some of the important reasons:

1. CMMI version 1.1 contains improvements over version 1.0 (which formed the basis for our first edition).
2. CMMI is now a recognized and widely adopted model, so that some of the material concerning the creation of CMMI and its relationship to the legacy models is less important to current readers.
3. The pioneer case studies are somewhat out of date.
4. Even with the publication of the CMMI reference book, the need continues for a broader, more succinct view of CMMI, one that is readily accessible to executives, managers, and practitioners, as well as to the simply curious.

5. The readers of the first edition of *CMMI*^SM *Distilled* sent us thoughtful comments, suggestions, and requests.

Candidly, another major reason was that we were running out of copies of the last edition with which to impress friends and family members, and figured a new edition would be more fun than simply ordering more books.

Organization of the Book

The book is divided into four major parts.

Part I introduces integrated process improvement and provides a rationale for undertaking such an approach. This material is both a primer for the novice and ammunition to gain management support for the process improvement champion. It offers general guidance as well as specific hints on implementation, including pointers to support the migration from legacy process improvement activities and accomplishments. Part I also provides "Pearl of Wisdom" that are based on lessons learned from the pioneering organizations that blazed the trail toward integrated process improvement. If you wish to start your reading with the details of CMMI, you could save this first part for review at a later time.

Part II describes the work of the CMMI Team. The CMMI philosophy, architecture, and models are presented, and examples of the models are annotated in detail to provide a better understanding of their contents. This part also includes some of the rationale for specific CMMI decisions and help in navigating the rather daunting CMMI models.

Part III builds on the first two parts and offers the authors' practical guidance in the use of the CMMI products. It suggests heuristics for choosing models and representations appropriate for a specific organization. It also describes CMMI appraisals and explains how to tailor the CMMI products to fit an organization and enhance the probability of success in applying CMMI.

Part IV presents some musings on the future of CMMI. These informed speculations reflect some of the discussions held formally and informally during and since CMMI development. The ideas included are intended to invite discussion and spark innovation, but not, as the sportswriters say, "as the basis for any actual cash wager."

Like their predecessors, the CMMI models are by necessity large and complex products. This book, while not duplicating all their information, will help you understand the CMMI models and auxiliary materials. It provides a rationale for integrating process improvement, a guide to the structure and contents of the CMMI models, and some practical ideas for using the models effectively in your organization. We strongly encourage you to obtain copies of the models from the CMMI Web site (www.sei.cmu.edu/cmmi) and browse through them as you are reading this book, especially Parts II and III.[1] For readers who would like a flavor of the models, Appendixes A and B present a concise summary of CMMI-SW/SE/IPPD/SS content in both the continuous and staged representations.

The CMMI project is an ongoing effort, so any time-restricted book about CMMI will necessarily be overcome by events. The authors have strived to provide information that is both timely and of lasting value, but understand the reality of the CMMI environment. To that end, the publisher has agreed to support this volume with updates through its Web site (www.awprofessional.com) and, when appropriate, further editions.

Second Edition Highlights

So what is different in the new edition? Along with the technical changes made to incorporate CMMI version 1.1, you will find more material about how process improvement can affect business goals, how management can support CMMI adoption, and how organizations can take advantage of a broad experience base to ease CMMI implementation. We've added material on the realized return on investment of process-improvement initiatives. For those who would like a 30,000-foot view, there is a new overview of the model that links the components to business practices and outcomes. Chapter 10 has been totally revised, presenting a more practical discussion based on experience with the latest version of SCAMPI.

Of course our discussion of CMMI evolution has been updated to reflect our latest understanding of how the model will continue to adapt and remain relevant for a long time to come. Most importantly, the previous edition's well-deserved paean to the author team has been

---

1. The models, formatted for easier reference in one volume, are now included in the SEI series book *CMMI®: Guidelines for Process Integration and Product Improvement*, by Mary Beth Chrissis, Mike Konrad, and Sandy Shrum.

replaced by a new poem, celebrating the model and its potential to provide guidance for a new generation of improving organizations.

Acknowledgments

Numerous people helped with the development of the second edition, and we are indebted to them for all their good efforts. First were the readers who gave us suggestions for improvement and identified errata, with special thanks going to Ron Radice, Suzanne Garcia, and Mike Phillips. Second were those who shared their experiences with us to bring you better examples and clearer exposition, especially Kathleen Dangle. Third, and certainly not least, were our amazing wives (Pam, Debbi, and Jo) who, in addition to providing occasional relief from family obligations, read various draft versions of our revised text, offering valuable improvement suggestions. We love you all even more.

Our hope for you, our readers, is that you will find benefit in this new edition and improvements that are informative, useful, and appropriate to your needs.

—Dennis, Aaron, and Rich
Baltimore, Dallas, and Washington, D.C., July 2003

Preface to the First Edition

This book is about a new way of approaching process improvement for engineering development. Process improvement is a generally well-understood and accepted means of achieving quality and productivity gains for software development, and the recognition of its importance for other engineering disciplines is growing. The success and wide adoption of the Capability Maturity Model (CMM) for Software have inspired increased development of similar models in disciplines other than software. The resulting proliferation of models in engineering organizations has led to conflicts in process-improvement goals and techniques, considerable increases in required training, and confusion on the part of practitioners as to which of the various models applies to their specific needs.

The Capability Maturity Model Integration (CMMI) project, an ongoing effort by industry, the U.S. government, and the Software Engineering Institute (SEI) of Carnegie Mellon University, is attempting to address this situation. Started in 1998, CMMI is an effort to codify the tenets of model-based process improvement and provide a single, integrated framework for improving engineering processes in organizations that span several disciplines. By integrating the tools and techniques used to improve individual engineering disciplines, both the quality and the efficiency of organizational process improvement are enhanced.[1]

In the last quarter of 2000, after extensive stakeholder review and piloting, the first official CMMI products were released. These models

---

1. CMMI initially focused on development activities (that is, building things), with a special emphasis on systems and software engineering. Clearly, many aspects of process improvement apply more broadly, to other engineering as well as nonengineering disciplines. As you learn about CMMI, you may gain insight into how its process improvement framework might be extended and applied to other areas. We assume that the majority of readers are interested in the initial CMMI focus on the development of software-intensive systems, and hence we write from that perspective. We also invite readers to think about other potential applications within the engineering development world and beyond.

provide users with a choice of single or integrated disciplines and a choice of a staged or continuous representation. They include a wealth of engineering and process-improvement information, such as clear goals and extensive guidance on the best practices to achieve them. Most importantly, a well-defined framework outlines how additional disciplines may be brought into the product suite so as to minimize the development of incompatible models in the future.

Purpose of the Book

This book has a threefold purpose. First, we intend to help organizations understand how an integrated approach to process improvement can help mature their technical and management processes. Second, to support this integrated approach, we present a new set of tools developed by the CMMI project specifically designed for multidiscipline process improvement. Finally, we provide practical guidance in the selection and use of those tools. This guidance is based on lessons learned from organizations that have adopted integrated process improvement, as well as the knowledge and experience gained from the hundreds of professionals who were involved in the development of the CMMI Product Suite.

Audience for the Book

The intended audience for this book comprises executives, middle managers, team leaders, acquisition specialists, process-improvement champions, and the often overlooked and overworked process-improvement practitioners. Executives, who may have deferred process improvement in the past because the scope of their business exceeded the boundaries of a single model, will find an approach and tools to mitigate their concerns. Middle managers and team leaders will find information on the effects of process improvement on their responsibilities and the cross-discipline nature of their environments. Process-improvement champions will find a means to enlarge their base of support and focus their efforts in a way that heightens the chances of adoption and success. Finally, individuals who are charged with implementing process improvement will find help in applying models in the real world. It is our hope that when unsuspecting project and program managers are instructed to "implement that CMMI stuff," this book will provide sufficient information to save both their careers and their sanity.

While applicable to any organization involved with rigorous, time-critical development of complex systems, this book will hold special interest for system developers and systems integrators who supply the U.S. government. The federal government participated in the CMMI development work, thereby supporting the efforts of its suppliers (both external and internal) to improve process performance. In October 1999, the U.S. Department of Defense established the requirement that its large program development contractors demonstrate full compliance with a maturity level 3 as measured by the CMM for Software (or equivalent).[2] More recently, it has indicated its intention to have CMMI-SE/SW identified as an equivalent evaluation tool.[3] Given the considerable interest at all levels in adding the acquisition discipline to CMMI, the authors believe that CMMI will likely see application in improving government system acquisition organizations, as well.

Our Intentions

The authors have all been active in process improvement in the real world. We bring considerable practical experience to this effort, together with our ideas on improving the way process improvement is accomplished. Together we struggled through the creation of the CMMI products, benefiting from the wide variety of views brought by the CMMI Product Development Team. Generally, this book describes the products and positions of the nearly 100 other experienced practitioners and researchers that made up that team. In some places, however, we express our own opinions. In those cases where the text may not reflect the consensus of the team, we have identified our unorthodoxy.

It is our hope that this book reflects the tremendous accomplishments of the entire CMMI Product Development Team. Most of all, we want you to obtain a clearer understanding of the practice and benefits of integrated process improvement based on CMMI products. Through the information in this book, we hope to help make your process-improvement initiatives successful.

---

2. "Software evaluations for ACAT 1 programs," memorandum from Dr. J. S. Gansler, Under Secretary of Defense (Acquisition and Technology), Oct. 26, 1999.
3. "Use of CMMI evaluations by the Department of Defense," memorandum from Dr. Delores M. Etter, Deputy Under Secretary of Defense (Science and Technology), Dec. 11, 2000.

Acknowledgments

The authors would like to acknowledge the help and support of the CMMI Product Development Team and the CMMI Steering Group. The members of those groups, past and present, may not agree with everything that we say here, but this book would not exist without their devoted efforts over several years on behalf of CMMI. Additionally, several individuals were key to the actual development of this book. They include Karl Arunski, Roger Bate, Denise Cattan, Jeffrey Dutton, Delores Etter, Jack Ferguson, Craig Hollenbach, Linda Ibrahim, Mike Phillips, Sarah Sheard, and Joan Weszka.

Peter Gordon, Asdis Thorsteinsson, and other Addison-Wesley personnel were invaluable in helping us meld the significantly different styles of the three authors into coherent, readable prose. The reviewers engaged by the publisher, including several from the Software Engineering Institute, provided us with many useful improvement suggestions.

Finally, the authors would like to thank our families (and especially Pam, Debbi, and Jo), who put up with crabby spouses and parents, absences from home, and frenetic holidays so that this book could make its production schedule. We love you all.

—Dennis, Aaron, and Rich
Baltimore, Dallas, and Washington, D.C., January 2001

The Tower of Babel
Gustave Dore (1832–1883)
© 2000–2001 www.arttoday.com

Part I

Integrated Process Improvement

In the biblical story of the Tower of Babel, God caused a construction project to fail by interrupting communication through the creation of multiple languages. In the modern story of process improvement, we have created multiple languages to serve various organizational disciplines through divergent process-improvement models. As with the Tower of Babel story, this diversity poses a threat to communication. Capability Maturity Model Integration (CMMI) and integrated process improvement in general strive to reverse this situation by providing a single language through which multiple disciplines can share process-improvement activities and a unified focus on process-improvement objectives.

Part I Contents

1

Chapter 2. Implementing Integrated Process Improvement

In which the authors present valuable guidance concerning the best manner in which such endeavors should be undertaken so as to increase the likelihood of success.

Chapter 1

Why Integrated Process Improvement?

> *It is not necessary to change. Survival is not mandatory.*
> **W. Edwards Deming** (1900–1993)

> *The complexity of practice has always dwarfed the simplicity of theory.*
> **Robert Britcher,** *The Limits of Software* (1999)

Since you are reading (or at least browsing through) this book, either you are interested in process improvement and Capability Maturity Model Integration (CMMI), or you have been told to get interested in it. Perhaps your management chain or a major customer has indicated that they would like you to be at least a CMMI "level 3" organization. You think: "Should I really be interested? Will it make it easier for me to do my job? What is level 3? What is CMMI?" This book will help you answer these questions.

Chapter 1 will begin by reviewing the business context for any process-improvement initiative, and why that manager or customer may be encouraging you. To understand the rationale for change, it's important to look at some shortcomings of traditional process improvement when faced with the engineering paradigm of the twenty-first century. The engineering world has changed in at least three important ways since the introduction of model-based process improvement.

First, the environment within which engineering is performed has become increasingly complex. Efforts are larger, involve more people, cross corporation boundaries, are distributed far and wide, and must adhere to continually compressing implementation schedules to meet customer needs and heightened expectations.

Second, the way in which engineering work is performed has evolved. Cross-discipline teams, concurrent engineering, highly automated processes, and multinational standards have all affected engineering practice. These changes in turn cause modifications to the role of the engineering manager.

Third, the success of the Software Engineering Institute's (SEI's) Capability Maturity Model for Software has led to a proliferation of models, each of which addresses process improvement from the aspect of a particular discipline. Organizations have adopted multiple improvement models to address their critical processes.

All of these changes highlight the need to integrate process-improvement efforts. The myriad disciplines and processes involved in contemporary engineering are closely intertwined. The overhead and confusion resulting from the application of multiple models are too costly in terms of business expenses and resource allocation. As a consequence, a means of addressing process improvement across a number of disciplines within a single framework is needed. This chapter discusses how changes in the engineering world have influenced the effectiveness of traditional process-improvement strategies and how organizations can benefit from applying an integrated approach in order to reach their business objectives.

Model-Based Process Improvement

Model-based process improvement involves the use of a model to guide the improvement of an organization's processes. Process improvement grew out of the quality management work of Deming,[1] Crosby,[2] and Juran[3] and is aimed at increasing the capability of work processes. Essentially, process capability is the inherent ability of a process to produce planned results. As the capability of a process increases, it becomes predictable and measurable, and the most significant causes of poor quality and productivity are controlled or eliminated. By steadily improving its process capability, the organization "matures." Maturity improvement requires strong management support and a consistent long-term focus. In addition, it necessitates fundamental changes in the way managers and practitioners perform their jobs.

One means of achieving this focus has been the use of a capability model. Models provide a common set of process requirements that capture best practices and practical knowledge in a format that can be used to guide priorities. By using a model, organizations can modify or create processes using practices that have been proven to increase process capability. They may also employ models to conduct an appraisal of process capability for two purposes: to establish a baseline for improvement and to measure progress as improvement activities proceed.

Generally, model-based process improvement begins with management commitment and an appraisal. The findings from this appraisal, in turn, feed action plans. When these plans have been completed, further appraisals are performed and the cycle continues. The goal is for the organization to mature so that it continuously monitors and improves its processes, consistently produces high-quality products, is agile within its marketplace, and adjusts quickly to customer needs.

---

1. Deming, W. Edwards. *Out of the Crisis*. Cambridge, MA: MIT Center for Advanced Engineering, 1986.
2. Crosby, P. B. *Quality Is Free: The Art of Making Quality Certain*. New York: McGraw-Hill, 1979.
3. Juran, J. M. *Juran on Planning for Quality*. New York: MacMillan, 1988.

1.1 Business Objectives and Process Improvement

First of all, let's talk about your organization, and how you or your management might like it to perform. Organizations generally have many different business objectives, such as:

- Produce quality products or services.
- Create value for the stockholders.
- Be an employer of choice.
- Enhance customer satisfaction.
- Increase market share.
- Implement cost savings and best practices.
- Gain an industry-wide recognition for excellence.

To have a strong competitive edge in a rapidly evolving marketplace, you might like to take advantage of opportunities and avoid simply reacting to change. You may also like to improve your ability to predict costs and revenues, and find ways to raise productivity and lower expenses. This could help you to anticipate problems and develop ways to address them early.

In order to meet any of these objectives, you must have a clear understanding of what it takes to produce your products or services. To improve, you need to understand the variability in the processes that you follow, so that when you adjust them, you'll know whether the adjustment is advantageous. In short, you'll want to manage your business using accurate data about both products and processes.

But wait; how do you know that your data is reasonable or accurate? Can you compare information between projects? Generally, there has to be some consistency in the work you do in order to make valid comparisons. You want to be able to measure your success and make sure that the processes you follow add value to the products and services that you create. Of course, that implies a standard way of doing things and a baseline against which to measure.

Now we are getting down to the nitty-gritty. Does your organization have experience with developing and following a process, and can it support the development of common, standard processes? Can you determine the best ways to go about a particular task? Establishing standard processes that are appropriate and successful for your workplace and business is fundamental for process control and improvement. Unfortunately, this may not be within the scope of your position description or training. And what about that training?

Without good project management and fundamental technical skills, projects can't operate effectively enough to spend any time on improvement. Basic activities like planning and tracking need to be understood and encouraged. Version control and managing risks are essential disciplines that need to be addressed. And managing requirements so that you deliver value to your customer is a key business objective.

As you can see from the discussion above, getting to that competitive edge requires incremental improvements. That's where a process-improvement initiative really can help. Process-improvement activities focus on improving process capability and organizational maturity to help you advance the organization and accomplish its objectives. They can provide you with guidance on how to define and standardize processes, increase your work effectiveness, limit rework, measure the performance of the organization, and use the data to manage the business.

Of course, there is a cost associated with process improvement. Experience shows that it can take between 2 and 10 percent of normal engineering effort to support a major process-improvement initiative. However, experience also confirms a substantial positive return on investment (ROI) and improvement in key business indicators. Some representative examples include

- Tinker Air Force Base measured an ROI of 7 to 1 over seven years of software process improvement.[4]

- Northrop Grumman Information Technology after three years has reported in one of its units the operationally found defects down 60 percent, the ability to estimate monthly costs up 32 percent, and the ability to meet monthly cost goals up 40 percent.[5]

- IBM Global Services, India, report their ROI for process improvement is consistently 4 or 5 to 1.[6]

---

4. Butler, K., and W. Lipke, "Software Process Achievement at Tinker Air Force Base, Oklahoma," CMU/SEI-2000-TR-014, Pittsburgh: Software Engineering Institute, Carnegie Mellon University, September 2000.
5. Carter, L., et al. "The Road to CMMI: Results of the First Technology Transition Workshop," CMU/SEI-2002-TR-007, Pittsburgh: Software Engineering Institute, Carnegie Mellon University, February 2002.
6. Paulk, M., and M. Chrissis, "The 2001 High Maturity Workshop," CMU/SEI-2001-SR-014, Pittsburgh: Software Engineering Institute, Carnegie Mellon University, January 2002.

So, process improvement promises measurable benefits for organizations, particularly in the ability to estimate effort and the delivery of quality products. In the remainder of this chapter, we show how integrating process improvement across several disciplines can increase those benefits and add more.

Process Improvement and Golf

If you haven't got a handle on process improvement and how it can help your business, here's a way to think about it that may help. The process you use to produce a product or service may be likened to your golf swing. (Work with us here; pretend you are a duffer, even if you are not.) A golf swing is a complex sequence of closely coupled activities that you perform in an integrated manner to achieve a purpose—to send a golf ball to a specific place. As we all know, however, improving your golf swing is not an easy task. Neither is improving your business processes.

First, it's impossible to think of your golf swing all at once. You need to break it into pieces so you can concentrate on making adjustments that are under your control. Some of those pieces, like your grip and your stance (not to mention the club length, the flexibility of the shaft, the material in the club head, etc.), are fundamentals that have to be in place before any of the other pieces can be reliable. You have to take care of them before you can make any progress in other areas.

Second, you can't easily take a critical look at your own golf swing. You need an objective eye (the golf professional or a video camera) that can help evaluate what is right and what isn't. Of course, you also need some measures of correctness to use as a guide.

Third, as you improve the pieces of the swing (such as grip, stance, length of backswing, tempo), they begin to merge into a more integrated whole that you can begin to "groove" into predictable consistency. Once you find the swing that's comfortable on the 7 iron, it needs to be applied (with appropriate adjustment) to the other clubs in your bag.

Finally, it's only after you have consistency in your swing that you can begin to modify it for the situation at hand and really address the strategic parts of golf-club selection, shot placement, draws and fades, and other nuances many of us see only on television.

In many respects, organizational process improvement works the same way as improving your golf swing. Models can help to break your process into pieces, show you the fundamentals, and help you decide what to work on first. Experts in process improvement (e.g., champions, groups, and consultants) can help you evaluate your current processes and measure your improvement. The standard processes that you employ can provide standard data, and this becomes the basis for your projects to "groove" their activities. As a consequence, applying them to new areas and thinking strategically become the normal way to work.

And by the way, improving your organization may be easier than improving your swing; you have a lot of talented people who can work synergistically, and their efforts to improve are not limited to the weekends. Go get 'em, Tiger.

1.2 The Engineering Environment of the Twenty-First Century

Remember when there was one telephone company and one kind of phone service? When the only telephone-related worry you had was keeping long-distance calls under three minutes? When you understood not only the principles but also (perhaps) the mechanics of how the system worked?[7] Unfortunately (or fortunately, in some cases), the era of such relatively simple systems has ended. When you realize that your new telephone contains more software than the lunar landing module, Dorothy's plaintive "Toto, I don't think we're in Kansas anymore" may all too closely echo your feelings of consternation. Even technology-savvy engineers occasionally profess a sense of awe about the relentless pace of technological change. No one can deny that this change has brought new capabilities, new conveniences, and new complexity.

---

7. If you are too young to remember this time, ask a parent or other elder within your circle of friends. They'll appreciate the time to reminisce. However, if they begin to talk about the value of hard work, the buying power of the dollar, or walking 20 miles to school barefoot in the snow, make your escape quickly!

We are now on the rising edge of the system complexity curve, and there is little chance of moderation in the foreseeable future. The U.S. Department of Defense (DOD) has estimated that it will soon need to field systems utilizing as many as 40 million lines of software code. In some autonomous military systems, software will provide decision-making functions for reconnaissance and weapon delivery.

Complexity is related to more than purely software components. Many traditionally hardware modules now contain a large amount of micro-code that will inevitably interface in some manner with a software control system housed in yet another hardware device. In increasingly complex systems, the ability to differentiate between hardware and software functions may become nearly impossible, complicating design and maintenance tasks and significantly affecting our ability to calculate expected reliability. This complexity is readily evident in the products and systems being conceived, designed, and manufactured each day; moreover, it is mirrored in the activities of the acquiring and developing organizations, both in industry and government.

As systems grow more complex, the processes used to develop them will follow suit. The complexity of processes inevitably increases to keep pace with the number of individuals who are involved in performance. The theory and concepts of process improvement are elegant and understandable. When we apply them to increasingly complex systems, however, we find that, as Robert Britcher writes, "the complexity of practice has always dwarfed the simplicity of theory."[8] This result is particularly likely when the processes cut across organizational, discipline, corporate, or cultural boundaries.

With large and complex organizations, processes, and systems, process-improvement activities can easily become lost in the multiplicity of tasks, agendas, and personalities. Because each office or organization has its own responsibilities and diligently strives to improve its own practices, process improvement can evolve into a patchwork of unrelated and uncoordinated activities spread across a variety of organizations. Multiple groups and their executives may vie for

---

8. Britcher, Robert. *The Limits of Software*. Reading, MA: Addison-Wesley, 1999. This fascinating treatise on the philosophy and practice of software engineering is drawn from the author's work with IBM on the Federal Aviation Administration's (FAA) Advanced Automation System (AAS). AAS was terminated after expenditures of approximately $2 billion, based on the judgment that it could not be accomplished.

process-improvement resources. Process groups may select different and sometimes conflicting improvement models. Competition can emerge between groups, and the ownership of process improvement can become hotly debated. In the end, there is often more energy spent in the peripheral activities than in the improvement initiatives.

Lest you think that only large and complex projects lead to process-improvement problems, consider the small, entrepreneurial firm racing to meet a rapidly approaching market window. Such an organization finds it difficult, if not impossible, to address process improvement when time-to-market is so crucial to its survival. Such a firm often has personnel performing multiple engineering functions simultaneously; conceivably, it may have a different process for each individual in the company.

As another example, an information technology application services company may be forced to deal with an erratic customer who constantly changes requirements, priorities, and schedules, leaving little alternative except to function in a crisis development environment. Although neither type of organization described here has the financial or schedule resources to pursue traditional process improvement, each could benefit greatly from taking a more disciplined approach to engineering.

1.3 Concurrent Engineering and the Cross-Discipline Team

The way in which engineering and product development work is organized has undergone major changes in recent years. Much of this change has been aimed at eliminating the inefficiencies associated with stepwise development, where intermediate products are handed off to next-phase workers, who may have to do extensive rework to correct misunderstandings. Concurrent engineering, cross-discipline teams, cross-functional teams, integrated product teams (IPTs), and Integrated Product and Process Development (IPPD) all represent ways to address this problem and apply the necessary expertise at the appropriate time throughout the product or service life cycle. In practice, this trend means that designers and customers work with manufacturers, testers, and users to support the manufacturing organization in developing requirements. It has also been described as having "everyone at the table," implying that all critical stakeholders support all phases of product or service development.[9]

Understandably, the concept of concurrency has redefined the nature of organizational structure and development. It requires an enhanced management competency for dealing with "gray areas" and ambiguity, which is not easy for many managers, who are perhaps more versed in dealing with tangible facts and figures. The general acceptance and rapid deployment of cross-discipline or cross-functional teams in the engineering world has also proved a thorny issue for process improvement. The concept of functional departments, each with its own processes under its own control, strongly clashes with the highly interactive work style associated with cross-discipline teams.

To date, discrete process-improvement models have not effectively supported the "mixing bowl" environment of concurrent engineering. If the hardware engineering department is using one improvement model, the software developers a second, and the outsourcing and contracts departments yet a third, problems are inevitable. Separate "stovepipe"[10] models offer little chance of improving the processes used by a cross-discipline team, where every member is an actor in most of the processes and the separation between the disciplines has gone the way of the Berlin Wall.

Cross-discipline teams use integrated processes that are matched more closely to the ebb and flow of the life cycle than are the strict stages of classical development. They take advantage of evolutionary development approaches and innovative design techniques. Attempting to apply the discipline-specific models to such processes is analogous to requiring members of a jazz trio to strictly play their individual parts. Of course it's possible—but the outcome is not very satisfying. What is needed is a model that not only integrates the disciplines, but also integrates the processes themselves and supports effective work among various stakeholders, functional personnel, and management.

---

9. Of course, anything can be overdone. Programs with integrated product teams numbering in the hundreds can experience their own distinctive communication problems.

10. Stovepipe processes are usually organized by discipline and do not include the interfaces between those organizations.

1.4 A Proliferation of Models and Standards

If imitation is a measure of success, then the Capability Maturity Model (CMM) for Software is exceptionally successful—and for good reason. People in many disciplines were attracted to the elegance of the CMM concept and its close ties to quality management theory and practice. The general response was, "Hey, that's a great idea. Let's build something like that for *our* shop." Table 1-1 shows a number of the better-known CMM-like improvement models in use around the world, together with relevant international standards.

Table 1-1: *CMM-like Models*

Model	Description
CMM for Software	The original CMM developed at the Software Engineering Institute (SEI). In November 1986, the SEI, with assistance from MITRE Corporation, began developing a process maturity framework intended to assist organizations in improving their software processes. In September 1987, the SEI released a brief description of the process maturity framework and a maturity questionnaire (CMU/SEI-87-TR-23). The fully developed model (version 1.1) was released in 1993.
SE-CMM	The Systems Engineering Capability Maturity Model (SE-CMM) describes the elements of an organization's systems engineering process that are essential to good systems engineering. This model was developed by the Enterprise Process Improvement Collaboration (EPIC), which included industry, government, and academic members. It was merged in 1998 with the INCOSE SECAM to form the Electronics Industry Alliance's EIA 731. *(continued)*

Table 1-1: *CMM-like Models (continued)*

Model	Description
SA-CMM	A collaborative effort among the U.S. Department of Defense, the SEI, industry, and other U.S. government agencies, the Software Acquisition Capability Maturity Model (SA-CMM) supports benchmarking and improvements of the software acquisition process.
SECAM	The International Council on Systems Engineering (INCOSE) developed the Systems Engineering Capability Assessment Model (SECAM) as a checklist-based model. It has since been merged with the SE-CMM into EIA 731.
People CMM	This model addresses the ability of software organizations to attract, develop, motivate, organize, and retain talent.
EIA 731	This Systems Engineering Capability Model (SECM) supersedes the SE-CMM and SECAM; it was issued as an interim standard (EIA/IS 731) in 1998 and as a full standard (EIA 731) in 2002.
Systems Security Engineering CMM	This model represented an extension and enhancement of the SE-CMM by the U.S. National Security Agency (NSA); it provided additional practices and information concerning security of information systems.
IPD-CMM	The Integrated Product Development CMM (IPD-CMM) was published only in draft form. It was begun under the auspices of EPIC, but was superseded by the establishment of the CMMI project.

Model	Description
FAA-iCMM	The first truly integrated CMM, this model developed at the U.S. Federal Aviation Administration (FAA) integrates material from many sources: the SE-CMM, the SA-CMM, the CMM for Software, ISO 9000/2000, EIA 731, Malcolm Baldrige, ISO/IEC 15504, ISO/IEC 15288, ISO/IEC 12207, and CMMI. Now at Version 2, it is being used as a unified means of guiding process improvement across the entire FAA.
ISO/IEC 12207	An international standard on software life-cycle processes; it was first issued in 1995 and amended in 2002. (ISO is the International Organization for Standardization. IEC is the International Electrotechnical Commission.)
ISO/IEC 15288	An international standard on system life-cycle processes; it was issued in 2002.
ISO/IEC 15504	A draft international standard that defines the requirements for performing process assessment as a basis for use in process improvement and capability determination.
Project Framework	Developed as a proprietary product by ESI International, this model merges the CMM concept with the Project Management Institute's Project Management Body of Knowledge (PMBOK) to produce a management process-improvement tool.

All of the models described in Table 1-1 were created within an environment of evolving national and international standards and frameworks. As standards become used and accepted, maintaining harmonization between them and the improvement models becomes a

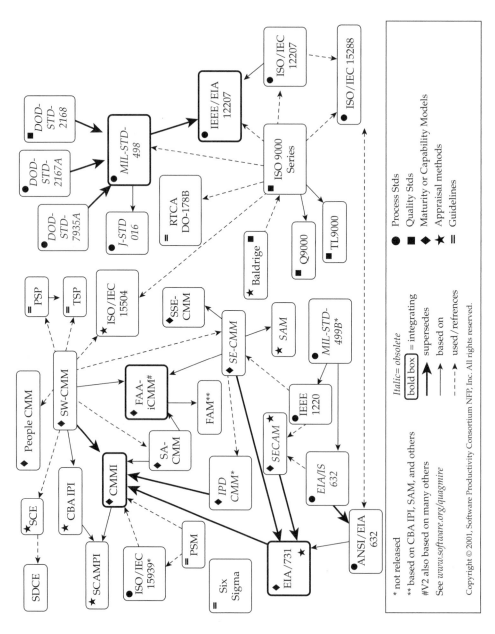

Figure 1-1: *The Frameworks Quagmire*

* not released
** based on CBA IPI, SAM, and others
#V2 also based on many others
See *www.software.org/quagmire*

Italic = obsolete
bold box = integrating

Process Stds
Quality Stds
Maturity or Capability Models
Appraisal methods
Guidelines

supersedes
based on
used/refrences

Copyright © 2001, Software Productivity Consortium NFP, Inc. All rights reserved.

ANSI/EIA 632 = Processes for Engineering a System, major modification of MIL-STD-499B, 1999.

Baldrige = Malcolm Baldrige National Quality Award, administered by the National Institute of Standards and Technology.

CBA IPI = CMM-Based Appraisal for Internal Process Improvement, released 1996.

CMMI = CMM Integration, SEI-facilitated work to integrate SW-CMM, SECM, and IPD-CMM content, v1.1 released.

DO-178B = Software Considerations in Airborne Systems and Equipment Certification, by RTCA, 1992.

DOD-STD-2167A = Defense System Software Development Standard, 1988.

DOD-STD-2168 = Defense System Software Quality Standard, companion to DOD-STD-2167A.

DOD-STD-7935A = DOD Automated Information System Documentation Standards, 1988.

EIA/IEEE J-STD-016 = Release name for interim commercial version of MIL-STD-498, released 1995.

EIA/IS 632 = Systems Engineering, minor modification of MIL-STD-499B, to make it more commercial (IS = Interim Standard).

FAA-iCMM = FAA's internal process improvement model, integrating ten different models and standards, v2.0 released 2001.

FAM = FAA Appraisal Method for iCMM.

IEEE 1220 = IEEE Standard for Application and Management of the Systems Engineering Process, 1998.

IEEE/EIA 12207 = U.S. implementation of ISO/IEC 12207, 1997.

IPD-CMM = Integrated Product Development CMM, a model that was not issued but whose content has been incorporated into the CMMI.

ISO 9000 Series = Series of more than 20 international standards and documents for quality systems, issued in 1994 and revised in 2000.

ISO/IEC 12207 = Software engineering—Software life cycle processes, international standard issued by ISO in 1995 and amended in 2002.

ISO/IEC 15288 = Systems engineering—System life cycle processes, international standard issued by ISO in 2002.

ISO/IEC 15504 = Information technology—Process assessment, international technical report issued by ISO in 1998–9 focused on software, with new version issued as standard and not limited to software available soon.

ISO/IEC 15939 = Software engineering—Software measurement process, international standard issued by ISO in 2002.

MIL-STD-498 = Software Development and Documentation military standard.

MIL-STD-499B = Systems engineering military standard, never released but used as a basis for EIA and IEEE systems engineering standards.

People CMM = CMM about developing software developers.

PSP = Personal Software Process, software development maturity guidance for individuals, from SEI.

Q9000 = U.S. adaptation of ISO 9000.

SA-CMM = Software Acquisition CMM, acquirer's mirror of SW-CMM.

SAM = SE-CMM Appraisal Method.

SCAMPI = Standard CMMI Appraisal Method for Process Improvement, released 2001.

SCE = Software Capability Evaluation, for outside audits using the SW-CMM.

SDCE = Software Development Capability Evaluation, an evolution of Software Development Capability/Capacity Review (SDCCR) and SW-CMM, by the U.S. Air Force.

SECAM = Systems Engineering Capability Assessment Model, produced by the Capability Assessment Working Group (CAWG) of the International Council on Systems Engineering (INCOSE).

SECM (EIA 731) = Systems Engineering Capability Model, a merger of SECAM and SE-CMM, issued in 1998 as an interim standard and in 2002 as a full standard.

SE-CMM = Systems Engineering Capability Maturity Model, from EPIC.

Six Sigma = Process improvement and management philosophy focused on reducing process output variation.

SSE-CMM = Security Systems Engineering CMM, an adaptation of SE-CMM for the discipline of security engineering.

SW-CMM = SEI's Capability Maturity Model for Software, 1993.

TL9000 = Set of requirements for telecommunications, based on ISO 9000.

TSP = Team Software Process, software development maturity guidance for teams, from SEI.

continuing challenge, particularly across disciplines. In describing the complexity of this environment, Sarah Sheard of the Software Productivity Consortium has coined the term "the frameworks quagmire."[11] Figure 1-1 shows her depiction of the proliferation and heritage of the various systems and software engineering standards, life-cycle models, quality awards, and process-improvement models. In this diagram, the arrows show where one model or standard contributed to the development of another.

As you can see in Figure 1-1, the development of these frameworks bears a striking resemblance to the bloodlines of the European monarchies in the middle centuries of the last millennium. This incestuous nature leaves many organizations to ponder the real value of moving from well-established standards to newly evolving ones. The difficulty and complexity of using multiple process-improvement models, in addition to the appropriate standards for organizations with multi-discipline requirements, is a strong rationale for integrating process improvement.

1.5 The Benefits of Integrated Process Improvement

In the preceding sections, we enumerated many factors that complicate process improvement. It is our assertion that many of these obstacles can be overcome by integrating process improvement through a common model. Of course, you may need to be convinced that this endeavor is worthwhile for your organization. At the end of the day, what are the real benefits of integrated process improvement?

Fundamentally, process-improvement integration has a major impact in four areas: cost, focus, process integration, and flexibility. Some of these changes are more easily quantified than others, but all represent real advantages.

---

11. The Software Productivity Consortium is a nonprofit partnership of industry, government, and academia. Its goal is to develop processes, methods, tools, and supporting services to help its members and affiliates build high-quality, component-based systems and continuously advance their systems and software engineering maturity pursuant to the guidelines of the major process and quality frameworks. Membership is open to all U.S.- and Canadian-based companies, government agencies, and academic organizations. Sarah Sheard can be reached at sheard@software.org. Also see www.software.org/quagmire.

1.5.1 Cost Benefits

Cost improvement is probably the easiest benefit to understand. There is always a cost to integration, but the savings from process-improvement integration can be significant. By applying a single model, organizations that would otherwise use multiple models can reduce the cost of:

- Training in multiple models and appraisal methods.
- Performing multiple appraisals within the same organizations (and possibly with the same practitioners).
- Maintaining redundant process assets in a repository.
- Maintaining or purchasing expertise in multiple models.

The better odds of success that arise from integrated process improvement also make it more likely that the organization will achieve cost savings resulting from higher quality, better predictability, and all the other benefits of improved processes.

1.5.2 Clarity of Focus

Within the diverse world of engineering organizations, particularly when projects cut across organizational boundaries, it is difficult to achieve the critical mass necessary to bring about real improvement within individual organizations. This problem can be characterized as stemming from a lack of focus and a need to unify the disparate activities. That is, the pressures from outside the group are too strong, the costs too high, or the resources too thinly applied to both improve local processes and interface them with other organizations or disciplines. Budget changes, the business environment, internal politics, and mergers and acquisitions all take their toll by consuming resources that could be applied to improvement.

An integrated process-improvement program can clarify the goals and business objectives of the various initiatives. By integrating process-improvement activities across a wider range of disciplines, it becomes easier to rally the troops—both practitioners and executives—to the process-improvement banner. Having a single process-improvement focus can unify and reinforce vision, efficiently marshal and apply scarce resources, and provide a common language for improvement across various disciplines. In particular, a single model with common terminology and common appraisal methods provides this kind of focus.

A word of caution is appropriate at this point. Not every model (such as the CMM for Software) can become the focus for process improvement. If the focus doesn't include all of the disciplines critical to organizational success, it will miss the breadth actually sought by process improvement. An integrated model allows personnel in each discipline to identify with the processes and feel that they have a stake in the now-focused process-improvement program.

1.5.3 Process Integration and Lean Organizations

One of the less obvious benefits of integrated process improvement is the "integrating" effect it has on organizations. When processes are defined across organizational and discipline boundaries, new understanding and mutual education often occur, resulting in the streamlining of the critical workflow and the elimination of redundant or unneeded activities.

Stovepipe process improvement often assumes that interfaces between organizations work effectively; rarely is one process aware of closely related or redundant activities in a sister stovepipe. By working on improving processes across the board, the organization essentially obtains a bonus reengineering effort as a by-product of the process-improvement initiative. This streamlining supports the Lean concept, which strives for increased value to the customer by eliminating waste in the production of products.[12]

1.5.4 Flexibility and Extension into New Disciplines

A final benefit provided by integration is the ability to add disciplines as the business or engineering environment changes. Adding a new individual model results in a great deal of redundancy and often-conflicting representations in the common process-improvement practices. Adding a discipline within an integrated program simply means a few more process areas and perhaps the reinterpretation of other areas, but the fundamental process-improvement structure and terminology remain the same.

---

12. Womack, James P., and Daniel Jones. *Lean Thinking*. New York: Simon and Schuster, 1996.

1.6 Conclusions

This chapter presented arguments that integrated process improvement is the right, practical, and obvious way to go to address a wide range of business objectives. It identified changes in the engineering environment, discussed the integration of work process across the product life cycle, and described a cacophony of competing standards—three factors that strongly suggest the need for integrated process improvement. Finally, it defined the benefits of such an approach beyond the simplification of an organization's improvement efforts.

Any change requires letting go of old ways of doing business, even ways that in the past may have been successful to some degree. This can affect not only the way in which those directly involved in projects do their job, but also the way in which managers at all levels understand their role. To maximize the chance for true improvement, managers need to lead the effort to make process improvement a way of life across the organization, even in the face of the constant need to meet profit objectives and deal with short-term problems.

Chapter 2 offers some practical advice on taking the plunge and implementing an integrated process-improvement program. By providing some guiding principles of how process-improvement integration works in large and small organizations, we hope to ease your implementation of this beneficial approach.

But what if your organization isn't complex or multidisciplinary? Single-model process improvement is better than no process improvement, and it may work perfectly well in some organizations. Nevertheless, we invite you to look carefully at the CMMI Product Suite before returning to your single-model effort.

The integration of disciplines in CMMI has produced a better model in a number of ways, even when applied just to a single discipline; you may realize advantages by using it. Indeed, because of the legacy of the CMM for Software, there is a version of the CMMI model that is targeted just for software: CMMI-SW. Besides, as a result of learning CMMI you'll be a lot better informed if your new CEO starts preaching the benefits of cross-discipline teams.

Chapter 2

Implementing Integrated Process Improvement

Do what you can, with what you have, where you are.
Theodore Roosevelt (1858–1919)

We find by experience (our own or another's) what is hurtful or helpful.
Giovanni Battista Lamperti, *Vocal Wisdom* (1895)

I have but one lamp by which my feet are guided,
and that is the lamp of experience.
Patrick Henry, Speech before the Virginia Convention (1775)

The two questions that are most frequently raised at integrated process seminars and presentations are

> *How do I pull it all together?*

and

> *What do I do with my existing process-improvement investments?*

Both old hands and novices may be overwhelmed by what they see as the complexity of integrating their often-disparate process-improvement activities. This chapter presents some practical advice for implementing integrated process improvement. The advice is based on the experience of some of the Capability Maturity Model Integration (CMMI) authors and others who have used a variety of methods to integrate their process-improvement activities. The chapter doesn't attempt to summarize or repeat the information found in the wealth of process-improvement and change management books now available. Rather, it points out critical strategies that can facilitate process-improvement integration.

The first section of this chapter addresses the issues of starting a new process-improvement initiative in an integrated way. It is intended for organizations that have not yet implemented formal process improvement and hence will be starting out with a clean slate. Building the needed support systems, networks, and sponsors, and the way in which this activity differs from single-discipline process improvement, is addressed in the second section. The third section is intended for organizations that are currently pursuing process improvement. It suggests ways to incorporate legacy processes and current process-improvement initiatives into an integrated process-improvement structure, without losing the organization's existing investments. The fourth section focuses on the use of appraisals to provide encouragement and energy to the improvement process, without leading to a "checklist mentality." The fifth section looks at process-improvement activities that are not model-based, and that may be ongoing concurrently with CMMI in an organization. Finally, the sixth section presents lessons learned from several organizations in the form of "Pearls of Wisdom."

2.1 Starting Integrated Process Improvement

You have successfully convinced your organization to initiate a new integrated process-improvement program. Or perhaps your organization has informed you that your raise or bonus now depends on such an event. In either case, you need to understand a few key principles about starting process improvement. Although these principles apply to any process-improvement effort, they are especially valuable when embarking on an integrated process-improvement path.

Key Integrated Process-Improvement Principles

1. *Maintain executive support.* Strong consistent support is crucial.

2. *Pick your targets carefully.* Don't underestimate the effort needed, because process improvement is hard work.

3. *Leverage best practices.* Use what is available and "steal with pride."

4. *Align process improvement with business objectives.* Leverage existing objectives or create new ones to support process improvement.

2.1.1 Principle 1—Maintain Executive Support

One of the most critical factors for all process improvement is the strength of executive support. As key stakeholders, the leaders of the organization must be strong, consistent, and visible to build a consensus among practitioners that the endeavor is not merely the management approach *du jour.* (Whatever happened to total quality management?) Executive buy-in and support is critical to obtain the resources for process-improvement activities and to ensure the rewards for the innovation and additional hard work that are fundamental parts of any change strategy. Particularly when initiatives cut across organizations, executives need to bridge the organizational gaps and soothe the damaged egos that inevitably arise in multidisciplinary endeavors. Leadership must achieve consensus among both middle management and the practitioners; otherwise, process improvement will become a paper exercise that produces hollow artifacts and lackluster performance.

For these reasons, it is essential to get commitment from executives early and often. Help them construct the "elevator speech" they need to counter the push back from middle management.[1] Executives should understand that if they take actions that run counter to process-improvement tenets, the message would be heard just as loudly as

---

1. By an "elevator speech," we mean a two- or three-minute summary of the goals, costs, and benefits of your project. This sales pitch should be short enough to give effectively in the space of an elevator ride.

public denigration of the program. Help them to develop an ongoing communication strategy, achievable goals, and good metrics for their own performance plans that can trickle down to their direct reports. Above all, make sure that upper management is notified of early successes, which they can use to defend the program when the first wave of cash-flow issues, schedule adjustments, or other similar crises that can impact organizational priorities appears.

In short, concentrate on keeping your executives aware, involved, and excited. You will then be well on your way to a successful integrated process-improvement program.

2.1.2 Principle 2—Pick Your Targets Carefully

Many process-improvement programs fail because they make poor estimates of what they can reasonably accomplish in a given amount of time.[2]

Process improvement can be difficult work, especially across organizations with strong personalities and well-defined cultures (a description that fits most organizations we know). For this reason, carefully consider your initial process-improvement goals. Select achievable objectives that can immediately show a benefit to the organization. This point may seem obvious, but it is less widely recognized that progress in a difficult area might be readily achievable; indeed, the greatest value for a new improvement program can often be achieved by attacking a tough problem first. Consider an initial goal of improving at least one cross-discipline or cross-organizational process—you not only bring more of the stakeholders into the early planning, but also often find significant reengineering gains that can pay for some of the later process-improvement work.

One important task that often becomes lost in the early excitement—and, if not addressed, nearly always comes back to haunt process-improvement teams—is the early design and use of a measurement program. Make sure that you establish a baseline against which to compare your process-improvement activities. You don't want a year to

---

2. For an analysis of the reasons why process improvement efforts may fail, see the following: Hayes, W., and D. Zubrow. *Moving On Up: Data and Experience Doing CMM-Based Process Improvement (CMU/SEI-95-TR-008).* Pittsburgh: Software Engineering Institute, Carnegie Mellon University, 1995; and Goldenson, D., and J. Herbsleb. *After the Appraisal: A Systematic Survey of Process Improvement, Its Benefits, and Factors That Influence Success (CMU/SEI-95-TR-009).* Pittsburgh: Software Engineering Institute, Carnegie Mellon University, 1995.

pass and have only anecdotal data to defend your successes against any naysayers left in power. No matter how good your persuasive skills, you must have convincing data that process improvement is affecting the organization's bottom line (or at least someone's bottom line). Otherwise, your program may soon find itself below the budget cut-off threshold, with resume writing being the only process improved.

2.1.3 Principle 3—Leverage Best Practices

For some reason, process-improvement champions are often creative types. Don't let your creativity blind you to the fact that many solid, proven process assets are available.[3] Suzanne Garcia, a self-professed process-improvement guerrilla, cajoled the students in her Software Engineering Institute (SEI) classes to "steal with pride!" This instruction doesn't mean stooping to industrial espionage or illegal acts. Rather, it entails searching for what's working and then building on those methods.

If your company has organizational process assets that could be applied to your new process-improvement program, use them. Network with process-improvement groups that operate at both national and local levels.[4] Sometimes consultants can provide assets that have been developed for similar organizations and domains at a fraction of the cost of custom development. Of course, just as with commercial-off-the-shelf (COTS) products, you must ensure that anything you obtain will meet your requirements (or else be willing to change your requirements to fit the product).

---

3. Appendix D lists some of these resources. One especially useful resource is the Software Engineering Information Repository (SEIR), which provides a forum for the contribution and exchange of information concerning software engineering improvement activities. Registered members of SEIR can ask questions, provide tips, and contribute (deposit) experiences or examples to assist one another with their implementation efforts. As part of this process, SEIR members are building a knowledge base in this repository for their future use. The Web site for SEIR is http://seir.sei.cmu.edu/.

4. One important process improvement group for systems engineering is the International Council on Systems Engineering (INCOSE), which operates both at the national level and through local chapters. Another is the Software Process Improvement Network (SPIN), made up of individuals who want to improve software engineering practices. These individuals are organized into regional "SPINs" that meet and share their experiences in initiating and sustaining software process improvement programs. See www.sei.edu/collaborating/spins.

SEI books, reports, conferences, and classes can all provide a wealth of good ideas. Read the journals and surf the Web. Somewhere among the naughty ads, shopping invitations, and stock come-ons, you may find a process description that eliminates a considerable chunk of your process development work. By focusing your efforts and creative energies on established best practices, you will be more effective and successful in your role as a process-improvement champion.

2.1.4 Principle 4—Align Process Improvement with Business Objectives

No step is more critical than closely coupling your process-improvement activities with corporate or organizational goals. In the long run, if process improvement will not affect the bottom line, then neither practitioners nor management will see it as valuable. When you develop your plan, look for existing goals and objectives to support and bring focus to your activities. Efficiency and quality goals are often good candidates, for example.

If you cannot identify clearly related business goals, determine how corporate objectives are developed. Then get your team or your sponsor involved in creating a specific objective that will support process improvement.

2.2 Building an Integrated Improvement Infrastructure

It is critical to establish roles and responsibilities for those individuals who will lead, carry out training for, and perform the process-improvement activities. This infrastructure becomes even more critical when the organization is approaching process improvement in an integrated fashion. Generally, a cadre of process champions will provide the core energy, the experience, and the initial sweat and blood to get process improvement off the ground. These people, however, may not represent all the stakeholders or power centers that will have an important role in the fully integrated environment.

It is almost always necessary to convene a steering group of interested or "volunteered" parties to handle issues that may arise during the process-improvement activities. In many cases, this group may simply represent an extension of the software engineering process group (SEPG) concept into an engineering process group (EPG)—or just a process group (PG) if the effort extends beyond engineering development—with membership that spans the broadened process-improvement landscape.[5]

Be aware of the political ramifications of integrating process-improvement activities when forming your process group. Make sure that all of the organizations involved have a place at the table; their participation will help counter the idea that the initiative is "something being done to them" against their wishes. Hold open meetings and advertise the outcomes. Also, keep a sense of equity throughout the effort—everyone should share in the rewards as well as the work.

The steering group should not be limited to practitioners and process-improvement specialists. It will prove much more effective if middle management is included and if executive management is represented or chairs the group. In this way, the process group can adequately deal with resource and other management issues.

A process group that comprises mostly managers probably will not get the nitty-gritty work done. To achieve its goals, it will need subgroups, committees, or work teams to coordinate the training, build better processes, maintain process assets, and perform all the other tasks involved in process improvement. Make sure that sufficient resources and guidance are available to allow these groups to function reasonably autonomously. Otherwise, you'll end up with your steering group micromanaging process improvement, and chaos waiting at the doorstep.

For both the steering group and the work teams, it is important to recognize that there is also a process for team development. It takes time for a team to get up to speed, to define and understand roles, responsibilities, expectations, and outcomes, in addition to the wants and needs of the various team members. Strong leadership can help steer the course through both smooth and rough waters.

Training is probably the most expensive—and most important—aspect of the infrastructure. With integrated process improvement, the required

---

5. SEPGs are a fundamental part of software process improvement, and the SEI has developed considerable literature describing their activities. The SEI and a regional SPIN co-sponsor an annual Software Engineering Process Group Conference. Check the SEI Web site, http://www.sei.cmu.edu, for more information on SEPGs and SPINs.

training goes beyond simple process definition, facilitation, and model comprehension courses, reaching into the various disciplines involved. Software and systems engineers may need to be cross-trained. They certainly need to understand the fundamentals of one another's discipline to define effective processes that involve both.

Although most organizations have internal resources that can provide much of this training, others may need to look into local university courses or professional training resources. Whatever way you acquire it, the quality, timeliness, and relevance of the training can have enormous implications for the success of your program.

2.3 Integrating Legacy Processes and Initiatives

Many organizations have already spent a great deal of time, effort, and money in establishing process-improvement programs using one or more of the legacy models. How do you leverage that investment when moving to CMMI? Organizations that already have successful process-improvement programs may have an easier task than those creating one from scratch, for three fundamental reasons. First, they probably have an entire improvement infrastructure in place and merely need to extend it to include the new disciplines or organizations. Second, they may have existing leadership support for this type of improvement and a fundamental appreciation of process improvement. Third, and most importantly, members of the initiative should have real success stories that they can use in promoting process improvement in those areas of the company not involved with the legacy efforts. This good news may not convince everyone, but it should at least win a hearing and will certainly provide executives with some of the support they need to pursue the program.

While establishing objectives is key to novice process-improvement champions, identifying the barriers to achieving desired objectives might be the equivalent challenge in moving from a legacy model(s) to an integrated approach. You should have a good feel for the location of the pockets of resistance in your organization. Work carefully to provide these skeptics with the first benefits, if possible. Be sure to include them when setting goals and identifying initial processes, and perhaps even include them on the process-improvement teams.

To win over doubters, you may need to return to the early days of your process-improvement experience and actively market the new integrated approach. Although this book will provide some of the raw material for that marketing, ultimately it is your responsibility to show how integrating processes and process improvement will benefit the organizations involved. Be upbeat about the opportunity. Have meetings between the "new member" organizations and some of your process-improvement leads, in which you give concrete examples of how process improvement works and its effects on the rank and file. Be honest about risks and barriers, and be proud of your achievements. After all, if you hadn't been successful, you wouldn't be considering an integrated approach.

One danger arises when you assume that disciplines new to the process-improvement effort will be able, in a relatively short time, to achieve the same level of process maturity as the disciplines that have been using the legacy models for many years. While the use of the legacy models will facilitate the efforts to bring new disciplines into the integrated approach, a multiyear adoption schedule will likely still be needed.

Another risk (or possible benefit) relates to the process-improvement program's effects on your customers and suppliers (or, more generally, your business partners). In some instances, your partner may be considering the same type of integrated process improvement. If so, you can cooperate in the experience, share lessons learned, and work together in defining processes that are common to both organizations or that span the partnership interface. In other instances, you will need to let your partners know how your process changes will affect them. Although the impact may be negative, it is more likely that your partners will also reap benefits as your organization performs better.

Most of the organizations that have been using the CMMI Product Suite have developed a mapping between their existing process-improvement assets and the CMMI. This mapping, which is likely to require a large effort, provides a good sense of the "delta" between where you are and where integration will take you. It can be used to monitor progress and to market integration by showing how little additional work is necessary to gain the benefits of integrated process improvement. It can also be of great benefit as you collect the objective evidence you need for an appraisal.

2.4 Using Appraisals

Appraisals are the Dr. Jekyll and Mr. Hyde of model-based process improvement. On the one hand, they provide diagnostic support and document hard-earned progress. On the other hand, they can be used as a weapon to force compliance, support preformed management opinions, or limit access to contract opportunities. Obtaining a specific process area capability level or maturity level by a particular date is often used as a goal. While this tactic can be very effective when applied rationally, it can also lead to the dreaded scourge of all true process-improvement advocates—the checklist mentality. Integrated process improvement broadens the range of potential victims of this syndrome, especially for processes across organizational boundaries. Fortunately, some good ways exist to prevent organizations from falling into this trap.

One way to prevent the emergence of a checklist mentality is to make sure everyone understands that appraisals are intended to support process improvement, and they are temporal in nature. Unlike your grades in high school, they don't necessarily end up on your "permanent record." Rather, they highlight strengths that will help you succeed and identify weaknesses that could damage your business.

Another strategy is to ensure that appraisals are timed so that they are not "big bang" events but rather represent the culmination of a methodical improvement plan. To prevent the appraisal from being viewed as a "final exam," some organizations have implemented a series of mini-appraisals along the way, each of which supports the improvements needed before the milestone appraisal occurs. In this way, an appraisal is seen as a way of helping achieve the goals, rather than a goal in and of itself.

2.5 Process Improvement without Models

As advocates of model-based, integrated process improvement strive to build bridges with diverse parts of their organization, no doubt they will encounter other process-improvement initiatives that are not model-based. In aerospace companies, for example, there is a growing amount of support for "Lean" thinking, and the Lean Aerospace Initiative.[6] Many of the process models (see Table 1-1, in Chapter 1) are directed primarily toward developing and sustaining a product, with a central focus on systems and software engineering. In contrast, Lean has a broader focus on the full product life cycle across the enterprise.

Lean was created to facilitate the production of aerospace products that not only performed well, but also were affordable, through the reduction and elimination of non-value-added activities. It addresses all functions involved in production, such as manufacturing, finance, inventory management, and scheduling. Using techniques such as "value stream mapping," waste may be identified and targeted for removal. For the production of complex products, Lean defines the organizational characteristics that would encourage adaptive improvements and reductions in cost.

So the effort to integrate process improvement in an organization may well involve more than just using an integrated model. Indeed, it should be well understood that the use of a model is not the only way for an organization to approach process improvement. Champions of process improvement need to be open to various approaches and apply the tools that make the most sense in individual circumstances.

In most process-improvement models there is the expectation that processes are first defined and then followed. A similar point may be made in the world of standards. For example, one of the key concepts of an organization that is compliant with the ISO 9000 Quality Management System standard is this: "Say what you do, and do what you say." To meet the requirements of the standard, you need to establish and document how the quality of products and services is attained, and then carry out the procedures and plans as documented. A commitment from organizational management in the form of a quality policy and quality objectives is expected, along with the resources to maintain the quality management system. Measurement and analysis is needed to ensure that products meet requirements and that the quality management system is working.

---

6. There is information on the Web about Lean and the Lean Aerospace Initiative at http://lean.mit.edu/.

A quality management system that meets the requirements of the ISO 9000 standard has various parallels to a model-based process-improvement effort. Process improvement may be directed to business objectives other than quality, but frequently a concern with quality is central. A goal of both CMMI and ISO 9000 is to prevent product defects by identifying the root causes of problems and fixing the processes that contributed to them.[7]

There are many organizations that would like to see more synergy among activities such as CMMI, Lean, and ISO 9000. For example, is it essential that a CMMI appraisal and an ISO 9000 audit be independent events (and investments) within an organization that is working to meet the requirements of both? Probably not. Can the tools of Lean be integrated better into the activities that promote continuous process improvement using CMMI? Probably so. As CMMI moves further into the enterprise, we hope and expect that the champions for process improvement will bring activities such as CMMI, Lean, and ISO 9000 more into line.

2.6 Pearls of Wisdom on Integrating Process Improvement

We have already stressed the importance of several key factors in making integrated process-improvement work, including strong executive support and leadership; making use of best practices, process-improvement champions, and teams that are well prepared for their tasks; and an appraisal strategy that addresses the process-improvement goals of the organization. In this final section of the chapter, we present an additional collection of thoughts on integrated process improvement gleaned from the experience of pioneers and practitioners in many fields. We've divided them into two categories—those that describe practical approaches to integrated process improvement and those that document the benefits and opportunities that result.

---

7. When you use "ISO" and "process" in the same sentence, most people would think of ISO 9000 and quality management. Take note, however, that ISO/IEC 15288 on system life-cycle processes was issued in 2002 after many years of development. It defines 25 life-cycle processes in four categories: enterprise processes, project processes, technical processes, and agreement processes. Quality Management is one of the enterprise processes. We suspect that before long ISO/IEC 15288 will be seen as the primary process standard, and ISO 9000 will be seen as addressing one of those 25 processes.

2.6.1 Practical Advice

- Explicitly identify, recognize, and map legacy process-improvement investments to the integrated effort so they will not be marginalized or duplicated.

- Select and tailor the model to the business. Use local language to describe activities rather than "model-ese."

- An integrated process-improvement group is essential to success.

- Enthusiasm is a plus, but manage "experts and zealots" carefully—they can sometimes raise more barriers than they overcome.

- Integrate process-improvement reviews into project management reviews.

- Capture the hearts of middle managers.

- The devil's in the details—make sure that implementation is as strong and coherent as the vision.

- Train to organizational processes rather than to models, so that model changes in the future will have smaller effects on the organization.

- Continuous appraisal of projects emphasizes proactive process improvement, replaces the audit philosophy, and decreases the fear factor.

- Maintain a consistent appraisal team for consistent findings.

- Process teams of real process users can force the process definitions to be user-friendly and address real-world multidiscipline concerns.

- A well-designed cost accounting system facilitates the collection of useful process metrics data, particularly for cross-functional activities.

- Make a focused, continuing effort to identify common process opportunities.

- Using a "workshop" approach to process engineering can result in a tenfold increase in productivity for typical meetings.

- The early use of pilot projects with a draft version of an integrated process allows for testing and fine-tuning of the process. A good cross-section of projects gives early feedback on where improvements are needed.

- Don't try to integrate disciplines that differ widely in their process maturity.

- Fight the "Not invented here" syndrome. "Steal with pride" is a better motto.
- Focus on the development of a straightforward and consistent method for tailoring standard processes, especially for organizations that include highly diverse project domains.
- John Donne was right—"No man is an island." Remember that any change in an integrated environment will probably affect at least one other group.

2.6.2 Benefits and Opportunities

- Integrated process improvement identifies many cross-organizational issues and provides a unique opportunity to address them.
- Integrated process improvement prevents suboptimization of processes in a cross-discipline environment.
- Integrated process improvement yields more accurate project planning and reduced cycle time.
- Integrated process improvement increases buy-in from all affected organizations.
- Integrated process improvement provides an opportunity to implement integrated engineering assets.

Chesapeake Bay Area
LandSat 5 Thematic Mapper (1998)
NASA—Goddard Space Flight Center
Scientific Visualization Studio

Part II

The CMMI Models

The Chesapeake Bay is a highly productive economic engine. It is also a fragile ecosystem. Its best use and long-term prospects depend on making decisions that are based on an understanding of the complex relationships that exist between nature and humans.

Similarly, CMMI products are complex structures containing multiple layers of information. To achieve the highest benefit, CMMI users need to be aware of this complexity and the subtle relationships between and across the information layers. In Part II, we discuss the CMMI architecture and components, to help the reader more clearly understand how CMMI is structured, and how its parts relate to each other and to integrated process improvement as a whole.

Part II Contents

Chapter 3. The CMMI Concept

> *In which the reader is introduced to CMMI—its contents, objectives, limitations, accomplishments, and history.*

Chapter 4. CMMI Content

> *In which we describe the various elements and materials found in the CMMI models. Their relative importance is discussed to some extent, and the locations of the materials are elucidated.*

Chapter 5. CMMI Representations

In which the authors describe the two model representations—staged and continuous—and explain how they are accomplished within CMMI. A discussion of how the continuous representation can approximate the staged representation is presented.

Chapter 6. CMMI Dimensions for Measuring Improvement

In which the authors explain the manner by which the CMMI models—in both representations—guide and measure the improvement of processes. Both the capability and maturity dimensions are addressed. The concept of generic practices is introduced and their role in CMMI is explained.

Chapter 7. CMMI Process Areas

In which the CMMI process dimension is described in detail, so that the practitioner may understand the relationship between the goals, practices, and improvement dimensions.

Chapter 3

The CMMI Concept

*It must be remembered that there is nothing more difficult to plan,
more uncertain of success, nor more dangerous to manage than the
creation of a new order of things. For the initiator has the enmity
of all who would profit by the preservation of the old institutions, and
merely lukewarm defenders in those who would gain by the new order.*
Machiavelli, *The Prince* (1513)

*In this age, which believes that there is a short cut to everything,
the greatest lesson to be learned is that the most difficult
way is, in the long run, the easiest.*
Henry Miller, *The Books in My Life* (1957)

The implementation of integrated process improvement in an organization is possible using two or more single-discipline models. There are many advantages, however, in having just one model that covers multiple disciplines. For this reason, the U.S. Department of Defense—specifically, the Deputy Under Secretary of Defense (Science and Technology)—teamed up with the National Defense Industrial Association (NDIA) to jointly sponsor the development of Capability Maturity Model Integration (CMMI). Working with the Software Engineering Institute (SEI) at Carnegie Mellon University, this effort produced the first integrated CMMI models in 2000, together with associated appraisal and training materials; 2002 saw the release of CMMI version 1.1.

This chapter begins with an overview of the kinds of information and guidance found in CMMI models. For those not familiar with any of the source models, it provides a good introduction to CMMI's scope and usefulness. We follow the overview with a discussion of CMMI objectives and history. Next is information on the source models that were used in creating CMMI. Finally, we describe the CMMI project organization.

3.1 An Overview of CMMI

The CMMI Product Suite contains an enormous amount of information and guidance to help your organization improve its processes. But how does this information help? To answer this question, we note that essentially two kinds of materials are contained in the CMMI models:

1. Materials to help you evaluate the content of your processes— information that is essential to your technical, support, and managerial activities.

2. Materials to help you improve process performance—information that is used to increase the capability of your organization's activities.

We start with a brief look at each of these.

3.1.1 Process Content

CMMI provides guidance for your managerial processes. For example, you should establish and maintain a plan for managing your work, and make sure everyone involved is committed to performing and supporting the plan. When you plan, you should establish exactly how you develop and maintain cost, schedule, and product estimates. When you do the work that you plan, you should compare the performance and progress to the plan and take corrective actions if you find actual and planned results out of sync. You should establish and maintain agreements with your suppliers and make sure that you both satisfy them. There is information on managing project risk and on creating and managing teams, as well.

CMMI guidance on technical matters includes ways to develop, elaborate, and manage requirements, and to develop technical solutions that meet those requirements. It reminds you that the integration of product components depends on good interface information, and it needs to be planned and verified. You should make sure that the products and services you develop are consistent with the requirements and satisfy the customer's needs through verification and validation practices.

Support processes for technical and managerial activities are also addressed. You should always manage the versions and configurations of work products as well as end products and services. You should have methods of ensuring that the processes you have defined are being followed and the products you are developing meet the quality specifications you have established. You need to decide what information is important to you and establish ways to measure and track it. In some cases, you need to plan ways to resolve issues formally. You may need to figure out the root cause of serious problems with your products or key processes.

3.1.2 Process Improvement

Now let's look at improving the processes that you've established. The improvement information in CMMI models includes the creation of a viable, improvable process infrastructure. To build this infrastructure, CMMI includes ways to get your organization to focus more on defining and following its processes. Through training and standardization you can make sure everyone knows their roles and how to execute them in the process. You learn to use the measurement data you collect to improve your process performance, innovate when processes need to evolve, and ensure your ability to meet changing needs.

Processes need to be planned just like projects, and it helps if the organization has given some weight and validity to it through policy. You need to make sure that resources are available for trained, empowered people to perform the process. Those with an interest in a process need to be identified and involved. Work products and the process documentation should be controlled, and the progress against the process plan tracked, as well. There should be someone responsible for objectively evaluating that the process is being followed, and management should be briefed periodically on the process performance.

Processes become more capable when they are standardized across the organization and their performance is monitored against historical data. This way you can detect variation in performance early enough to address it less expensively. And ultimately, the process should be continuously improving through identifying the root causes of variability and innovative ways to fulfill its objectives.

3.1.3 CMMI and Business Objectives

In Chapter 1 we identified some common business objectives found in organizations. Based on this brief overview of CMMI's process content and concern with process improvement, how could you expect CMMI to specifically help your organization to meet such objectives? Let's look at each objective individually.

- *Produce quality products or services.* The process-improvement concept in CMMI models evolved out of the Deming, Juran, and Crosby quality paradigm: Quality products are a result of quality processes. CMMI has a strong focus on quality-related activities including requirements management, quality assurance, verification, and validation.

- *Create value for the stockholders.* Mature organizations are more likely to make better cost and revenue estimates than those with less maturity, and then perform in line with those estimates. CMMI supports quality products, predictable schedules, and effective measurement to support management in making accurate and defensible forecasts. This process maturity can guard against project performance problems that could weaken the value of the organization in the eyes of investors.

- *Be an employer of choice.* Watts Humphrey has said, "Quality work is not done by accident; it is done only by skilled and motivated people."[1] CMMI emphasizes training, both in disciplines and in process. Experience has shown that organizations with mature processes have far less turnover than immature organizations. Engineers in particular are more comfortable in an organization where there is a sense of cohesion and competence.

- *Enhance customer satisfaction.* Meeting cost and schedule targets with high-quality products that are validated against customer needs is a good formula for customer satisfaction. CMMI addresses all of these ingredients through its emphasis on planning, monitoring, and measuring, and the improved predictability that comes with more capable processes.

---

1. Humphrey, W. *Winning with Software*, Boston: Addison-Wesley, 2002.

- *Increase market share.* Market share is a result of many factors, including quality products and services, name identification, pricing, and image. Clearly, customer satisfaction is a central factor, and in a marketplace, having satisfied customers can be contagious. Customers like to deal with suppliers who have a reputation for meeting their commitments. CMMI improves estimation and lowers process variability to enable better, more accurate bids that are demonstrably achievable. It also contributes to meeting essential quality goals.

- *Implement cost savings and best practices.* Processes that are documented, measured, and continuously improved are perfect candidates for becoming best practices, resulting in cost savings for the organization. CMMI encourages measurement as a managerial tool. By using the historical data collected to support schedule estimation, an organization can identify and widely deploy practices that work, and eliminate those that don't.

- *Gain an industry-wide recognition for excellence.* The best way to develop a reputation for excellence is to consistently perform well on projects, delivering quality products and services within cost and schedule parameters. Having processes that conform to CMMI requirements can enhance that reputation. The results of CMMI appraisals can be compared across a company, a corporation, or an industry. Many organizations proudly advertise their CMMI-defined maturity rating alongside their ISO 9000 registration.

As you can see, CMMI comprises information that can make a significant impact on your organization and on the achievement of your business objectives. In the next sections we'll discuss a different set of objectives, those that led to the development of CMMI itself. In addition, we explore the models that were used as the basis for the information CMMI contains and something of the structure in place to manage it. More detail on CMMI contents is provided in subsequent chapters.

3.2 CMMI Objectives

While CMMI has many business-related benefits, the project as defined by its sponsors was directed toward the development of more efficient and effective process-improvement models. The CMMI project had both initial and longer-term objectives. The initial objective (represented in version 1.1 of the CMMI Product Suite) was to integrate three specific process-improvement models: software, systems engineering, and integrated product development.[2]

This integration was intended to reduce the cost of implementing multidiscipline model-based process improvement by:

- Eliminating inconsistencies.
- Reducing duplication.
- Increasing clarity and understanding.
- Providing common terminology.
- Providing consistent style.
- Establishing uniform construction rules.
- Maintaining common components.
- Assuring consistency with ISO/IEC 15504.
- Being sensitive to the implications for legacy efforts.

The longer-term objective was to lay a foundation for the later addition of other disciplines (such as supplier sourcing, manufacturing, acquisition, or safety and security) to CMMI. Figure 3-1 illustrates these objectives and the product line approach developed by the CMMI Team.[3]

To facilitate both current and future model integration, the CMMI Team created an automated, extensible framework that can house model components, training material components, and appraisal materials. Defined rules govern the potential addition of more disciplines into this framework.

From the start, the CMMI Team had to find an acceptable balance between competing requirements relating to change. The task of integration, which by its very nature requires change from each of the original single-discipline models, meant that all model users could expect new ways of thinking about process improvement to be needed in a CMMI environment. At the same time, an equally strong requirement called for protecting the investments in process improvement made by

---

2. CMMI-SW designates the CMMI model that contains the discipline of Software; CMMI-SE/SW designates the model that contains the disciplines of Systems Engineering and Software; CMMI-SE/SW/IPPD indicates the model that adds materials for Integrated Product and Process Development to CMMI-SE/SW. Extending the name with /SS indicates inclusion of the Supplier Sourcing material.

3. By the phrase "CMMI Team" we include all who were and are involved in the CMMI project, including the Steering Group, the Product Development Team (and later the Product Team), and the Stakeholder Group. See Section 3.4 for a description of the CMMI Project Organization.

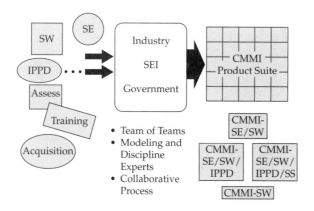

Figure 3-1: *The CMMI product line approach*

former users of those models, which meant controlling the introduction of new materials for each discipline. Judging from the significant rate of adoption throughout the world, we believe the CMMI Team has achieved an appropriate balance between old and new.

CMMI Milestones

1997	CMMI initiated by U.S. Department of Defense and NDIA
1998	First team meeting held
1999	Concept of operations released
	First pilot completed
2000	Additional pilots completed
	CMMI-SE/SW version 1.0 released for initial use
	CMMI-SE/SW/IPPD version 1.0 released for initial use
	CMMI-SE/SW/IPPD/SS version 1.0 released for piloting
2002	CMMI-SE/SW version 1.1 released
	CMMI-SE/SW/IPPD version 1.1 released
	CMMI-SE/SW/IPPD/SS version 1.1 released
	CMMI-SW version 1.1 released

3.3 The Three Source Models

To truly appreciate the significance of the CMMI accomplishments, you need to understand a bit of the history that led up to the development of the CMMI Product Suite. Of primary importance are the stories of the source models. Table 3-1 summarizes the three source models for CMMI-SE/SW/IPPD.

Table 3-1: *Source Models for CMMI-SE/SW/IPPD*

Model Discipline	Source Model
Software	SW-CMM, draft version 2(c)
Systems Engineering	EIA/IS 731
Integrated Product and Process Development	IPD-CMM, version 0.98

3.3.1 The CMM for Software

The character of software development sometimes seems closer to mathematics and art than it does to most other engineering disciplines. Software is inherently an intangible, intellectual development medium. No laws of physics govern its behavior; it is both marvelously and dangerously malleable. For this reason, it is critical that mature disciplines and processes be applied when working with software.

Software engineering and process management have been intimately associated since the pioneering work of Ron Radice and Richard Phillips in Watts Humphrey's group at IBM in the 1980s.[4] Basing their work on the tenets of the quality movement, Radice and Phillips led the effort to capture the best practices of successful software developers and then organize those best practices in a way that helped struggling organizations get a handle on their processes and improve them. Given the nature of software development, it was not surprising that the large majority of the practices related to management discipline and processes.

---

4. Radice, R. A., and R. W. Phillips. *Software Engineering, an Industrial Approach, Vol. 1.* Englewood Cliffs, NJ: Prentice Hall, 1988. Radice, R. A., J. T. Harding, P. E. Munnis, and R. W. Phillips. "A Programming Process Study." *IBM Systems Journal*, 2/3, 1999.

> ## *Software Engineering*
>
> As defined in IEEE Standard 610.12, *software engineering* is the application of a systematic, disciplined, quantifiable approach to the development, operation, and maintenance of software—that is, the application of engineering to software.[5]

In 1986, Watts Humphrey, the SEI, and the Mitre Corporation responded to a request by the U.S. federal government to create a way of evaluating the software capability of its contractors. The group used IBM's concepts to create a software maturity framework, a questionnaire, and two appraisal methods. Over the next few years, this work was continued and refined.

In 1991, the SEI published the CMM for Software version 1.0, a model that describes the principles and practices underlying software process maturity. The CMM is organized to help software organizations improve along an evolutionary path, growing from an ad hoc, chaotic environment toward mature, disciplined software processes. The CMM was used and evaluated for two years, then revised and released as version 1.1 in 1993.[6] A similar revision was planned for 1997 as version 2.0;[7] this version was developed but never released as an independent model. However, the good work did not go to waste: The proposed revision was used as the source for the CMMI integration effort. In addition, two documents regarding software appraisals were used: the CMM Appraisal Framework, version 1.0,[8] and the CMM-Based Appraisal for Internal Process Improvement (CBA IPI): Method Description.[9]

---

5. *IEEE Standard Glossary of Software Engineering Terminology. IEEE Standard 610.12–1990.* New York: Institute of Electrical and Electronics Engineers, 1990.

6. Paulk, Mark C., et al. *Capability Maturity Model for Software, Version 1.1 (CMU/SEI-93-TR-24; also ESC-TR-93-177).* Pittsburgh: Software Engineering Institute, Carnegie Mellon University, February 1993. Paulk, M. et al., *The Capability Maturity Model: Guidelines for Improving the Software Process,* Reading, MA: Addison-Wesley, 1995.

7. For more on the history of the CMM for Software, see Paulk, Mark C. "The Evolution of the SEI's Capability Maturity Model for Software." *Software Process Improvement and Practice,* 1995, pp. 3–15.

8. Masters, S., and C. Bothwell. *CMM Appraisal Framework (CMU/SEI-95-TR-001).* Pittsburgh: Software Engineering Institute, Carnegie Mellon University, February 1995.

9. Dunaway, D., and S. Masters. *CMM-Based Appraisal for Internal Process Improvement (CBA IPI): Method Description (CMU/SEI-96-TR-007).* Pittsburgh: Software Engineering Institute, Carnegie Mellon University, April 1996.

The IEEE definition of software engineering extends software engineering's scope beyond the primary material contained in the CMM for Software to include software-related topics such as requirements elicitation, installation, operation, and maintenance. The CMMI model covers these areas in more detail through inclusion of appropriate material from EIA 731.

3.3.2 The Systems Engineering Capability Model

Systems engineering integrates all of the system-related disciplines so that systems meet business and technical needs in the most effective way, while striving to minimize local optimization and maximize return on investment. Another way of envisioning systems engineering is as the application of a set of rigorous engineering techniques to the solution of a complex technical problem.

Systems Engineering

INCOSE defines *systems engineering* as "an interdisciplinary approach and means to enable the realization of successful systems."[10]

It is difficult to fully understand the scope of systems engineering without looking at the various specialty disciplines associated with it. In *Essentials of Project and Systems Engineering Management*, Howard Eisner lists 30 key elements of systems engineering. These elements include such diverse areas as mission engineering, architectural design, life-cycle costing, alternatives analysis, technical data management, operations and maintenance, integrated logistics support, and reengineering.[11]

The systems engineering material in CMMI has a complex history. In a modern-day "Tale of Two Capability Models," two organizations undertook to model systems engineering practices. In August 1995, the Enterprise Process Improvement Collaboration (EPIC), a group of

---

10. INCOSE Winter Workshop 1996, January 1996.
11. Eisner, Howard. *Essentials of Project and Systems Engineering Management.* New York: Wiley Interscience, 1997.

industry, academic, and government organizations, released the Systems Engineering Capability Maturity Model (SE-CMM). EPIC enlisted the SEI and architect Roger Bate to lead the development. The team pulled its systems engineering expertise primarily from aerospace and defense industry corporations and from the Software Productivity Consortium. The result was a model based on the appraisal model architecture contained in draft versions of ISO/IEC 15504 that addressed engineering, project, process, and organization practices.[12]

Around the same time that the SE-CMM was under development, INCOSE created a checklist for evaluating the capabilities of systems engineering organizations based on various engineering standards. Over time, this checklist evolved into a full-blown capability model known as the Systems Engineering Capability Assessment Model (SECAM). SECAM extended the SPICE concepts of a continuous model but focused more specifically on systems engineering practices than the SE-CMM, using ANSI/EIA 632, "Processes for Engineering a System," as the fundamental reference.

Needless to say, an environment with two models developed by two reputable organizations that purported to address the same issues was ripe for a model war. Which model would emerge as the "standard" by which organizations could be evaluated? After a year of heated discussions, in 1996 EPIC and INCOSE agreed to work together under the auspices of the Government Electronic and Information Technology Association (GEIA) of the Electronic Industries Alliance (EIA), with the goal of merging the two models into a single EIA standard. The result was the interim standard EIA/IS 731, Systems Engineering Capability Model (SECM).[13] By issuing the interim standard, the systems engineering community could apply a single, common description of systems engineering processes to the CMMI project.

---

12. In January 1993, an international working group (WG 10) was formed as part of Subcommittee 7 (SC7) of the ISO/IEC Joint Technical Committee 1 (JTC1) to create a standard for software process assessment. Piloting of working drafts was accomplished through a project called SPICE (Software Process Improvement and Capability dEtermination). The combined effort of WG 10 and the SPICE project resulted in the development of ISO/IEC 15504 as a draft standard. At the time of writing the Second Edition of this book, the draft standard is nearing approval as an international standard, and it has been refocused to address "Process Assessment" generally, not limited just to software process assessment.

13. *EIA Interim Standard, Systems Engineering Capability-EIA/IS 731* (Part 1: Model, EIA/IS 731–1, version 1.0; Part 2: Appraisal Method, EIA/IS 731–2, version 1.0), 1999. This was converted to a full standard, EIA 731, in 2002.

Systems engineering in CMMI remains heavily influenced by EIA 731. While echoes of the controversy between SECM and SE-CMM found voice in CMMI discussions, the resulting systems engineering content reflects an even stronger evolution of the original concepts. It preserves some of the innovations of EIA 731 while providing a more consistent underlying architecture compatible with the emerging ISO standards.[14] EIA 731 includes both the SECM model (Part 1) and an appraisal method (Part 2).

3.3.3 The Integrated Product Development CMM

The source model for Integrated Product and Process Development (IPPD) was a draft of the Integrated Product Development CMM, known as IPD-CMM version 0.98. This model had been developed almost to the point of its initial formal release when the CMMI project began in 1998.

From the outset, the CMMI Steering Group wanted to include the concept of Integrated Product and Process Development in the CMMI Product Suite. This concept was fundamental to many of the large member corporations of NDIA, and it was strongly supported by the Department of Defense (DOD).[15] Unfortunately, the definition of IPPD used in the CMMI requirements document was derived from the DOD's experience with integrated operation of government system acquisition programs—and acquisition was not an initial discipline for CMMI. This discrepancy led to some difficulty in addressing the IPPD tenets within the CMMI scope. Adding to the confusion was a lack of consensus in the industry (and among members of the development team) regarding the fundamental concepts and best practices of integrated product development. Because it represented a relatively new means of organizing and accomplishing engineering work, there were nearly as many definitions as there were organizations.

This problem was not unique to CMMI. Indeed, the team established by EPIC to develop the IPD-CMM, which was supported by many of the same members of the SE-CMM team, struggled with IPPD concepts for more than two years before being subsumed into the CMMI effort. The final draft IPD-CMM was established as a source document for CMMI, but the draft never achieved the status of a finished product.

---

14. For example, see ISO/IEC 15504 and ISO/IEC 15288.
15. The U.S. Air Force played a significant role in the development of the IPD-CMM.

Integrated Product and Process Development

CMMI defines *Integrated Product and Process Development* as a systematic approach to product development that achieves a timely collaboration of relevant stakeholders throughout the product life cycle to better satisfy customer needs.

IPPD emphasizes the involvement of stakeholders from all technical and business functions throughout the life cycle—customers, suppliers, and developers of both the product and product-related processes, such as testing and evaluation, manufacturing, support, training, marketing, purchasing, financial, contracting, and disposal processes. Clearly, implementing IPPD affects more than an organization's engineering processes and practices. Because it is essentially a way of doing business, it may radically change organizational structure and modify leadership behavior.

3.4 CMMI Project Organization

During the development phase that led to the initial CMMI materials, the project was organized with a Steering Group, a Product Development Team, and a Stakeholder Group. In all, it involved the efforts of over 200 people during a period of more than six years. The three groups comprised representatives from industry, government, and the SEI. Representatives of the disciplines whose models were to be integrated into CMMI were included in all three groups.

The Steering Group produced a list of requirements for CMMI, which was reviewed by the Stakeholder Group and subsequently used by the Product Development Team to guide its creation of the CMMI products. The Product Development Team was a cross-discipline group created for the initial development work; it was charged with ensuring that the viewpoints and interests of each discipline were adequately considered in the integration process. The Stakeholder Group reviewed the initial draft CMMI materials, with its work being followed by a public review of a second round of draft materials, prior to the version 1.0 release in late 2000. Taking advantage of early feedback from version 1.0 users, and responding to over 1,500 change requests, version 1.1 of the Product Suite was released in 2002.

The CMMI Team

The following organizations supplied members to the CMMI Team: ADP Inc., AT&T Labs, BAE Systems, Boeing, Comarco Systems, Computer Sciences Corporation, Defense Logistics Agency, EER Systems, Ericsson Canada, Ernst and Young, General Dynamics, Harris Corporation, Honeywell, IBM, Institute for Defense Analyses, Integrated System Diagnostics, KPMG Consulting, Litton PRC, Lockheed Martin, MitoKen Solutions, Motorola, Northrop Grumman, Pacific Bell, Q-Labs, Raytheon, Rockwell Collins, Science Applications International Corporation, Siemens, Software Engineering Institute, Software Productivity Corporation, Sverdrup Corporation, TeraQuest, THALES, TRW, U.S. Federal Aviation Administration, U.S. National Reconnaissance Office, U.S. National Security Agency, U.S. Air Force, U.S. Army, and U.S. Navy.

The cross-discipline team that produced the initial CMMI models included members with backgrounds in software engineering, systems engineering, and Integrated Product and Process Development. Most engineering organizations maintain these skills, but the manner in which they are aligned and interact varies across organizations. Thus the CMMI Team not only had to resolve differences among the three source models, but also had to bridge the cultural, linguistic, and professional differences separating engineering specialties and organizations. The bridges that had to be built in constructing the CMMI models serve as precursors of those that users of the models will need to construct to successfully support integrated process improvement and process appraisal.

During the CMMI development effort, the team actively sought to keep balanced membership across the three disciplines. This move was supported by the strong interest espoused by the software and systems engineering communities. Thanks to the wide acceptance of the CMM for Software, strong advocacy was provided by the SEI and organizations that had used the model, understood its value, and wanted to see that value preserved in the integrated CMMI models. Likewise, in the systems engineering world, the International Council on Systems Engineering (INCOSE) advocated inclusion of systems engineering practices. Even the Integrated Product and Process Development community was represented on the CMMI Team, albeit with members voicing a somewhat wider range of views on how IPPD should be handled than did the more established discipline representatives. In the end, this team of experienced and active people, each of whom brought his or her specific expertise and preferences to the table, came together to create the CMMI Product Suite.

Once the development phase of the initial CMMI Product Suite was completed, a new organizational structure was established. That is, the CMMI Product Development Team evolved into the CMMI Product Team. This team has access to expert groups for software, systems engineering, IPPD, supplier sourcing, appraisals, and the core CMMI components. A configuration control board was established to guide CMMI evolution, and the SEI was named as the Steward of the CMMI Product Suite. In its role as Steward, SEI is responsible for maintenance and support of CMMI. As time goes on, new cross-functional teams of experts will be required to handle revisions of existing products and the subsequent work of adding disciplines to the CMMI framework.

Figure 3-2 shows the current CMMI project organization.

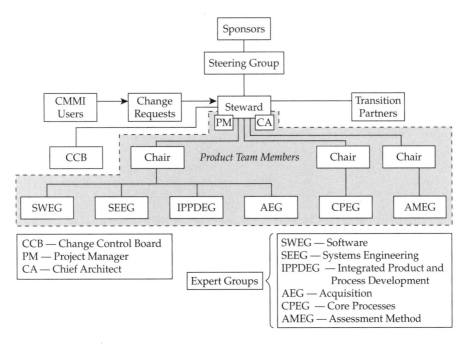

Figure 3-2: *Current CMMI project organization*

Chapter 4

CMMI Content

All that is gold does not glitter,
Not all who wander are lost.
J. R. R. Tolkien, *The Fellowship of the Ring* (1954)

I have gathered a posie of other men's flowers,
and nothing but the thread that binds them is mine own.
John Bartlett, Preface to *Familiar Quotations* (1901)

What's in a Capability Maturity Model Integration (CMMI) model, and how can your organization use it? At several hundred pages in length, the CMMI models seem formidable even to the most experienced process-improvement champion. With just a little understanding of how the models are put together and what kind of material is presented, however, you can begin to navigate the depths of CMMI with confidence. This chapter describes the types of information you can find in the CMMI models and notes the location where you can find it. You will also learn to interpret the importance of the various types of information.

4.1 Process Areas

The fundamental organizational feature of all the CMMI models is the "process area." Not everything related to processes and process improvement is included in a process-improvement model. Like its predecessor models, CMMI selects only the most important topics for process improvement and then groups those topics into "areas." This classification results in CMMI version 1.1 models with a relatively small set of process areas: 22 in CMMI-SE/SW and CMMI-SW, 24 in CMMI-SE/SW/IPPD, and 25 in CMMI-SE/SW/IPPD/SS.

We will discuss the CMMI process areas in detail in Chapter 7. For now, to introduce the concept of a process area, let's look at one and see what it covers. For our example, we'll use Requirements Management.

Within both systems and software engineering, it is widely believed that the management of the product requirements is a central area of concern during any development effort. Experience has demonstrated that a failure to adequately identify the requirements and manage changes to them is a major cause of projects not meeting their cost, schedule, or quality objectives. This experience justifies collecting information related to the management of requirements into a major model component—that is, a process area. Users of the model should, therefore, focus on this process area to establish the process area capability relating to the management of requirements.

As stated in the model, the *purpose* of the Requirements Management process area is "to manage the requirements of the project's products and product components and to identify inconsistencies between those requirements and the project's plans and work products." In addition to this *purpose*, the process area has *goals* that describe the results of a successful requirements management process and *practices* that can help achieve these goals. There is also a great deal of explanatory and "how to" material meant to provide some concrete help with managing requirements. That's pretty much a process area in a nutshell.

While the source models all had concepts similar to what CMMI includes as a process area, they (of course) used different names for them. The first task was to define the set of process areas for the integrated model—that is, which to pick, which to merge, which to drop? On the surface, this endeavor might seem straightforward. In reality, the subtleties of the interactions within and among process areas made this task one of the most perplexing challenges faced by the CMMI Team. One significant contributor to this challenge was the way in which engineering development was treated in the source models.

The Software CMM focused primarily on process management. Among the "key process areas" in the model, only one specifically targets the core engineering tasks, which range from the analysis of software requirements at the front end of development, to software integration and testing at the concluding end. This key process area was called Software Product Engineering in the Software CMM, and it dealt with tasks specific to software development. All of the other SW-CMM key process areas were written such that they could easily be applied to development work other than software. Along with the success of the Software CMM in improving software development, this flexibility may explain the interest in applying the CMM concepts to disciplines beyond software; much of what was believed to be good with the Software CMM had a utility that was not restricted to just the software area.

For systems engineers, a more detailed examination of the engineering development steps was deemed necessary to apply these modeling concepts to their broader scope of responsibility. In the Systems Engineering Capability Model (EIA 731), 7 of the 19 "focus areas" (more than one third of the focus areas) fall within the systems engineering technical category. Clearly, for the team of systems engineers who created this model, the capability of an organization in the technical areas deserved equal footing with its capability in process management and support areas.

To achieve an integrated model that addressed both systems engineering and software concerns, compromise and change would clearly be necessary. The CMMI Team decided to include six engineering process areas that applied to both systems and software. This choice was made to preserve the value of past efforts to improve systems engineering, and it reflected the judgment that many in the software community would, in fact, welcome more attention on the engineering tasks. The result might expand the scope of concern for past users of the software model, but it should in no way reduce or undercut the value of prior process-improvement efforts for software.

Due to this and other decisions to keep the valued parts of each of the source models, the resulting integrated model was larger than any one of its sources. This expanded scope will certainly be of value in providing additional guidance for process improvement. Nevertheless, it increases the challenge in providing process appraisal methods that are accurate and reliable, yet not overly time-consuming, expensive, and intrusive. We will say more about this appraisal issue (and others) in Chapter 10.

4.2 Content Classification

Any process-improvement model must, of necessity, include a scale relating to the importance and role of the materials contained in the model. In the CMMI models, a distinction is drawn between the terms "required," "expected," and "informative." The most important material is *required;* these items are essential to the model and to an understanding of what is needed for process improvement and demonstrations of conformance to the model. Second in importance is the *expected* material; these items may not be fully essential, and in some instances they may not be present in an organization that successfully uses the model. Nevertheless, expected material is presumed to play a central role in process improvement; such items are a strong indicator that the required components are being achieved. Third in importance (and largest in quantity) is *informative* material; these items constitute the majority of the model. The informative materials provide useful guidance for process improvement, and in many instances they may offer clarification regarding the intended meaning of the required and expected components.

If you are seeking only a quick overview of a CMMI model, one recommended approach is to review all of the required material. This strategy may be thought of as an "executive overview" level. For a still high-level but slightly more detailed review, you could focus on the combined required and expected materials. This approach may be considered a "manager overview" level. With either type of review, the best place to look is Appendix D (Required and Expected Model Elements) of the CMMI-SE/SW/IPPD/SS, version 1.1, model, or Appendixes A and B of this book. Here the first two categories of model components are joined (with a very minimal amount of informative material) to present only the most essential elements of the model.

4.3 Required Materials

The sole required component of the CMMI models is the "goal." A goal represents a desirable end state, the achievement of which indicates that a certain degree of project and process control has been achieved. When a goal is unique to a single process area, it is called a "specific goal" (SG). In contrast, when a goal may apply across all of the process areas, it is called a "generic goal" (GG). Table 4-1 lists four examples of specific goals.

Each process area has between one and four specific goals; the entire CMMI-SE/SW/IPPD/SS model (version 1.1) includes a total of 55 specific goals.

Table 4-1: *Specific Goals for Four Process Areas*

Process Area	Specific Goal
Requirements Management	REQM SG 1: Requirements are managed and inconsistencies with project plans and work products are identified.
Project Monitoring and Control	PMC SG 2: Corrective actions are managed to closure when the project's performance or results deviate significantly from the plan.
Organizational Process Performance	OPP SG 1: Baselines and models that characterize the expected process performance of the organization's set of standard processes are established and maintained.
Causal Analysis and Resolution	CAR SG 2: Root causes of defects and other problems are systematically addressed to prevent their future occurrence.

As is evident from the four examples in Table 4-1, a goal statement is fairly succinct. In each case we should inquire what it might mean in practical terms by looking into the model in greater depth. This effort does not (either explicitly or implicitly) increase the amount of required material in the process area, but it may provide for a better understanding of the specific goal statements.

In contrast to a specific goal, a generic goal has a scope that crosses all of the process areas. Because their application is so broad, the wording of a generic goal tends to be somewhat more abstract than the wording of a specific goal. Consider, for example, GG 2: "The process is institutionalized as a managed process." To better understand what this statement means, let's start with the CMMI Glossary (CMMI-SE/SW/IPPD/SS, version 1.1, Appendix C). There we find the definition of "institutionalization." In Chapter 3, we find the definition of a "managed process." Both definitions are provided in Table 4-2.[1]

Taken together, these two definitions provide much more detail than the short statement of the generic goal itself. Nevertheless, even with these definitions, questions about practical meaning may linger. What

Table 4-2: *Definitions Related to CMMI Generic Goal 2*

CMMI Glossary Term	CMMI Definition
Institutionalization	The ingrained way of doing business that an organization follows routinely as part of its corporate culture.
Managed process	A "managed process" is a performed process that is planned and executed in accordance with policy; employs skilled people having adequate resources to produce controlled outputs; involves relevant stakeholders; is monitored, controlled, and reviewed; and is evaluated for adherence to its process description.

---

1. In the book *CMMI: Guidelines for Process Integration and Product Improvement* (Chrissis, M., M. Konrad, and S. Shrum, Boston: Addison-Wesley, 2003), all of the terminology and definitions are found together in the Glossary.

are the key features of the "ingrained way of doing business"? How is a process "evaluated for adherence to process description"?

Although the goal is the only required element in a CMMI model, no statement of any goal—specific or generic—can be fully understood without exploring more of the model. The first expansion of that understanding comes by looking at the expected components.

4.4 Expected Materials

The only expected component of the CMMI models is the statement of a "practice." A practice represents the "expected" means of achieving a goal. Every practice in the CMMI models is mapped to exactly one goal. A practice is not a required component, however; a specific organization may possess demonstrated means of achieving a goal that do not rely on the performance of all the practices that are mapped to that goal. That is, "alternative" practices may provide an equally useful way of reaching the goal. With the models that preceded CMMI, the use of alternative practices was rare. Whether that will hold true in the future with the CMMI models remains to be seen. While CMMI practices (as a class) are not required, they act as strong indicators that the goals to which they are mapped are being met. However, alternative practices are acceptable when organizations need adequate flexibility in special or unusual situations.

When a practice is unique to a single process area, it is called a "specific practice" (SP). When a practice may apply across all of the process areas, it is called a "generic practice" (GP).

Table 4-3 details several examples of specific practices, together with the goal to which they are mapped. Note that a goal, which represents an end state, is always written in the passive voice, whereas a practice, as a means to achieve the goal, is always written in the active voice.

Between two and seven specific practices are mapped to each specific goal; the entire CMMI-SE/SW/IPPD/SS version 1.1 model includes a total of 189 specific practices, which are mapped to the 55 specific goals.[2]

---

2. The continuous representation includes 189 specific practices; the staged representation includes 185. The discrepancy arises because, when the continuous representation includes both a "base" practice and an "advanced" practice on the same topic, only the advanced practice appears in the staged representation. See Section 7.3 on the Engineering process areas for further information.

Table 4-3: *Specific Practices Associated with Specific Goals*

Specific Goal	Specific Practice
REQM SG 1: Requirements are managed and inconsistencies with project plans and work products are identified.	REQM SP 1.1-1[3]: Develop an understanding with the requirements providers on the meaning of the requirements.
PMC SG 2: Corrective actions are managed to closure when the project's performance or results deviate significantly from the plan.	PMC SP 2.1-1: Collect and analyze the issues and determine the corrective actions necessary to address the issues.
OPP SG 1: Baselines and models that characterize the expected process performance of the organization's set of standard processes are established and maintained.	OPP SP 1.2-1: Establish and maintain definitions of the measures that are to be included in the organization's process performance analyses.
CAR SG 2: Root causes of defects and other problems are systematically addressed to prevent their future occurrence.	CAR SP 2.2-1: Evaluate the effect of changes on process performance.

When the specific practices mapped to a specific goal are taken as a unit, they provide additional insight into how the goal should be understood. Table 4-4 shows one goal together with its full complement of practices. In this example, establishing and maintaining work-product baselines involves identifying configuration items, implementing a configuration and change management system, and establishing baselines for both internal and external use.

In contrast to a specific practice, a generic practice has a scope that crosses all of the process areas. For example, one generic practice that is

---

3. The numbering for this practice is SP 1.1-1 in the continuous representation, and SP 1.1 in the staged representation. The addition of "-1" in the continuous representation indicates a capability level, which is not used in the staged representation. Chapter 6 describes the two representations and the concept of capability level.

Table 4-4: *Specific Goal and Specific Practices for Configuration Management*

Specific Goal	Specific Practices
Configuration Management (CM) SG 1: Baselines of identified work products are established.	CM SP 1.1-1: Identify the configuration items, components, and related work products that will be placed under configuration-management. CM SP 1.2-1: Establish and maintain a configuration management and change management system for controlling work products. CM SP 1.3-1: Create or release baselines for internal use and for delivery to the customer.

mapped to the generic goal to institutionalize a managed process (GG 2) addresses the training of people. Consider GP 2.5: "Train the people performing or supporting the process as needed." In other words, an organization and its projects are expected to provide the training that is needed when it follows a managed process in such a way that the process becomes institutionalized. For each process area in a CMMI model, needed training is expected, based on the application of this generic practice.

4.5 Informative Materials

CMMI models contain 10 types of informative components.

1. Purpose. Each process area begins with a brief statement of purpose for the process area. Generally, a purpose statement consists of one or two sentences that summarize or draw together the specific goals of the process area. Consider the purpose statement from Risk Management:

> *The purpose of Risk Management is to identify potential problems before they occur, so that risk-handling activities may be planned and invoked as needed across the life of the product or project to mitigate adverse impacts on achieving objectives.*

The three specific goals in Risk Management address preparations, identification and analysis of risk, and mitigation as needed. In this way, the purpose statement provides a quick, high-level orientation for the entire process area.

2. Introductory Note. A section including multiple introductory notes that apply to the entire process area follows the purpose statement. Typically, these notes present information on the scope of the process area, its importance, the way in which it reflects recognized best practices, unique terminology used in it, and the interaction of it with other process areas.

3. Reference. Explicit pointing from one process area to all or part of another process area is accomplished with a reference. In CMMI, a reference is simply an indicator noting that, to obtain more information on some topic, one should look in another process area.

4. Names. In CMMI, all required and expected components (goals and practices) are given a name, which provides a convenient handle for referring to the component. Table 4-5 lists examples of names from the Measurement and Analysis (MA) process area. Thus, in training classes or in discussion, we can refer to the "align activities" goal or the "specify measures" practice in Measurement and Analysis. Although this name provides a convenient shorthand, do not confuse the name of the model component with the component itself. The components form the basis for process improvement and process appraisal—not the names.

Table 4-5: *Names from the Measurement and Analysis Process Area*

Component	*Name*	*Required or Expected Material*
MA SG 1	Align Measurement and Analysis Activities	Measurement objectives and activities are aligned with identified information needs and objectives.
MA SP 1.2-1	Specify Measures	Specify measures to address the measurement objectives.

5. Practice-to-Goal Relationship Table. Using the names for goals and practices, the relationship table in each process area maps each specific and generic practice to its related specific or generic goal, respectively.

6. *Notes.* Whereas the general notes at the beginning of a process area are labeled as "introductory notes," there are also (plain) notes attached to other model components, such as goals, practices, and subpractices. They represent a rich source of information that should prove valuable in planning and conducting process-improvement efforts. In the model, examples are highlighted by a box outlining the note.

7. *Typical Work Products.* When a practice is performed, there will often be outputs in the form of work products. In the Model Terminology chapter of the CMMI Model (Chapter 3) a work product is defined (in part) as follows:

> *Any artifact produced by a process. These artifacts can include files, documents, parts of the product, services, processes, specifications, and invoices.*

The items identified in a list of typical work products are examples; they should not be considered essential to the performance of the process, and the list should not be thought of as exhaustive. The intention is merely to provide initial guidance regarding the type of work products that may be produced by a practice. During an appraisal, however, you will be required to produce evidence proving that your process produces outputs and to show examples of those outputs to get credit for institutionalization of the process area.

8. *Subpractices.* For many practices in the CMMI models, subpractices provide a decomposition of their meaning and the activities that they might entail as well as an elaboration of their use. Unlike practices (which are expected model components), subpractices appear in the model for information purposes only.

9. *Discipline Amplifications.* One of the most distinctive aspects of CMMI as compared with prior source models is the fact that the CMMI model components are discipline-independent. The advantage of this approach derives from the ability of different disciplines to use the same components, which promotes common terminology and understanding across various disciplines. The limitation on discipline-independent components becomes apparent, however, when one considers that generalization can entail the removal of content. For example, the CMM for Software included a practice that made explicit reference to developing estimates of software size. In contrast, CMMI speaks more generally about producing estimates for the attributes of work products and tasks (see Project Planning, SP 1.2-1).

To maintain the usefulness of the discipline-specific material found in its source models, CMMI provides discipline amplifications that are introduced with phrases such as "For software engineering," or "For systems engineering." For example, in the Project Planning process area, the specific practice on establishing estimates of project attributes has a discipline amplification for software engineering that mentions software size and examples of size measures. It also has a discipline amplification for systems engineering that mentions the number of functions and the number of interfaces as important attributes to include in the estimate. Amplifications are informative material, so they are not required in an appraisal. Nevertheless, the appraisers may use them as guidance on how to interpret the practice for specific disciplines and to gain a better idea of how the practice will affect the process-improvement activities.

10. *Generic Practice Elaborations.* Whereas discipline amplifications provide details for each specific discipline, generic practice elaborations provide details regarding the application of a generic practice in a given process area. For example, in the Product Integration process area, the generic practice on establishing an organizational policy is elaborated with these words:

> *This policy establishes organizational expectations for developing product integration sequences, procedures, and an environment, ensuring interface compatibility among product components, assembling the product components, and delivering the product and product components.*

Sometimes, in a given process area, a generic practice and a specific practice may seem to address a similar topic. For example, the generic practice may deal with planning the process, and a specific practice may focus on planning a particular aspect of the process. In such a circumstance, a generic practice elaboration is used to comment on the distinction intended between the generic and specific practices.

4.6 Document Map

Figures 4-1 and 4-2 show where to find the various types of information described in the continuous and staged representations, respectively. The illustrations are from the downloadable models.[4]

---

4. The model is formatted differently in *CMMI: Guidelines for Process Integration and Product Improvement*. See Section 5.4 for more information.

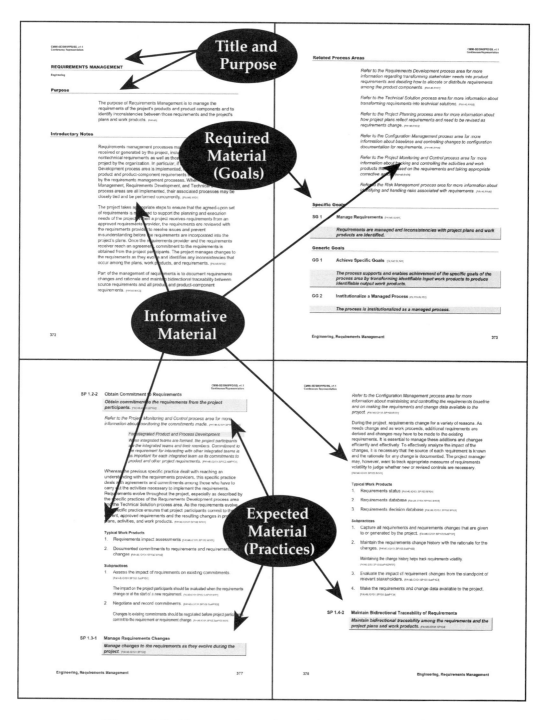

Figure 4-1: *Document map for continuous representation*

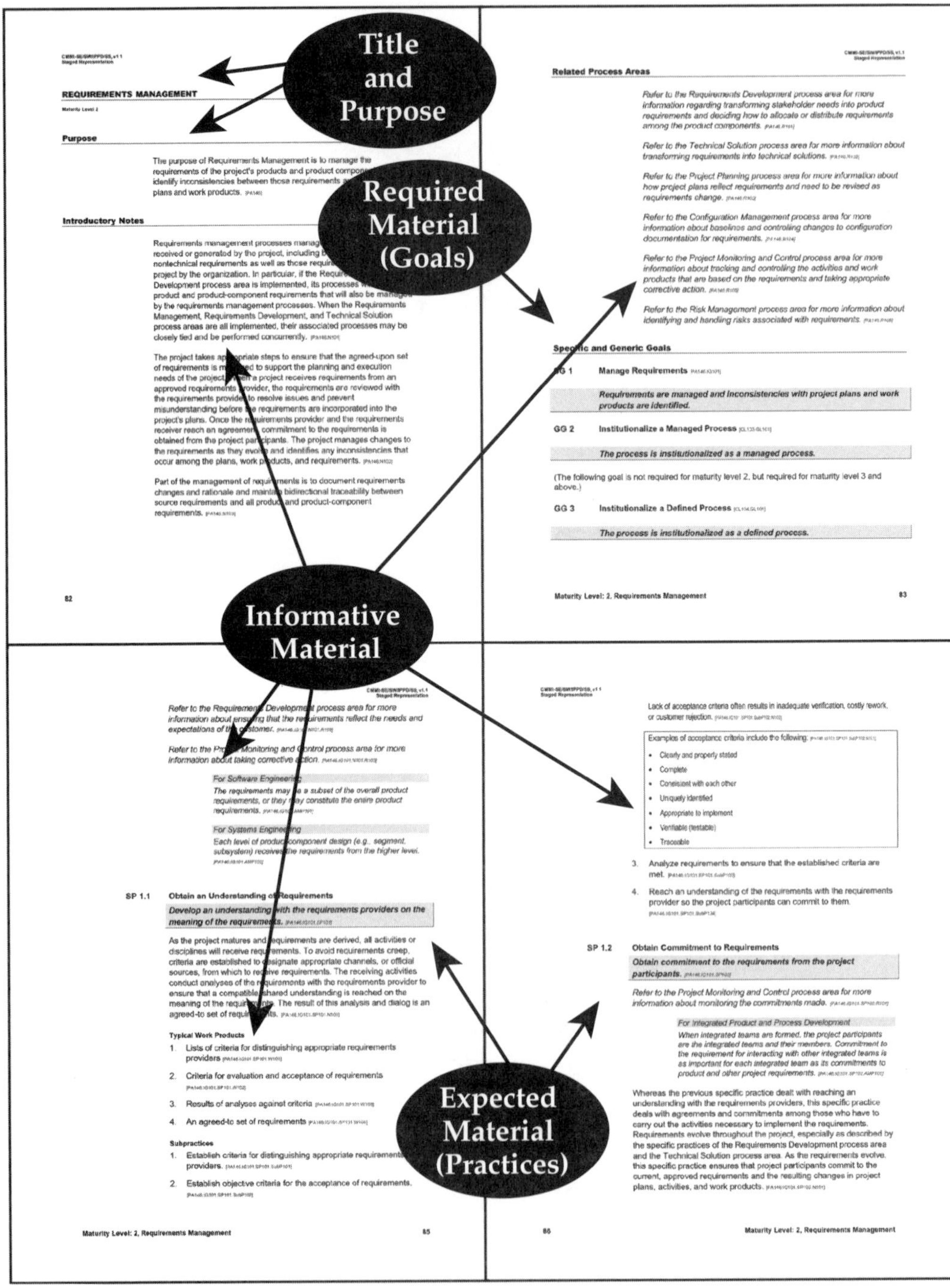

Figure 4-2: *Document map for staged representation*

Chapter 5

CMMI Representations

If we cannot now end our differences,
at least we can help make the world safe for diversity.
John Fitzgerald Kennedy (1963)

We tend to see our own experiences as the normal process,
so we are often amazed that anyone could have taken a different path.
But when we do meet up, it's always fascinating to
compare notes about the different ways to get there.
Daniel Gilly, *Unix in a Nutshell* (1992)

A fundamental choice faces the user of a Capability Maturity Model Integration (CMMI) model today: Do you use the continuous or staged representation? The question relates to the architectural structure of the model. One source model for CMMI, the CMM for Software, was a "staged" model. Another source model, the Systems Engineering Capability Model, was a "continuous" model. The third source, the Integrated Product Development (IPD) CMM, was a "hybrid" that combined features of both the staged and continuous.

One way to think about the architectural options is to focus on process improvement. An organization may choose to approach process improvement from the perspective of either process area capability or

71

organizational maturity. Simply put, a process area capability perspective focuses on establishing baselines and measuring improvement results in each area individually. This approach is supported in a continuous representation, with its use of the key term "capability." In contrast, an organizational maturity perspective emphasizes sets of process areas that are intended to define proven stages of process maturity across an organization. This approach is employed in a staged representation, with its use of the key term "maturity."

While many may have wished that the CMMI Team had selected a single architectural representation for its integration task, that decision was judged to be premature and "too hard" for the initial integration effort. The fundamental problem related to the lack of consensus regarding which approach to process improvement would be better, and hence which architecture would be preferable.[1] Each side had many strong proponents, so the CMMI Team made the judgment that the risk of losing support for CMMI would be too great if it summarily eliminated either representation or tried to find a single "hybrid" solution. Hence the CMMI models (version 1.1) for each combination of disciplines are presented with two representations, continuous and staged. Note, however, that the CMMI Team put a great deal of effort into ensuring the logical equivalence of the two representations.

5.1 Staged Models

A staged model provides a predefined road map for organizational improvement based on proven grouping and ordering of processes and associated organizational relationships. The term "staged" comes from the way that the model describes this road map as a series of "stages" that are called "maturity levels." Each maturity level has a set of process areas that indicate where an organization should focus to improve its organizational process. Each process area is described in terms of the practices that contribute to satisfying its goals. The practices describe the infrastructure and activities that contribute most to the effective implementation and institutionalization of the process

---

1. The phrase "religious war" comes to mind. This disagreement is unfortunate, as both approaches have positive aspects. Good news—since the initial CMMI version 1.0 release in 2000, there seems to be more willingness to appreciate the values inherent in each approach.

areas. Progress occurs by satisfying the goals of all process areas in a particular maturity level.[2]

The CMM for Software is the primary example of a staged model. Figure 5-1 shows the CMM for Software and its five stages, and Table 5-1 shows the key process areas within each stage.

The key process areas at level 2 of the CMM for Software focus on the software project's concerns related to establishing basic project management controls. Level 3 addresses both project and organizational issues, as the organization establishes an infrastructure that institutionalizes effective software engineering and management processes across all projects. The key process areas at level 4 focus on establishing a quantitative understanding of both the software process and the software work products being built. Level 5 covers the issues that both the organization and the projects must address to implement continual, measurable software process improvement.

Appraisals against a staged model evaluate the organization as a whole by determining how many of the process areas have been achieved—that is, how many goals have been met. Based on the satisfied key process areas, the organization may be assigned a single maturity level. When you hear that a corporation "is at level 3," for example, it means that the organization has conducted an appraisal and has satisfied all goals associated with the process areas included in levels 2 and 3 of a staged model.

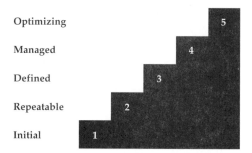

Figure 5-1: *The Software CMM stages*

---

2. The concept of five stages or maturity levels goes back to Crosby in *Quality Is Free*, which described a five-level scale with "world-class" as level 5. Actually, Crosby's proposed scale is closer to capability levels in a continuous model than to maturity levels in a staged model, because he applied a similar scale across many areas. Section 5.2 describes the capability levels in a continuous model.

Table 5-1: *The Software CMM Version 2(c) Key Process Areas*

Level	Focus	Key Process Areas
Level 5: Optimizing	Continuous process improvement	Organization Improvement Deployment Organization Process & Technology Innovation Defect Prevention
Level 4: Managed	Quantitative management	Statistical Process Management Organization Process Performance Organization Software Asset Commonality
Level 3: Defined	Process standardization	Peer Reviews Project Interface Coordination Software Product Engineering Integrated Software Management Organization Training Program Organization Process Definition Organization Process Focus
Level 2: Repeatable	Basic project management	Software Configuration Management Software Quality Assurance Software Acquisition Management Software Project Control

Level	Focus	Key Process Areas
		Software Project Planning
		Requirements Management
Level 1: Initial	Competent people and heroics	None

5.2 Continuous Models

Continuous models provide less specific guidance on the order in which improvement should be accomplished. They are called continuous because no discrete stages are associated with organizational maturity. EIA 731 is an example of a continuous model.

Like the staged models, continuous models have process areas that contain practices. Unlike in staged models, however, the practices of a process area in a continuous model are organized in a manner that supports individual process area growth and improvement. Most of the practices associated with process improvement are generic; they are external to the individual process areas and apply to all process areas.[3] The generic practices are grouped into capability levels (CLs), each of which has a definition that is roughly equivalent to the definition of the maturity levels in a staged model. Process areas are improved and institutionalized by implementing the generic practices in those process areas.

In a continuous model such as EIA 731, goals are not specifically stated, which puts even more emphasis on practices. The collective capability levels of all process areas determine organizational improvement, and

---

3. EIA 731 introduced the concept of advanced practices. These technical practices within a process area (called a focus area in 731) are associated with higher capability levels and so augment the generic practices. CMMI models include a version of the advanced practice mechanism.

an organization can tailor a continuous model and target only certain process areas for improvement. In other words, they create their own "staging" of process areas.

In a continuous appraisal, each process area is rated at its own capability level. An organization will most likely have different process areas rated at different capability levels. The results can be reported as a capability profile, like that shown in Figure 5-2.

The capability profile may include just the level number ratings, as in Figure 5-2, or it may also contain detailed information at the goal or practice levels. The latter option provides more specific information in graphical form by highlighting the findings (weaknesses and strengths) with different colors. Profiles have generally been implemented via a spreadsheet.

Capability profiles can also be used to define a target for process-improvement activities in an organization. Because a target profile shows the desired capability profile at a specific point in time, it can be used to show progress on the process-improvement journey.

Another way to use capability profiles is to organize the process dimension so that it represents the staged maturity levels. For example, a series of profiles may be used to set goals for the organization or to evaluate the results of an appraisal using equivalent staging (Section

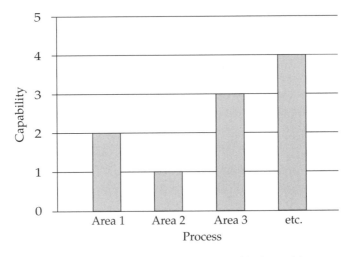

Figure 5-2: *Capability level profile (simple)*

5.3.3 describes the application of this concept to CMMI). In addition, capability profiles can be defined for subsets of process areas when different parts of the organization own the processes related to them. Alternatively, the same process areas may be included in multiple owners' target profiles. When the entire organization undergoes an appraisal, the process areas are rated as a whole.

5.3 CMMI Model Representations

The CMMI Team was given an unprecedented challenge: Create a single model that could be viewed from two distinct perspectives, continuous and staged. This mandate meant that each representation should include the same basic information for process improvement: A CMMI process appraisal that addressed the same scope should result in the same findings, no matter which model representation was used during the appraisal.

5.3.1 Selection of Process Areas

As described in Chapter 4, a major challenge centered on the selection of the process areas for CMMI.[4] A second, even thornier issue was whether the process areas in the two representations would need to be (or should be) identical.[5] The team employed a well-defined set of criteria in identifying process areas. That is, a process area was defined as containing a related set of activities that, if performed, would result in a high probability of significant improvement in the area and thus aid in the achievement of business objectives for the organization.[6]

---

4. The CMMI Team did not start with a blank slate. Its task was not to create a new model from scratch, but rather to integrate (initially) three existing models. Each of these models already had process areas identified, and these areas made up the initial set of candidates. The team took into consideration the hopes or expectations among users of the CMMI source models that process areas to which they were accustomed would continue in CMMI.

5. In this section we invite the reader to enter (briefly) this "briar patch," not to share the pain (well, maybe a little), but to provide some insight. You can, of course, decline the invitation. The bottom line (which you need to know) is that the two CMMI representations have the same process areas.

6. A variety of other criteria for what makes a good process area exist, including the following: A process area tells you what to do, not how to do it or who should do it; it can be implemented in multiple organizational and product contexts; and it has sufficient cohesion and granularity to be separately implemented, rated, and improved.

For example, the inadequate definition or management of project requirements is frequently mentioned in trying to understand what went wrong in a given program. Furthermore, a set of recognized activities exists that, if performed, would go a long way toward correcting what might have gone wrong with requirements. As a consequence, it should come as no surprise that CMMI includes two process areas related to this topic: Requirements Development and Requirements Management. No debate occurs regarding whether process areas such as Requirements Development or Requirements Management would be appropriate in both a staged representation and a continuous representation. Whichever architectural representation was to be adopted for the model, both areas would be of critical importance.

Suppose, however, that the CMMI Product Development Team had been asked to proceed differently. That is, suppose it had been asked not to develop one model with two representations, but rather just one model representation (for example, continuous, staged, or some hybrid). It is not clear that the resultant list of process areas would have been exactly identical for each of the various possible model representations. In other words, the process areas needed in a staged representation and the process areas needed in a continuous representation are not necessarily the same.

For example, in a staged model the process areas exist at a single maturity level only; they do not span levels. In the CMM for Software, for instance, Requirements Management is a process area staged at maturity level 2 (as it is in the CMMI staged representation); no parts of the Requirements Management process area exist at higher maturity levels. Thus, as an organization works to achieve maturity levels 3, 4, or 5, it need not tackle additional tasks that come from the Requirements Management process area.

Of course, the organization should not ignore the maturity level 2 process areas as it moves ahead to higher maturity levels. To be an organization at maturity level 3 means (in general) that the processes used on projects are tailored from the organization's standard set of processes. This approach includes the management of requirements; a standard set of processes should exist for doing requirements management across the organization, and individual projects should derive their specific processes for requirements management from that standard set.

In CMMI, the Integrated Project Management (IPM) process area, which is staged at maturity level 3, requires an organization to return to the process areas from maturity level 2 (such as Requirements Management) and perform them in a manner consistent with maturity level 3 requirements. In IPM, a goal for a project is to use a defined process that is tailored from the organization's set of standard processes.

Moving from the staged to the continuous representation, a generic practice at capability level 3 (GP 3.1) also sets the expectation for a defined process. In Requirements Management, for example, GP 3.1 reads: "Establish and maintain the description of a defined requirements management process." By performing that practice, and the comparable generic practice in other process areas staged at maturity level 2, the organization may raise each process area to capability level 3 when viewed from the perspective of the continuous representation. The continuous representation does not require an independent mechanism, such as the first goal in IPM to raise maturity level 2 process areas to the corresponding maturity level 3 defined level.

Also, if you look at IPM from a continuous viewpoint, some practices may look like they really belong (perhaps as "advanced" practices) in the Project Planning or Project Monitoring and Control process areas.

We will not explore in detail all of the architectural nuances that might distinguish the two representations. Rather, we will simply note that the CMMI Team had a choice: allow the process areas to be different in the two representations, or keep them the same. The former option (different process areas) would have allowed for the construction of "better" or "purer" staged or continuous representations, but at the cost of potential confusion to those who might need to deal with two representations having different process areas. The latter option (same process areas) would enhance the sense that the two representations are really just one CMMI model with two views, but at the cost of potentially confusing duplication or positioning of material in the model, which would be needed to allow both representations to work. The decision was made to have the same process areas in both representations for CMMI.

Although the CMMI Team decided not to have a single CMMI representation in the initial release, the decision to have the same process areas in the two representations will support any future movement toward hybridization. This merger, of course, could be accomplished only with some degree of inelegance and duplication, as exemplified by the IPM requirement for use of a defined process described both by a goal and a generic practice.

5.3.2 Organization of Process Areas

The 25 process areas of CMMI-SE/SW/IPPD/SS are divided into four maturity levels in the staged representation and four process categories in the continuous representation. Tables 5-2 and 5-3 show these two structures, respectively.

Table 5-2: *Staged Groupings*

Staged Grouping	Acronyms	Process Areas
Maturity level 2	REQM	Requirements Management
	PP	Project Planning
	PMC	Project Monitoring and Control
	SAM	Supplier Agreement Management
	MA	Measurement and Analysis
	PPQA	Process and Product Quality Assurance
	CM	Configuration Management
Maturity level 3	RD	Requirements Development
	TS	Technical Solution
	PI	Product Integration
	VER	Verification
	VAL	Validation
	OPF	Organizational Process Focus
	OPD	Organizational Process Definition
	OT	Organizational Training
	IPM	Integrated Project Management
	RSKM	Risk Management
	IT	Integrated Teaming
	ISM	Integrated Supplier Management
	DAR	Decision Analysis and Resolution
	OEI	Organizational Environment for Integration

Staged Grouping	Acronyms	Process Areas
Maturity level 4	OPP	Organizational Process Performance
	QPM	Quantitative Project Management
Maturity level 5	OID	Organizational Innovation and Deployment
	CAR	Causal Analysis and Resolution

Table 5-3: *Continuous Groupings*

Continuous Grouping	Acronyms	Process Areas
Process Management	OPF	Organizational Process Focus
	OPD	Organizational Process Definition
	OT	Organizational Training
	OPP	Organizational Process Performance
	OID	Organizational Innovation and Deployment
Project Management	PP	Project Planning
	PMC	Project Monitoring and Control
	SAM	Supplier Agreement Management
	IPM	Integrated Project Management
	RSKM	Risk Management
	IT	Integrated Teaming
	ISM	Integrated Supplier Management
	QPM	Quantitative Project Management

(continued)

Table 5-3: *Continuous Groupings (continued)*

Continuous Grouping	Acronyms	Process Areas
Engineering	REQM	Requirements Management
	RD	Requirements Development
	TS	Technical Solution
	PI	Product Integration
	VER	Verification
	VAL	Validation
Support	CM	Configuration Management
	PPQA	Process and Product Quality Assurance
	MA	Measurement and Analysis
	DAR	Decision Analysis and Resolution
	OEI	Organizational Environment for Integration
	CAR	Causal Analysis and Resolution

5.3.3 Equivalent Staging

To reinforce the concept of one model with two views or representations, CMMI provides a mapping to move from the continuous to the staged perspective. For maturity levels 2 and 3, the concept is straightforward and easy to understand. If an organization using the continuous representation has achieved capability level 2 in the seven process areas that make up maturity level 2 (in the staged representation), then it can be said to have achieved maturity level 2 (Figure 5-3).

Similarly, if an organization using the continuous representation has achieved capability level 3 in the seven process areas that make up maturity level 2 and the 14 process areas that make up maturity level 3 (a total of 21 process areas in CMMI-SE/SW/IPPD/SS), then it can be said to have achieved maturity level 3 (Figure 5-4).

For maturity levels 4 and 5, a similar mechanism is not available to define an equivalent staging. For example, maturity level 4 in the

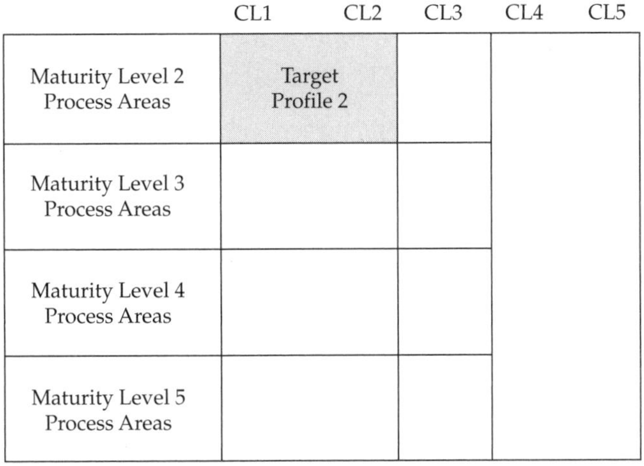

	CL1	CL2	CL3	CL4	CL5
Maturity Level 2 Process Areas	Target Profile 2				
Maturity Level 3 Process Areas					
Maturity Level 4 Process Areas					
Maturity Level 5 Process Areas					

Figure 5-3: *Target profile 2*

staged representation does not require that level 4 kinds of activities go on in each and every process area. Nor is quantitative management of processes or subprocesses required for any given process area. One organization that achieves maturity level 4 may do quantitative management in one set of areas, and another organization may handle quantitative management in another set of areas; there may be no overlap between the two sets, and yet both organizations may operate at

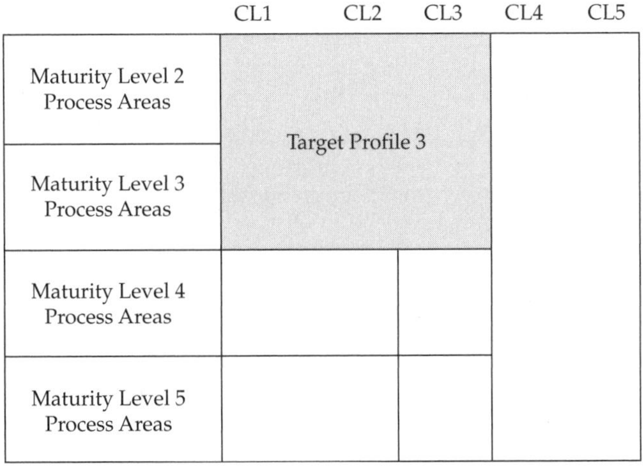

	CL1	CL2	CL3	CL4	CL5
Maturity Level 2 Process Areas					
Maturity Level 3 Process Areas	Target Profile 3				
Maturity Level 4 Process Areas					
Maturity Level 5 Process Areas					

Figure 5-4: *Target profile 3*

maturity level 4. Thus, in Figure 5-5, we cannot highlight any particular process area as being capability level 4 and claim that it is required for an equivalent staging to maturity level 4.

Instead, to obtain an equivalent staging for maturity level 4, we require that an organization meet the goals up through capability level 3 in the process areas that are staged at maturity level 4. This idea may sound confusing, but it is correct. Table 5-4 details the three goals of the two maturity-level 4 process areas. To achieve capability level 3 in these two process areas means two things:

1.   The three specific goals in Table 5-4 are met: The project is quantitatively managed, subprocesses are statistically managed to meet quality and process performance objectives, and baselines and models for expected process performance exist.

2.   A defined process is used for the activities performed to achieve these goals.

These items are exactly what would need to be established for maturity level 4, based on the CMMI staged representation. Consequently, to be rated at maturity level 4, some subprocesses in some process areas must be statistically managed, but it is not possible to specify in advance which process areas are targeted. In a real-life capability profile for an organization at maturity level 4, the capability level of at least one process area would be at level 4.

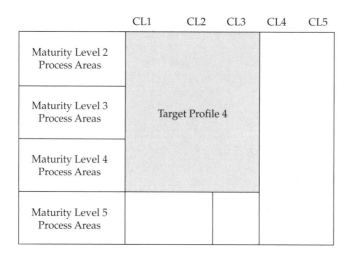

Figure 5-5: *Target profile 4*

Table 5-4: *Maturity Level 4 Process Areas and Goals*

Process Area	Specific Goals
Quantitative Project Management (QPM)	SG 1: The project is quantitatively managed using quality and process-performance objectives. SG 2: The performance of selected subprocesses within the project's defined process is statistically managed.
Organizational Process Performance (OPP)	SG 1: Baselines and models that characterize the expected process performance of the organization's set of standard processes are established and maintained.

The equivalent staging for maturity level 5 is handled in a similar way (Figure 5-6). In this manner, the user of the continuous representation could establish a maturity-level rating, if desired, for any maturity level (1 through 5).

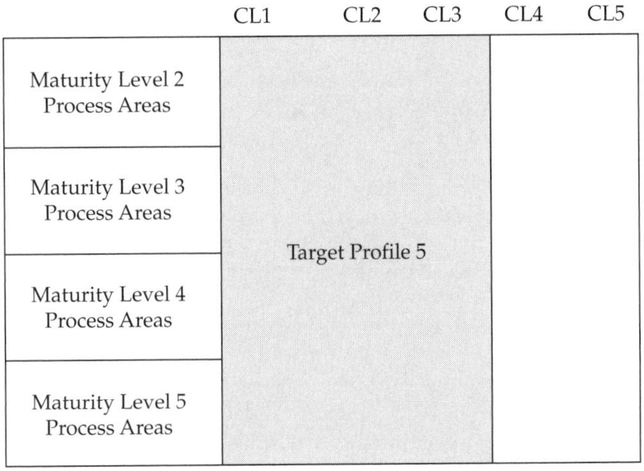

Figure 5-6: *Target profile 5*

For CMMI, if an organization wanted to have a single-number rating of a maturity level, it could choose a CMMI staged representation. Of course, because of this equivalent staging comprising a set of four target profiles, the organization could also choose a CMMI continuous representation.

5.4 A Single CMMI Source

To close this chapter in which we have explained the two CMMI representations, we wish to note a novel approach taken with regard to representations in the CMMI guidelines book.[7]

The authors of that book wished to make the entire model available to their readers, but were confronted with the dilemma of which versions to use (of the eight currently available—four discipline combinations, each in two representations). Their solution was to use none of them, but at the same time use all of them: create a single CMMI "source" that collects together all of the CMMI model "information."

There are several benefits to the approach they followed. Because the models are large documents, with each needing about 450 pages in book format, reproducing multiple versions would have resulted in a book that was thicker, heavier, and more expensive. While the authors have gained an obvious benefit in avoiding unnecessary repetition of model information that is overwhelmingly identical or similar, we should not focus on just the practical issue of publication. With the relevant model information in a single unified format, with everything presented together, readers can learn in depth about CMMI models without being forced to prematurely select a particular version. In other words, their approach produced a real win-win.

Eventually model users will need to select which version (or versions) of the model from the CMMI Product Suite they will use; we will discuss considerations related to that decision later in Chapter 9. When the time comes to make a selection, the information in the chapter you are now concluding, which focuses on what distinguishes the two representations, should provide you with the basic understanding that you will need to make an informed choice.

---

7. Chrissis, M., M. Konrad, and S. Shrum. *CMMI: Guidelines for Process Integration and Product Improvement*. Boston: Addison-Wesley, 2003.

Chapter 6

CMMI Dimensions for Measuring Improvement

Catch, then, oh catch the transient hour;
Improve each moment as it flies!
Samuel Johnson, *Winter. An Ode* (1709–1784)

Anyone who isn't confused really doesn't understand the situation.
Edward R. Murrow (1908–1965)

Chapter 5 presented some basic information about the two representations (continuous and staged) that are provided for every Capability
Maturity Model Integration (CMMI) model. This chapter continues
to explore the relationships between the two representations by taking
a more detailed look at how the capability and maturity dimensions
are implemented in CMMI.[1] Essentially, the differences in the two

---

1. At some point in our description of the two CMMI architectural representations, you may ask,
"Which representation should I use?" When that point comes, you may wish to turn to Chapter 9,
on picking a representation. In Chapter 6, we focus on building a good understanding of these
structures and their implementation in CMMI.

representations reflect the methods used to describe the process dimension for each capability or maturity level. Rest assured that while the mechanics of the descriptions may differ, both representations achieve the same improvement purposes through the use of generic goals and practices as required and expected model elements.

Continuous models describe improvement through the capability of process areas, singly or collectively. A capability level includes a generic goal and its associated generic practices that are added to the specific goals and practices within the process area. When the organization meets the process area-specific goals and generic goals, it achieves the capability level for that process area.[2]

Staged models describe the maturity of organizations through successful implementation of ordered groups of process areas. These groups, or stages, improve processes together, based on achievements in the previous stage. Each process area in the staged model includes the appropriate generic goals and practices for its stage.

The remainder of this chapter discusses in detail the characteristics and mechanisms used by CMMI in defining the capability dimension, the maturity dimension, generic practices, and staging. Chapter 7 addresses the process dimensions for both representations.

6.1 Capability Dimension

The capability dimension is used in the continuous representation of CMMI, just as it was in CMMI's predecessor source model, EIA 731 (see Section 3.3.2). In this section we describe the levels and summarize the mechanism of capability improvement. Section 6.3 offers a more detailed discussion of the individual generic practices.

CMMI includes six levels of process area capability, imaginatively called capability levels (CLs), and numbered 0 through 5. These CLs indicate how well the organization performs in an individual process area. As shown in Figure 6-1, capability level 0 (CL 0) indicates that the processes are Not Performed, which means that one or more of the specific goals of the process area are not satisfied. The capability levels

---

2. If a continuous model contains advanced practices, then for a capability level to be achieved, all advanced practices specified at or below that level must also be met.

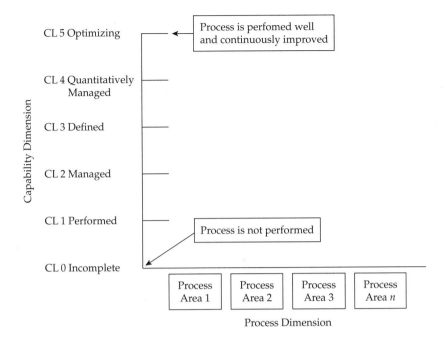

Figure 6-1: *Capability dimension*

increase up to capability level 5 (CL 5), where the process is performed well and is being continuously improved.

Table 6-1 shows the generic goal statements for each capability level. As the table shows, no generic goal exists for CL 0 (Not Performed). A process area is at CL 0 when it fails to reach CL 1. The reason for not having a goal is that this level simply signifies "not yet CL 1."[3]

Capability level 1 is called Performed, and the generic goal for this level focuses on the achievement of the specific goals of the process area. One generic practice is mapped to the CL 1 generic goal. It specifies that the base practices of the process area are performed at this level of capability. Even though 1 is a lowly number, reaching CL 1 represents a significant achievement for an organization; if a process area is at CL 1, then the specific goals of the process area are satisfied.

---

3. It is highly recommended that when describing an organization's capability as 0 that the words "not yet level 1" be substituted—no one wants to be considered as being at level 0.

Table 6-1: *Generic Goals*

Capability Level	Generic Goal
CL 0	No goal.
CL 1	GG 1: The process supports and enables achievement of the specific goals of the process area by transforming identifiable input work products to produce identifiable output work products.
CL 2	GG 2: The process is institutionalized as a managed process.
CL 3	GG 3: The process is institutionalized as a defined process.
CL 4	GG 4: The process is institutionalized as a quantitatively managed process.
CL 5	GG 5: The process is institutionalized as an optimizing process.

The added capabilities for CL 2 through CL 5 depend on the specific practices within a process area being performed at their capability level; only when they are performed can they be improved by satisfying higher-level generic goals. Figure 6-2 illustrates how a process increases in capability.

Capability level 2 is called Managed, and its generic goal focuses on institutionalization as a managed process. Ten generic practices are mapped to the CL 2 generic goal. A managed process has increased capability over a performed process; the ten generic practices provide a definition for that increased capability. In general, a process operating at CL 2 has an organizational policy stating which processes will be used. The projects follow a documented plan and process description. They apply adequate and appropriate resources (including funding, people, and tools) and maintain appropriate assignment of responsibility and authority.

In addition, the organization and the projects allow for training of the people performing and supporting the process. Work products are placed under appropriate levels of configuration management. All

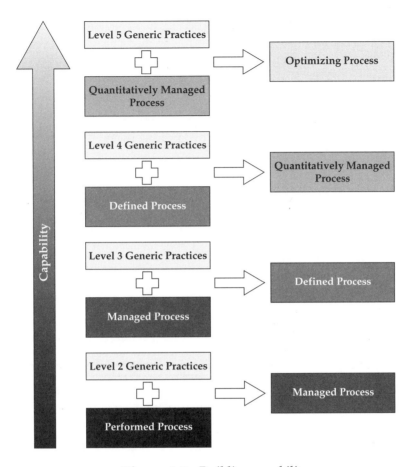

Figure 6-2: *Building capability*

relevant stakeholders are identified and involved as appropriate. Personnel monitor and control the performance of the process and take corrective action when needed. They objectively evaluate the process, its work products, and its services, addressing any noncompliance with corrective actions. The activities, status, and results of the process activities are reviewed with appropriate levels of management, and corrective action is taken if necessary. Thanks to this robust set of generic practices at CL 2, mostly targeted at individual projects, a managed process represents a significant advance relative to a performed process.

Capability level 3 is called Defined, and the generic goal for this level focuses on institutionalization as a defined process. In layman's terms, for each process area considered, each project in an organization will have a managed process (like that created under CL 2) that is tailored from an organization's standard processes using standard tailoring guidelines.[4] Two generic practices are mapped to the CL 3 generic goal. Besides the establishment of defined processes, process assets and process measurements must be collected and used for future improvements to the process.

Whereas capability level 2 targets the capability of individual process instances,[5] capability level 3 focuses on organizational standardization and deployment of the processes. Process performance is stabilized across the projects because processes are standardized across the organization; the standard processes are tailored for each instance in which that process is needed. Personnel can readily apply their process-based knowledge and skills across multiple instances of the process without expensive retraining. The organization supports the use of the process by providing process asset libraries and tailoring guidelines.

Capability level 4 is called Quantitatively Managed, and its generic goal focuses on institutionalization as a quantitatively managed process. Without getting into the finer points of statistical process control, a CL 4 process is a defined process (like that created under CL 3— see how this inheritance works?) that uses statistical and other quantitative methods to control selected subprocesses. For example, if you know that defects for a certain product are historically less than 5 percent of the total volume and your process measures (as instituted at CL 3) deviate from that percentage significantly, you can be fairly certain that a problem exists and should be investigated.

Because of the overhead involved and to make general common sense, the process measures selected for CL 4 relate to individual subprocesses—not necessarily all processes or even entire processes. Obviously, the organization should quantitatively manage only those subprocesses that are important to its business needs and objectives.

Capability level 5 is called Optimizing, and the generic goal for this level focuses on institutionalization as an optimizing process. CL 5 is a bit tricky, because it essentially requires the organization to constantly adapt the quantitatively managed subprocesses established at CL 4 based on their measures and established objectives for quality and process performance. This requirement doesn't just mean fixing problems

---

4. This example assumes the process area considered is a project-related process area—that is, from the Project Management process area category.

5. Usually, each instance of the process is associated with a project.

(such as the quality anomaly cited earlier), but entails analyzing trends, surveying technical practice, addressing common causes of process variation, and then determining how best to adapt the process to changing business needs. This procedure could result in either evolutionary or revolutionary action.

6.2 Maturity Dimension

The maturity dimension of a CMMI model is described in the staged representation. Five levels of maturity exist, each of which indicates the process maturity of the organization. Figure 6-3 shows the maturity levels (MLs) and their characteristics.

Note the overlap in the names for maturity levels 2 through 5 and the names for capability levels 2 through 5. Although these capability levels and maturity levels have the same names, a fundamental difference separates them: Capability levels are independently applied to any individual process area, whereas a maturity level specifies a set of process areas whose combined set of goals must be achieved.

Furthermore, generic goals and practices follow different inclusion rules in the staged representation than they do in the continuous representation. They are included in the process areas according to the level where the process area is staged. Process areas staged at maturity

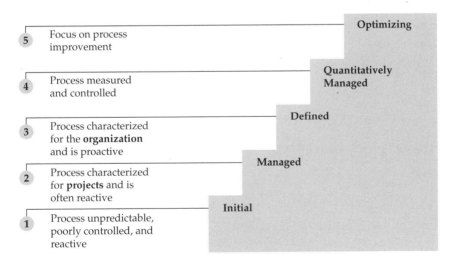

Figure 6-3: *Staged maturity levels*

level 2 use the CL 2 generic goal and its associated generic practices. Process areas staged at maturity levels 3 through 5 include the CL 3 generic goal, plus the generic practices from both capability levels 2 and 3. CL 1, 4, and 5 generic goals and practices are not used in the maturity-level definitions—no process areas are staged at level 1, and the generic goals for levels 4 and 5 are addressed by the specific goals and practices of the four process areas staged at those levels.

Note that maturity level 1 has a different name (Initial) from that assigned to capability level 1 (Performed). In the staged representation, ML 1 is similar to CL 0 in its negative connotation; that is, an organization at ML 1 is one that has not reached ML 2. No goals need to be met to qualify for ML 1. Unlike CL 1, ML 1 does not connote any significant achievement for an organization.

Figure 6-4 shows the structure of a maturity level. In the staged representation, each process area exists at a maturity level. The process areas required for each staged level were shown in Chapter 5. In Chapter 7, we will describe each of the process areas.

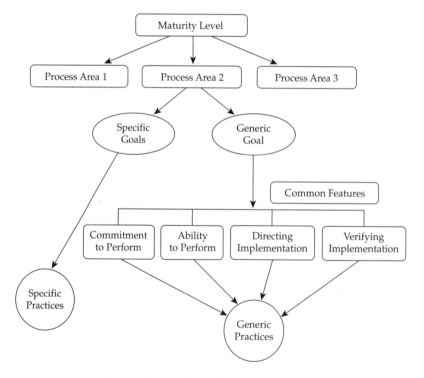

Figure 6-4: *Maturity level structure*

6.3 Generic Practices in the Capability Dimension

In the previous two sections, we saw how generic goals and practices are used to define both capability levels and maturity levels. The continuous representation includes 17 generic practices grouped by capability levels 1 through 5. As stated earlier, only the capability level 2 and 3 generic practices are included in the staged representation. These 12 generic practices are grouped by their Common Feature category, using a terminology that was carried over from the CMM for Software. This section takes a more detailed look at the full set of generic practices used in the continuous representation. Section 6.4 scrutinizes the partial set of generic practices used in the staged representation.

6.3.1 Capability Level 0 Generic Practices

Capability level 0 does not have any generic practices. It is the Not Performed level, which means that the specific goals for a process area are not satisfied.

6.3.2 Capability Level 1 Generic Practice

Table 6-2 shows the capability level 1 generic practice. When GP 1.1 is applied to a process area, the base specific practices of the process area are performed.[6] Most of the specific practices in the CMMI models are base practices, with the only exceptions involving some advanced practices in the Engineering process areas.

Table 6-2: *Generic Practice from Capability Level 1*

Name	Generic Practice
GP 1.1 Perform Base Practices	Perform the base practices of the process to develop work products and provide services to achieve the specific goals of the process area.

---

6. In the CMMI continuous representation, a *base practice* is a specific practice that resides at CL 1; it is distinguished from an advanced practice that resides at CL 2 or higher. Section 7.3 provides further discussion of base and advanced practices.

6.3.3 Capability Level 2 Generic Practices

Table 6-3 shows the capability level 2 generic practices.

Table 6-3: *Generic Practices from Capability Level 2*

Name	Generic Practice
GP 2.1 Establish an Organizational Policy	Establish and maintain an organizational policy for planning and performing the process.
GP 2.2 Plan the Process	Establish and maintain the plan for performing the process.
GP 2.3 Provide Resources	Provide adequate resources for performing the process, developing the work products, and providing the services of the process.
GP 2.4 Assign Responsibility	Assign responsibility and authority for performing the process, developing the work products, and providing the services of the process.
GP 2.5 Train People	Train the people performing or supporting the process as needed.
GP 2.6 Manage Configurations	Place designated work products of the process under appropriate levels of configuration management.
GP 2.7 Identify and Involve Relevant Stakeholders	Identify and involve the relevant stakeholders as planned.
GP 2.8 Monitor and Control the Process	Monitor and control the process against the plan for performing the process and take appropriate corrective action.
GP 2.9 Objectively Evaluate Adherence	Objectively evaluate adherence of the process against its process description, standards, and procedures, and address noncompliance.
GP 2.10 Review Status with Higher-Level Management	Review the activities, status, and results of the process with higher-level management and resolve issues.

When GP 2.1 is applied to a process area, it establishes an organizational policy that requires planning and execution of the process area. Organizational policies need not be labeled with the term "policy," but senior management sponsorship must be documented in a manner that requires planning and the use of the processes associated with the process area.

Implementing GP 2.2 establishes the requirements and objectives for the processes associated with the process area, and it forms the basis for process planning. This GP has five subpractices that provide information on how this feat could be accomplished, dealing with management sponsorship, documenting the process, planning for performing the process, reviewing the process with relevant stakeholders, and revising it as necessary.

This "Plan the Process" generic practice can create confusion when it is applied to the Project Planning process area, as it seems to entail a need to "plan the plan." This result is desired; the planning of the activities for the Project Planning process area is a logical and necessary set of tasks in any project. The process for planning a project is one that, like any other process, should be planned.[7]

Another potential source of confusion is the fact that some process areas include a goal or specific practice to establish a strategy or a plan. This concept differs from the generic practice, because a specific practice for planning addresses detailed product or product-component strategies and plans—not planning across the full scope of process area activities. For example, in the Risk Management process area, SP 1.3-1 establishes and maintains the strategy to be used for risk management and SP 3.1-1 develops risk mitigation plans for the most important risks to the project. In contrast, the generic practice expects that all of these activities will be planned, along with the other risk management practices.

GP 2.3 is a favorite of all project and program managers. When applied to a process area, it ensures that adequate resources are allocated for carrying out the processes associated with the process area. This practice includes developing the work products of the process area and providing the services associated with the process, as well as the need for funding, facilities, people, and tools.

---

7. Only one level of "recursion" exists. Nothing in the model requires one to "plan to plan the plan."

When a project applies GP 2.4 to a process area, responsibility and authority are assigned to perform the processes associated with that area. The three subpractices cover assigning responsibility for personnel who are in charge of the process as well as workers who perform the tasks of the process, and confirming that those individuals understand their responsibilities.

Ensuring that process participants are trained correctly is the focus of GP 2.5. It includes training of the people performing and supporting the process so that both groups understand the process sufficiently to perform or support it. The Organizational Training process area provides guidance on how to develop an organizational training program that supports this generic practice. The generic practice and the process area differ, however, in that the process area provides training practices at the organizational level, whereas the generic practice addresses training for each process. Of course, a project may choose to rely on organizational training assets to the extent that they are available.

When a project applies GP 2.6 to a process area, it ensures that the appropriate level of configuration management is maintained for the process work products. Formal configuration management may or may not be expected, and a work product may be subject to different levels of configuration management at different points in time. The Configuration Management process area provides the specific practices needed to manage the selected work products for each project-related process area.

GP 2.7 requires involving all of the affected entities. The relevant stakeholders are specifically identified and drawn into the process associated with the process area.[8] The three subpractices identify stakeholders, let project planners know who these stakeholders are, and get the stakeholders involved. Although much of the CMMI material relevant to integrated product and process development is staged at maturity level 3, this CL 2 practice is important in both an integrated and a nonintegrated environment.

GP 2.8 monitors the plan for executing the process (which was defined in GP 2.2) and ensures that corrective actions are implemented when necessary. It has seven subpractices that provide more detailed information on how to monitor and control processes. The Project Monitoring

---

8. A relevant stakeholder is a person or role that is affected by or accountable for a process outcome, and whose involvement in a particular activity is planned.

and Control process area supports this generic practice by providing specific goals and practices for monitoring and taking corrective actions.

Objective evaluation of process and work product performance is provided to a process area through GP 2.9. While a quality assurance group or department may be used to perform the evaluations, CMMI does not assume any particular organizational structure. Note, however, that people not directly responsible for managing or performing the process should perform the evaluation. The Process and Product Quality Assurance process area supports this generic practice by providing guidance on how to accomplish objective evaluations.

When a project applies GP 2.10 to a process area, its higher-level management reviews the activities, status, and process results and resolves any outstanding issues related to process performance. Each level of management may have its own needs for information about the process performance. The reviews should be both periodic and event-driven.

6.3.4 Capability Level 3 Generic Practices

Table 6-4 shows the capability level 3 generic practices.

GP 3.1 supports institutionalization of processes by requiring that projects establish and maintain a defined process tailored from the organization's standard processes. Defined processes may be established for a project or an organizational group; although various parts of the organization may have different defined processes, all will be based on the standard processes. This tailoring provides flexibility to companies

Table 6-4: *Generic Practices from Capability Level 3*

Name	Generic Practice
GP 3.1 Establish a Defined Process	Establish and maintain the description of a defined process.
GP 3.2 Collect Improvement Information	Collect work products, measures, measurement results, and improvement information derived from planning and performing the process to support the future use and improvement of the organization's processes and process assets.

that have similar units that are organized differently, while ensuring that the standard processes remain truly standard across the enterprise.

GP 3.1 has five subpractices that support the establishment of the defined process that is associated with the process area. The Organizational Process Definition process area supports GP 3.1 by providing specific goals and practices related to the establishment of standard processes. The Integrated Project Management process area is also closely related to this generic practice. The notes in the model on individual specific practices offer more information on the use of these processes in an organization.

GP 3.2 represents a key to further process improvement, because it requires the organization to collect example work products, measures, and other data about the process for future use. Without such historical data, the process may become difficult to plan and impossible to manage quantitatively—the focus of CL 4. Three of the subpractices provide information on the contents of the process library. The fourth subpractice captures proposed improvements to the process assets. The Organizational Process Focus process area supports this generic practice by addressing process asset deployment and incorporating process-related experiences into the organizational process assets.

6.3.5 Capability Level 4 Generic Practices

Table 6-5 shows the capability level 4 generic practices.

Table 6-5: *Generic Practices from Capability Level 4*

Name	Generic Practice
GP 4.1 Establish Quality Objectives	Establish and maintain quantitative objectives for the process that address quality and process performance based on customer needs and business objectives.
GP 4.2 Stabilize Subprocess Performance	Stabilize the performance of one or more subprocesses to determine the ability of the process to achieve the established quantitative quality and process-performance objectives.

GP 4.1 expects an organization to use its business objectives to define process performance and quality objectives. All relevant stakeholders should be included in this activity, which entails making use of the CL 2 generic practice. Once established, quantitative objectives are allocated to the processes. The processes may be related to process areas or a set of process areas. The Quantitative Project Management process area encompasses quantitatively managing processes, so the information in that area is extremely useful in implementing this generic practice, especially in project-related process areas.

In implementing GP 4.2, the organization uses the quality and process-performance objectives to statistically manage selected subprocesses. A strong rationale for choosing the particular subprocesses should exist, and the organization needs to demonstrate how those subprocesses are managed to meet the intent of the generic practice. The Quantitative Project Management process area also supports this generic practice.

6.3.6 Capability Level 5 Generic Practices

Table 6-6 shows the capability level 5 generic practices.

Table 6-6: *Generic Practices from Capability Level 5*

Name	Generic Practice
GP 5.1 Ensure Continuous Process Improvement	Ensure continuous improvement of the process in fulfilling the relevant business objectives of the organization.
GP 5.2 Correct Common Cause of Problems	Identify and correct the root causes of defects and other problems in the process.

Implementing GP 5.1 drives the organization to select and deploy process and technology improvements that contribute to its ability to meet quality and performance objectives for the process. The Organizational Innovation and Deployment process area provides more information in terms of goals and practices on ways to implement this generic practice.

The root causes of defects in the process are identified and corrected through GP 5.2.[9] Without this practice, organizations would find it difficult to gain the agility needed to rapidly solve problems and to effectively evolve their processes. Goals and practices that can be applied in implementing GP 5.2 appear in the Causal Analysis and Resolution process area.

6.4 Generic Practices in the Maturity Dimension

The maturity dimension is used in the staged representation for the model. As discussed in Section 6.2, only the generic goals and practices from capability levels 2 and 3 are used in establishing the maturity dimension.

Although they are grouped as common features rather than as capability levels, the generic practices have the same meaning here that they have in the capability dimension. While this grouping mixes the generic practices of different capability levels, no special meaning is implied—it is simply a different way of grouping the practices. The nomenclature in Table 6-7[10] appears in the staged representation and provides a means to relate the generic practices of both representations.

Table 6-7: *Common Features and Generic Practices*

Commitment to Perform	
GP 2.1 (CO 1)	Establish and maintain an organizational policy for planning and performing the process.
Ability to Perform	
GP 3.1 (AB 1)	Establish and maintain the description of a defined process.
GP 2.2 (AB 2)	Establish and maintain the plan for performing the process.

9. The concept of a *root cause* is frequently misunderstood. Clearly, it is not a cause for which no preceding cause exists; only a god or the "big bang" would be a candidate to meet that definition. Rather, a root cause is an antecedent cause of a problem or defect such that, if it were removed, the problem or defect would be lessened or eliminated.

10. For brevity, Table 6-7 shows the generic practices for process areas that are staged at maturity levels 3 through 5.

Ability to Perform	
GP 2.3 (AB 3)	Provide adequate resources for performing the process, developing the work products, and providing the services of the process.
GP 2.4 (AB 4)	Assign responsibility and authority for performing the process, developing the work products, and providing the services of the process.
GP 2.5 (AB 5)	Train the people performing or supporting the process as needed.
Directing Implementation	
GP 2.6 (DI 1)	Place designated work products of the process under appropriate levels of configuration management.
GP 2.7 (DI 2)	Identify and involve the relevant stakeholders as planned.
GP 2.8 (DI 3)	Monitor and control the process against the plan for performing the process and take appropriate corrective action.
GP 3.2 (DI 4)	Collect work products, measures, measurement results, and improvement information derived from planning and performing the process to support the future use and improvement of the organization's processes and process assets.
Verifying Implementation	
GP 2.9 (VI 1)	Objectively evaluate adherence of the process against its process description, standards, and procedures, and address noncompliance.
GP 2.10 (VI 2)	Review the activities, status, and results of the process with higher-level management and resolve issues.

6.5 Organizational Capability Evolution

Users of staged models (especially the CMM for Software) often have difficulty in understanding how a continuous model measures organizational progress. When one is accustomed to a model in which process areas build on one another, it is not obvious how possibly unrelated process areas might be improved without some kind of staging. It may also be unclear when work should be carried out in a particular process area. Although the CMM for Software does not explicitly prohibit addressing higher-level key process areas before lower-level ones, it implies that this sequence should not be the normal way of proceeding. In EIA 731 (a continuous model), this implication would be meaningless; the focus areas in the Systems Engineering Capability Model (SECM) were not staged.

The following example describes how a user of a continuous CMMI model might approach a process area that is staged at ML 4. Consider Quantitative Project Management (QPM), which is an ML 4 process area. Obviously, it doesn't make sense for an organization to start its process improvement journey with this particular process area. In fact, cautionary statements in the Introductory Notes section of the process area warn against this approach. The continuous representation, however, does not dictate the time or state that must be reached before delving into this process area. Whenever work on QPM starts, and an organization establishes a QPM process, it may be rated at CL 1. By adding generic goals and practices, over time it may improve its capability to CL 5, if such improvement is deemed appropriate by the organization. In contrast, strict adherence to the staging in CMMI would mean that a user would not look at QPM until ML 4.[11] The bottom line is that while the continuous user has more freedom deciding when to start work on QPM, the wise user of either representation, staged or continous, will delay this effort until the basics of process improvement are in place. It should be clear to all that having quantitatively managed processes is an advanced capability and not a starting point.

---

11. In EIA 731, the practices in QPM are addressed as advanced practices in other focus areas.

Chapter 7

CMMI Process Areas

Never tell people how to do things. Tell them what to do and they will surprise you with their ingenuity.
General George S. Patton (1885–1945)

In theory, there is no difference between theory and practice. In practice there is.
Yogi Berra (1925–)

The CMMI-SE/SW/IPPD/SS model includes 25 process areas that define the process dimension of the model. These process areas are the same in both Capability Maturity Model Integration (CMMI) architectural representations. This chapter provides a brief description of each process area, focusing on its purpose, goals, and specific practices. It also points out some of the inherent relationships between the process areas, which are important in planning process-improvement activities.

In the continuous representation, the process areas are grouped by category: Process Management, Project Management, Engineering, and Support. The process areas in three of the four categories (Support is the exception) are related to one another. The Support process areas are independent of each other as well as all other process areas. In the staged representation, the process areas are grouped into maturity levels 2 through 5. Table 7-1 shows the process areas grouped by category and labeled with their maturity level (ML).

Table 7-1: *Process Areas by Category with Maturity Level*

Category	Process Area	Maturity Level
Process Management	Organizational Process Definition	3
	Organizational Process Focus	3
	Organizational Training	3
	Organizational Process Performance	4
	Organizational Innovation and Deployment	5
Project Management	Project Planning	2
	Project Monitoring and Control	2
	Supplier Agreement Management	2
	Integrated Project Management for IPPD	3
	Risk Management	3
	Integrated Teaming	3
	Integrated Supplier Management	3
	Quantitative Project Management	4
Engineering	Requirements Management	2
	Requirements Development	3
	Technical Solution	3
	Product Integration	3
	Verification	3
	Validation	3

Category	Process Area	Maturity Level
Support	Configuration Management	2
	Process and Product Quality Assurance	2
	Measurement and Analysis	2
	Decision Analysis and Resolution	3
	Organizational Environment for Integration	3
	Causal Analysis and Resolution	5

In our review of each process area, we will follow the groupings provided by the four categories of the continuous representation. This strategy should clarify the process area relationships that emerge when planning a successful process-improvement strategy.

7.1 Process Management Process Areas

The five process areas that make up the Process Management category contain the cross-project practices related to defining, planning, deploying, implementing, monitoring, controlling, verifying, measuring, and improving processes. They are[1]

- Organizational Process Definition (OPD).
- Organizational Process Focus (OPF).
- Organizational Process Performance (OPP).
- Organizational Innovation and Deployment (OID).
- Organizational Training (OT).

---

1. In the continuous representation of the model the order in which these process areas are presented is OPF, OPD, OT, OPP, OID. The order here is different to facilitate our explanation of relationships among the process areas.

Figure 7-1: *Process Management process area relationships*

As shown in Figure 7-1, a close relationship exists between four of these process areas. OPP builds on the capabilities in OPF and OPD. OID builds on the capabilities of the other process areas. This relationship is defined in the staged representation with OPF and OPD at ML 3, OPP at ML 4, and OID at ML 5. When using the CMMI continuous representation for process improvement, you should understand these relationships and plan your improvement projects accordingly. For example, you should not seek a capability level in OPP that is greater than what you have achieved in both OPF and OPD.

7.1.1 Organizational Process Definition

The purpose of Organizational Process Definition is to establish and maintain a usable set of organizational process assets. OPD (see Figure 7-2)[2] has one specific goal: to create and maintain organizational process assets. OPD and OPF work together in that the former provides guidance for an organization on creating processes and their supporting assets, while the latter provides guidance on identifying and planning process improvements.

---

2. We will begin our description of each process area with a context diagram and the purpose statement from the model. The context diagrams are drawn from the CMMI training materials: *Introduction to CMMI-SE/SW/IPPD/SS, Continuous V1.1 Modules.*

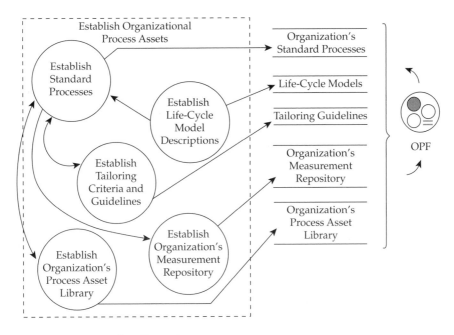

Figure 7-2: *Organizational Process Definition context diagram*

The OPD goal—creating and maintaining organizational process assets—is accomplished with five specific practices. The first establishes descriptions of life-cycle models that may be used by each project. These models are also used as the basis for establishing the organization's standard processes in the second practice. The third practice provides tailoring guidelines and criteria for the standard processes, which are in turn used by the projects during the planning phases of the project life cycle.

The fourth specific practice provides a repository for organizational process measurements, while the fifth is for establishing process assets that are used by the projects. An organizational measurement repository supports process performance and quantitative process management as the organization's capability and maturity improve. The repository also supports the use of historical data in establishing estimates. The process asset library supports projects in planning their project-unique processes through tailoring and implementing the standard processes, with resultant cost savings. This library may contain document templates, example plans, work products, policies, and other process enablers.

7.1.2 Organizational Process Focus

The purpose of Organizational Process Focus is to plan and implement organizational process improvement based on a thorough understanding of the current strengths and weaknesses of the organization's processes and process assets. OPF (see Figure 7-3) uses two specific goals to achieve this purpose: one for determining improvement opportunities and another for planning and implementing selected improvements. The specific practices mapped to each of these goals are shown in the context diagram.

For the first goal—determining process-improvement opportunities—the organization establishes and maintains its process needs and objectives. These pieces of information are used when appraising the processes, with the appraisal generating findings and ratings that are used along with improvement initiatives to identify the organization's needed process improvements. The organization can then select which improvements to make.

The second goal—planning and implementing those process-improvement activities—is carried out with four specific practices. The organization uses selected improvements to establish process action plans. Next, the

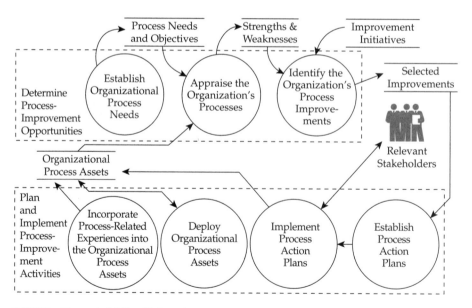

© 2002 by Carnegie Mellon University.

Figure 7-3: *Organizational Process Focus context diagram*

plans are implemented, resulting in process assets that are subsequently deployed and incorporated into the process asset library.

Note that the context diagram in Figure 7-3 (and others in this chapter) shows how typical work products of the practices may be used. In this book we will not attempt to discuss every specific practice or every arrow to or from a typical work product in the context diagram. For further information, refer to the model itself or take a formal CMMI training course. Our objective here is simply to introduce some of the important details within each process area.

7.1.3 Organizational Process Performance

The purpose of Organizational Process Performance is to establish and maintain a quantitative understanding of the performance of the organization's set of standard processes in support of quality and process-performance objectives, and to provide the process-performance data, baselines, and models to quantitatively manage the organization's projects. OPP (see Figure 7-4) has one specific goal: to establish these

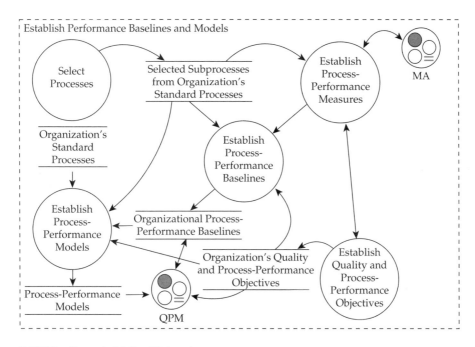

© 2002 by Carnegie Mellon University.

Figure 7-4: *Organizational Process Performance context diagram*

performance baselines and models. This "advanced" process area builds on both OPD and OPF by establishing expectations and objectives for the quantitative management of process performance.

Selected processes or subprocesses are analyzed, perhaps by examining both performance measures and product measures (for example, quality). Process-performance baselines and models are then established. The baselines measure the performance of the organization's standard processes at various levels of detail. Tailoring and other factors (such as product line, complexity, application domain, or team size and experience) can significantly affect the baselines. As a result, the organization may need several performance baselines.

7.1.4 Organizational Innovation and Deployment

The purpose of Organizational Innovation and Deployment is to select and deploy incremental and innovative improvements that measurably improve the organization's processes and technologies. The improvements support the organization's quality and process-performance objectives as derived from the organization's business objectives. OID (see Figure 7-5) adds further capability to OPD, OPF, and OPP with its

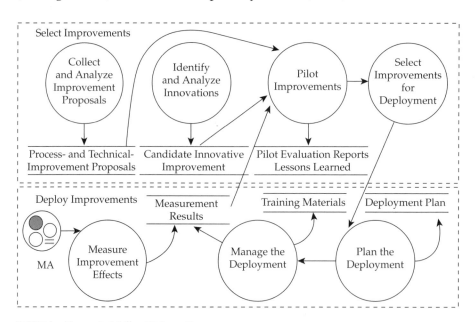

© 2002 by Carnegie Mellon University.

Figure 7-5: *Organizational Innovation and Deployment context diagram*

two goals: systematically selecting improvements and systematically deploying them.

The CMMI models include technology in the OID process area. Technology is also addressed, at least at the subprocess level and dealing with product technology, in the Technical Solution (TS) process area. In OID, both product- and process-related technology are deployed to improve the total organization.

The first OID goal—selecting improvements—involves collecting and analyzing process- and technology-improvement proposals. Innovations are identified and analyzed, evaluated through pilot projects, and then selected for deployment. The improvements may be incremental or innovative. The second goal—deploying improvements—includes planning the deployment and then measuring the effectiveness of the new process or technology as well as its effects on other management objectives.

7.1.5 Organizational Training

The purpose of Organizational Training is to develop the skills and knowledge of people so they can perform their roles effectively and efficiently. OT (see Figure 7-6) has two specific goals: one for establishing

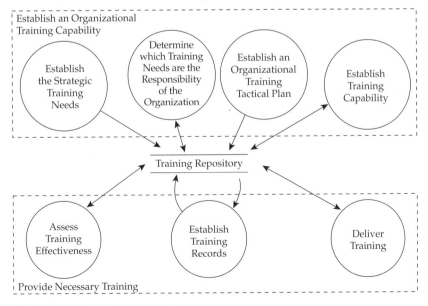

© 2002 by Carnegie Mellon University.

Figure 7-6: *Organizational Training context diagram*

an organizational training capability and another for providing necessary training. This process area does not build on the capability level of any other Process Management process area. Rather, OT focuses on the organization's strategic and cross-project training needs.

The first goal—establishing an organizational training capability—includes four specific practices. First, strategic training needs are established to guide the overall organizational training. Second, responsibility for each need is assigned, to either the organization or the project. Third, a tactical plan is established to ensure that training needs are met. This plan should explain how each of the organization's training needs will be addressed. The fourth practice addresses the actual establishment of the organization's training capability, such as developing or obtaining training materials.

Under the second goal, providing necessary training, the specific practices focus on delivery of training to the target audiences, measurement of the training's effectiveness, and creation of training records for the employees.

7.2 Project Management Process Areas

The Project Management process areas cover the activities related to planning, monitoring, and controlling the project. The CMMI-SE/SW model includes six project management process areas:[3]

- Project Planning (PP)
- Project Monitoring and Control (PMC)
- Integrated Project Management (IPM)
- Quantitative Project Management (QPM)
- Supplier Agreement Management (SAM)
- Risk Management (RSKM)

---

3. The ordering of these process areas in the continuous representation of the CMMI-SE/SW model is PP, PMC, SAM, IPM, RSKM, and QPM. In the CMMI-SE/SW/IPPD version the order is PP, PMC, SAM, IPM, RSKM, IT, and QPM. In the CMMI-SE/SW/IPPD/SS version the order is PP, PMC, SAM, IPM, RSKM, IT, ISM, and QPM. The order here is different to facilitate our explanation of relationships among the process areas.

The SE/SW/IPPD model includes one additional process area under Project Management and an expanded version of the Integrated Project Management process area:

- Integrated Project Management for IPPD (IPM)
- Integrated Teaming (IT)

The SE/SW/IPPD/SS model includes one additional process area under Project Management:

- Integrated Supplier Management (ISM)

This section describes the Project Management process areas in the CMMI-SE/SW model. Section 7.5 covers the process area in the IPPD model extension and Section 7.6 covers the process areas in the Supplier Sourcing model extension.

As shown in Figure 7-7, a close relationship exists between four of these process areas. IPM and QPM build on the capabilities of PP and PMC. This relationship is defined in the staged representation with PP and PMC at ML 2, IPM at ML 3, and QPM at ML 4. Likewise, Integrated Supplier Management (ISM) at ML 3 builds on Supplier Agreement Management at ML 2. When using the continuous representation for process improvement, you should understand this relationship and plan your improvement projects accordingly.

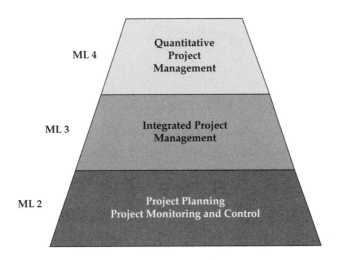

Figure 7-7: *Project Management process area relationships*

7.2.1 Project Planning

The purpose of Project Planning is to establish and maintain plans that define project activities. PP (see Figure 7-8) has three specific goals: to establish estimates, to develop a project plan, and to obtain commitments. PP and PMC work together, in that the former involves the creation of the project plans, and the latter involves tracking progress against the plans, thereby ensuring that any corrective actions are managed to closure.

In the first goal—establishing estimates for the project—the scope of the project is estimated based on a work breakdown structure, and project attributes for work products and tasks are estimated. To set the scope of the planning effort, a project life cycle is defined. Estimates of effort and cost can then be developed. These estimates are used as the basis for developing the project plans in the second goal, developing a project plan: Budgets and schedules are established, risks are identified, and plans are created for data management, resources, knowledge and skills needed, and stakeholder involvement.

For the third goal—obtaining commitment to the plan—the project reviews all of the plans that affect the project to understand project commitments, reconciles the project plan to reflect available and projected resources, and obtains commitments from relevant stakeholders responsible for performing and supporting plan execution.

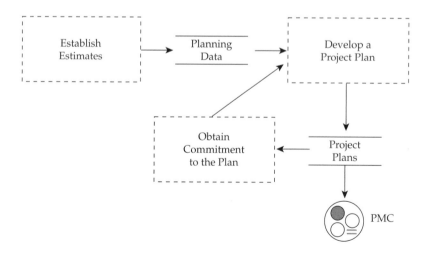

Figure 7-8: *Project Planning context diagram*

7.2.2 Project Monitoring and Control

The purpose of Project Monitoring and Control is to provide an understanding of the project's progress so that appropriate corrective actions can be taken when the project's performance deviates significantly from the plan. PMC (see Figure 7-9) has two specific goals: one on monitoring actual performance, and another on managing corrective actions.

The first goal—monitor the project against the plan—has five practices that identify what should be monitored and two practices that deal with reviews. The monitoring focuses on the following:

- Project planning parameters
- Commitments
- Project risks
- Data management
- Stakeholder involvement

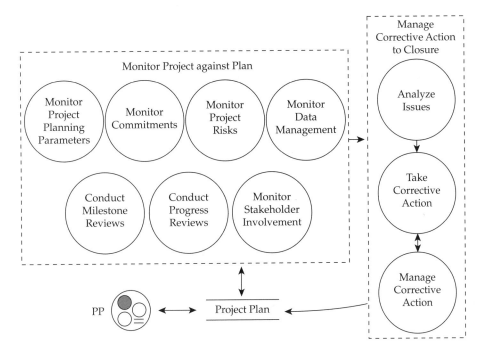

Figure 7-9: *Project Monitoring and Control context diagram*

These monitoring efforts are reviewed at both progress reviews and milestone reviews. Whenever these practices identify needed corrective actions, the second goal—managing corrective actions—provides specific practices to analyze the issues, take the necessary action, and manage the corrective action to closure. Note that other CMMI process areas (such as Verification, Supplier Agreement Management, and Configuration Management) refer to this PMC goal and its practices to obtain information about managing corrective actions.

7.2.3 Integrated Project Management

The purpose of Integrated Project Management is to establish and manage the project and the involvement of the relevant stakeholders according to an integrated and defined process that is tailored from the organization's set of standard processes. IPM (see Figure 7-10) has two specific goals in the CMMI-SE/SW model. Adding IPPD provides two more specific goals. The two basic specific goals relate to using a defined process for the project and coordinating activities with relevant

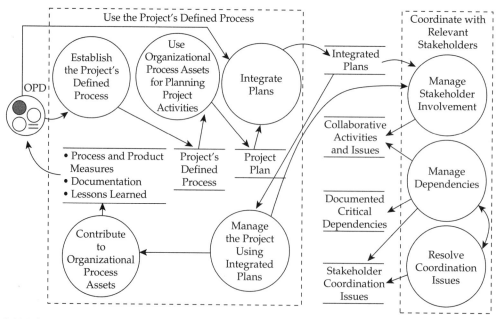

© 2002 by Carnegie Mellon University.

Figure 7-10: *Integrated Project Management (without IPPD) context diagram*

stakeholders. These goals build on the planning covered in PP, by making sure that the appropriate organizations and people are involved in managing the project. The organization's standard processes, which were developed in the Organizational Process Definition process area, are the basis for the project's defined process.

The first IPM goal—using a defined process for the project—has five practices. Establishing the project's defined process is the first step, with the organization's standard processes serving as a starting point. Next, the organizational process assets from the organizational process asset library are used for planning the project activities, integrating all plans to describe the defined process, and managing using the integrated plans. Finally, the project contributes its work products to the organization's process assets for use by future projects and process-improvement activities.

The second basic goal—coordination and collaboration with relevant stakeholders—has three practices, which focus on managing the involvement of stakeholders to satisfy commitments and resolve mis-

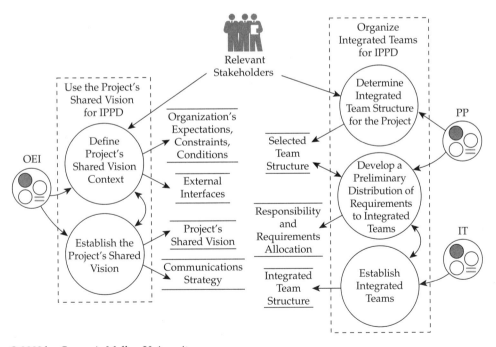

Figure 7-11: *Integrated Project Management for IPPD context diagram*

understandings, tracking critical project dependencies, and resolving outstanding issues.

The addition of IPPD brings two more specific goals: using the project's shared vision and organizing integrated teams. The first goal (Figure 7-11), which is dubbed SG 3 in the IPPD version, defines a shared vision context that is used to establish a shared vision for the project and evaluates the use and effectiveness of that vision. The second goal, called SG 4 in the IPPD version, organizes integrated teams by determining team structure for a project, developing a plan for distributing requirements to the team, and establishing the teams.

7.2.4 Quantitative Project Management

The purpose of the Quantitative Project Management process area is to quantitatively manage the project's defined process to achieve the project's established quality and process-performance objectives. QPM (see Figure 7-12) has two specific goals that build on the goals of PP,

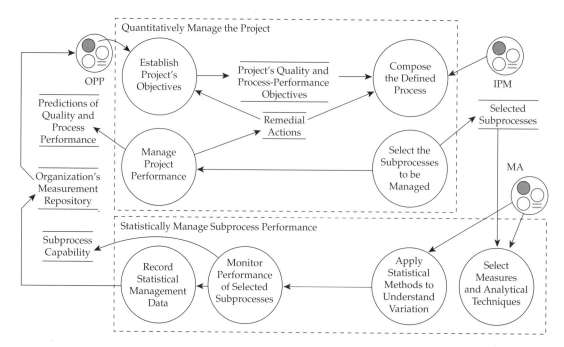

Figure 7-12: *Quantitative Project Management context diagram*

PMC, and IPM: using performance objectives to quantitatively manage the project and statistically managing selected subprocesses. The first goal—using performance objectives to quantitatively manage the project—is achieved by specific practices that establish performance objectives, analyze and select candidate subprocesses, and monitor the project's performance objectives to determine whether they have been satisfied. The second goal—statistically managing selected subprocesses—is achieved by specific practices that select measures and analytical techniques, understand variation, monitor the selected subprocesses, and record the resulting data in a measurement repository for the organization. In this way, QPM builds on PMC by ensuring that the organization uses statistical management practices as well as historical data to determine objectives and select the subprocesses that will be quantitatively managed.

7.2.5 Supplier Agreement Management

The purpose of Supplier Agreement Management is to manage the acquisition of products from suppliers for which there exists a formal agreement. SAM (see Figure 7-13) has two specific goals: one for

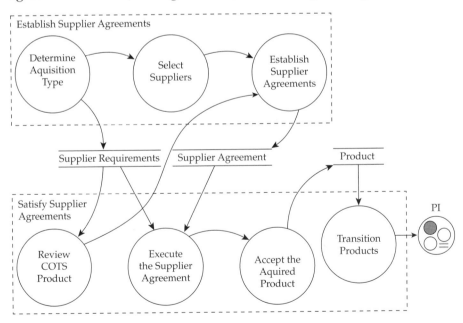

© 2002 by Carnegie Mellon University.

Figure 7-13: *Supplier Agreement Management context diagram*

establishing supplier agreements and another for satisfying them. This process area works in cooperation with the Technical Solution process area, in which the organization decides whether to make or buy products. Once a decision to buy is made, SAM creates the agreement and then manages it from the purchaser's viewpoint. Product-component requirements are developed in the Requirements Development process area.

In the first goal—establishing supplier agreements—the project analyzes the acquisition options to see how well they meet the needs and requirements. Suppliers are then identified and selected, and an agreement is established. In the second goal—satisfying supplier agreements—the project reviews commercial off-the-shelf (COTS) products, performs the activities mandated in the supplier agreements, ensures that the supplier agreement is satisfied before accepting the acquired products, and transitions the acquired products to the project for the integration effort.

7.2.6 Risk Management

The purpose of Risk Management is to identify potential problems before they occur, so that risk-handling activities may be planned and invoked as needed across the life of the product or project to mitigate adverse impacts on achieving objectives. RSKM (see Figure 7-14) actually builds on part of the PP process area, as a specific practice in PP identifies and analyzes project risks, and the project plan should document those risks. However, PP is less systematic and less proactive than the requirements noted in RSKM. Furthermore, RSKM could be applied outside of the project context to manage organizational risks (if desired). Several other process areas reference RSKM.

RSKM has three specific goals that involve preparation for risk management, identification and analysis of the risks, and handling and mitigation of risks as appropriate. The first goal—prepare for risk management—includes determining risk sources and the categories used for organizing risks by "bins," establishing the parameters used to analyze and categorize risks, and developing a risk strategy. The second goal—identification and analysis—focuses on determining the relative priority of the risks based on the analysis parameters. The third goal—handling and mitigation of the risks—encompasses developing and implementing risk mitigation plans.

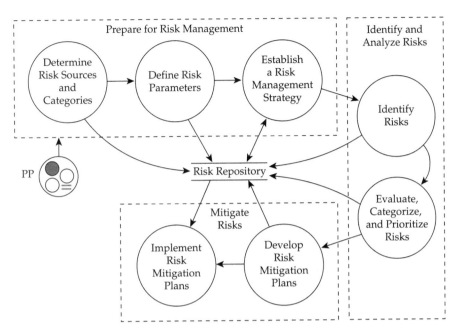

Figure 7-14: *Risk Management context diagram*

7.3 Engineering Process Areas

In both the Process Management and Project Management categories, (some of) the process areas build upon and presuppose others. In contrast, the Engineering category lacks one-directional, "build upon" relationships between process areas. Instead, it is assumed that all of the process areas are used together in an integrated manner. In CMMI, the Engineering process areas integrate engineering processes into a "product-oriented" set of process areas. Improving product development processes means targeting essential business objectives, rather than the more narrow objectives of specific disciplines. That is, the Engineering process areas are constructed to discourage the tendency toward a "stovepiped" set of processes.

The Engineering process areas apply to the development of any product or service in the engineering development domain (for example, software products, hardware products, services, or processes). They address all development using the term "product" rather than "system." This choice was made to avoid problems with that terminology. The process areas apply recursively at all levels of product development. The term "product component" designates the building blocks of the "product."

These process areas are constructed to apply to many different types of organizations, not just those responsible for the initial systems engineering and software development work. For example, a software maintenance organization that provides software updates to a system may not have been part of the initial development effort. Such a group may review the CMMI Engineering process areas and decide that Requirements Development doesn't apply to it; someone else handled those activities. In reality, any engineering change request is based on some need. That need should be elicited, new requirements should be determined based on it, and alternative solutions should be considered before the selected solution is designed, implemented, verified, and validated. In this way, the technical control based on these principles ensures that all maintenance actions are necessary and meet the user's needs.

The requirement for the model to support both continuous and staged representations, however, caused some problems. One architectural feature of CMMI is that only the Engineering process areas contain advanced practices—that is, specific practices assigned to a capability level greater than CL 1.[4] In the CMMI models that have been released to date, the advanced practices in the Engineering process areas are all at CL 2 or CL 3. Because the CMMI lacks advanced practices in process areas other than Engineering, the definition of the capability levels is complicated, especially in the Process Management and Project Management categories, where some of the process areas build on each other.[5]

---

4. The discussions on the CMMI Team regarding advanced practices were highly contentious. Some team members wanted no advanced practices; others wanted them throughout the model. The decision to put them in only the Engineering process areas represented a "middle-ground" decision based on the fact that many of the advanced practices in EIA 731 resided in these process areas. It also reflected the hope that practical application of CMMI models would enable the community to determine how useful advanced practices are for process improvement, thereby deciding the fate of this model construct.

5. The argument in favor of advanced practices states that they help define the capability levels within a process area and identify a clear path of process improvement. Specific goals become complicated, however, because they are defined as covering all specific practices at all capability levels. Thus a specific goal takes on an expanded meaning as one moves from one capability level to the next. Some find this flexibility problematic; others do not.

Six Engineering process areas exist:

- Requirements Management (REQM)
- Requirements Development (RD)
- Technical Solution (TS)
- Product Integration (PI)
- Verification (VER)
- Validation (VAL)

In this section, descriptions of the specific practices will identify advanced practices with the capability level in parentheses, such as "(CL 2)."

7.3.1 Requirements Management

The purpose of Requirements Management is to manage the requirements of the project's products and product components and to identify inconsistencies between those requirements and the project's plans and work products. REQM (see Figure 7-15) has one specific goal: to manage requirements and identify inconsistencies with plans and work products. It is the only Engineering process area that is staged at ML 2; all other Engineering process areas are staged at ML 3. The CMM

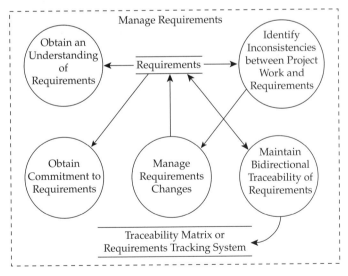

Figure 7-15: *Requirements Management context diagram*

for Software had a Requirements Management process area at ML 2 that led to the inclusion of this process area at ML 2 in CMMI.

REQM has five specific practices, including two advanced practices at CL 2. Neither of these advanced practices builds on a lower-level practice.[6] To achieve CL 1 in REQM with the CMMI continuous representation, the single specific goal of managing requirements can be met with just the three expected specific practices at CL 1 (that is, ignoring the other two specific practices). To achieve CL 2 in REQM, the goal must be met with all five expected specific practices. At either CL 1 or CL 2, if alternative practices were used to satisfy the goal, an expanded set of alternative practices would be needed for CL 2 compared with CL 1, so as to match the expanded expectation.[7]

Here and in other Engineering process areas we will present all specific practices as a group. We take the viewpoint of the higher capability levels and explicitly note all advanced practices.

To manage requirements, the person or team that receives them needs to develop an understanding of what they mean before doing anything with the requirements. It should obtain a commitment from the people who implement the requirements (CL 2). Once the requirements are received and understood, and a commitment is obtained, all changes to the requirements should be managed, including recording change histories and evaluating change impacts. The project should provide for bidirectional traceability of the requirement and the associated plans and work products (CL 2). Tracing the requirements provides a better basis for determining the ramifications of changes, and it ensures that all requirements have a parent and that the product design covers all high-level requirements. Finally, the project should identify inconsistencies between the requirements and the project plans and work products. Any corrective action required to fix inconsistencies is accomplished in the requirements development process, the project planning process, or possibly other processes.

---

6. Some Engineering process areas include a base practice that says to do something, plus an advanced practice that says to do the same thing better. In this way, an advanced practice "builds on" a lower-level practice. Not all advanced practices follow this pattern, as the examples here from REQM show.

7. When advanced practices are mapped to a goal, the satisfaction of the goal is not a binary affair. A basic way of satisfying the goal exists, as does a more advanced way of satisfying the same goal. Some critics have labeled this phenomenon "chameleonic goals."

7.3.2 Requirements Development

The purpose of Requirements Development is to produce and analyze customer, product, and product-component requirements. RD (see Figure 7-16) has three specific goals: developing customer requirements, developing product requirements, and analyzing and validating requirements to produce a definition of the required functionality. This process area contains all of the practices related to generating product and product-component requirements. It is recursive with TS, with alternative solutions being developed to help determine lower-level product requirements.

Figure 7-16 shows a simplified context diagram for RD, because this process area contains too many specific practices to include on one figure. Furthermore, Figure 7-16 does not really illustrate how the requirements are developed. The analysis tasks are performed concurrently with the development tasks. Processes developed from RD practices should be designed to meet the needs of the organization. They can represent several different product life-cycle models, such as waterfall, iterative, incremental, and multilevel models.

The development process needs a starting point, and RD's first goal provides it by developing customer requirements. The first two specific practices call for the collection (CL 1) and elicitation (CL 2) of

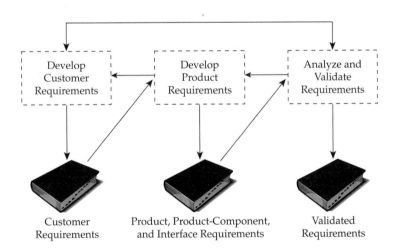

Figure 7-16: *Requirements Development context diagram*

stakeholder needs, expectations, constraints, and interfaces. Providing information on needs allows the customer (and other stakeholders) to describe the product's desired function, performance, appearance, and other characteristics. In the third specific practice, the stakeholders' needs, expectations, constraints, and interfaces are translated into customer requirements.

In the staged representation, only the second (elicit needs) and third (transform into customer requirements) specific practices are expected; the first specific practice (collect needs) is listed as informative only. Why does this difference arise if both representations are really two views of the same model? How can a specific practice be an expected item in one representation but not in the other? Actually, this discrepancy is not difficult to understand. When (as here) an advanced practice builds on a lower-level practice, which makes sense for distinguishing two capability levels in a continuous representation, only the advanced practice appears in the staged representation.

In a process area that exists at just one maturity level, it would be awkward to have two specific practices where one subsumes the other: (1) do x and (2) do x better. Because you cannot successfully perform the advanced practice and yet fail to meet the base practice, the latter is not needed in the staged world.

RD's second goal addresses the use of customer requirements to develop the product-level and product-component-level requirements. In some cases, these requirements may consist of a system and its subsystems, boxes, boards, software configuration items, software components, and modules. In other cases, they may include processes, subprocesses, or service-related products. The three specific practices focus on translating the customer requirements into the more technical form of product requirements, allocating the requirements to each component of the product, and identifying interface requirements. One way of handling interfaces is to treat them as if they were the same as the other requirements. Note, however, that a lack of attention to the interfaces often results in defects, which can lead to rework, cost overruns, and schedule slips.

In RD's third goal, the requirements are analyzed and validated as they are developed; this step is critical for the success of a product. The six specific practices that map to this goal involve preparation, analysis, and validation. To get started, a good way to undertake the analysis is to develop operational concepts and scenarios that detail the way the product will be used, stored, transported, and so forth. The operational concepts help define the requirements from a broad, in-use point of view, and they help establish a definition of the required functionality.

Analysis of requirements ensures that they are necessary and sufficient to meet the objectives of the higher-level requirements. In addition, requirements are analyzed to balance stakeholder needs and constraints (CL 3). Two specific practices address validating requirements—one at CL 1 and one at CL 2. The first base practice ensures that the resulting product will perform appropriately in its intended use environment. The second builds on the first, adding the use of multiple techniques to further reduce the risks of proceeding. Only the advanced practice is explicitly listed as expected in the staged representation.

7.3.3 Technical Solution

The purpose of Technical Solution is to design, develop, and implement solutions to requirements. Solutions, designs, and implementations encompass products, product components, and product-related life-cycle processes either singly or in combinations as appropriate. TS (see Figure 7-17) has three specific goals that address selecting product-component solutions, developing the design, and implementing the design. The context diagram in Figure 7-17 is high level, showing only the goals. In the first goal—selecting product-component solutions—alternative solutions are developed and analyzed, and the one that best

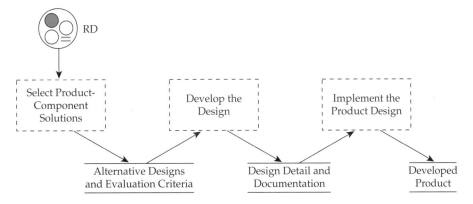

© 2002 by Carnegie Mellon University.

Figure 7-17: *Technical Solution context diagram*

satisfies the criteria is selected. The selected alternative may be used to develop more detailed requirements in the RD process area or designed in the second goal of TS. After the product components are designed, they are implemented together with support documentation in the third goal of TS.

The first TS goal includes four specific practices, the second of which (at CL 2) builds on the first: develop alternative solutions and develop detailed alternative solutions. CMMI characterizes a "detailed alternative solution" by means of a list of basic things to be included.[8] The specific practice to evolve the operational concepts and scenarios based on the alternative solutions (CL 2) helps determine which alternative to select, along with the other criteria that have been established. For the fourth specific practice, the engineer or team selects the solution that best satisfies the established criteria.

For the second goal—developing the product or product-component designs—five specific practices exist. The first specific practice develops a design for the product component. The second practice (at CL 3) develops a technical data package. The fourth specific practice (at CL 3) builds on the third (at CL 1): establish product-component interface solutions, and do so in terms of established criteria. In the final specific practice (at CL 3), the project evaluates whether the product components should be developed, purchased, or reused. If it decides to purchase a component, the SAM process area establishes the agreement and manages it.

The third goal—implementing the product components and generating associated support documentation—has two specific practices. For the first, the project implements the designs for all types of product components—software, hardware, and so on. For the second, it develops and maintains the end-use support documentation that describes how to install, operate, and maintain the product.

7.3.4 Product Integration

The purpose of Product Integration is to assemble the product from the product components, ensure that the product (as integrated) functions properly, and deliver the product. PI (see Figure 7-18) has three specific

---

8. This choice reduced the number of specific practices in the model; an alternative would have been to add additional specific practices to address the listed items individually.

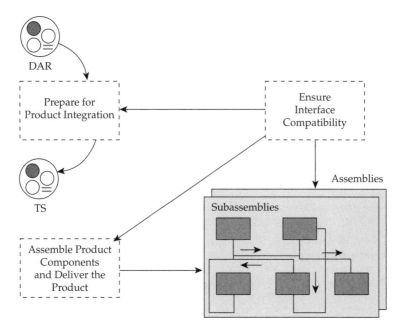

© 2002 by Carnegie Mellon University.

Figure 7-18: *Product Integration context diagram*

goals that address preparing for integration, ensuring interface compatibility, and assembling the product components for delivery.

The first goal—preparing for integration—includes three specific practices. First, the project develops the sequence for integration, which assists in the overall planning effort. Second, it establishes the environment for integration (CL 2). Finally, it defines the procedures and criteria for integration (CL 3).

The second goal—ensuring that the interfaces (both internal and external) are compatible—has two specific practices. First, the project reviews the interface descriptions for coverage and completeness. Note that interfaces to the environment are included in this practice. Then, it manages the interface definitions, designs, and changes for the product and product components to maintain consistency and resolve issues.

The third goal—assemble product components and deliver the product—has four specific practices. After the product components are implemented and unit testing is complete, the integration process begins. The lowest levels of the product are usually integrated first, with the product being assembled in successive stages. In CMMI, the delivery of the product occurs in the PI process area. First, the project confirms that each component has been properly identified and functions according to its description, and that the interfaces comply with their descriptions. This step helps avoid problems during assembly of the product components, which occurs in the next specific practice. Personnel then evaluate the assembly according to the procedures. Finally, they package the product and deliver it to the appropriate customer.

7.3.5 Verification

The purpose of Verification is to ensure that selected work products meet their specified requirements. VER (see Figure 7-19) has three specific goals that address preparing for verification, performing peer reviews on selected work products, and verifying selected work products.

The first goal—preparing for verification—has three specific practices. These three practices resemble PI's preparation specific practices: select the work products and the verification methods early in the project, establish the environment for verification (CL 2), and define the procedures and criteria for selected work products (CL 3). Verification planning is performed early in the project, because many of the activities associated with requirements development and design (such as analyses, reviews, and demonstrations) involve ensuring that the requirements are, in fact, verifiable.

The second goal—performing peer reviews on selected work products—has three practices. Peer reviews comprise a specialized verification

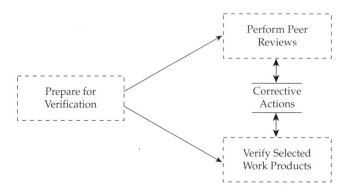

© 2002 by Carnegie Mellon University.

Figure 7-19: *Verification context diagram*

activity intended to reduce defects in selected work products. Among software developers, they are perceived to be a highly valued technique. In fact, the CMM for Software devoted an entire key process area to peer reviews. For the specific practices, the project first prepares for the peer reviews, then conducts them, and finally (at CL 2) analyzes the preparation, conduct, and results. Selection is a critical step in the preparation stage; the cost of conducting the reviews means that they should remain limited to key work products.

For the third goal—verifying selected work products—two specific practices exist. First, personnel perform verification according to the verification procedures, capturing results and associated action items. Then (at CL 2) they analyze the results and further identify needed corrective actions based on established verification criteria.

7.3.6 Validation

The purpose of Validation is to demonstrate that a product or product component fulfills its intended use when placed in its intended environment. VAL (see Figure 7-20) has two specific goals that address preparing for validation and validating the product or product components. The validation practices are similar to those used in verification, but the two process areas focus on different topics. Validation addresses those activities needed to show that a product fulfills its intended use when it is placed in its intended environment, whereas verification shows that the work products meet their specified requirements.

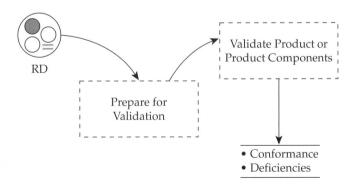

Figure 7-20: *Validation context diagram*

The first goal—preparing for validation—has three specific practices, which mirror those in PI and VER. First, the project selects the products and product components for validation. Next, it establishes the environment for validation (CL 2). Finally, personnel define the procedures and criteria for validation (CL 3).

The second goal—performing validation—has two specific practices. First, workers perform the validation according to the procedures to show that the product or product component performs as intended. Then, they capture and analyze the validation results, identifying any problems or unresolved issues.

7.4 Support Process Areas

The Support process areas provide essential processes that are used by other CMMI process areas; in addition they are used by the CMMI generic practices. In general, these process areas are targeted toward the project (except for Process and Product Quality Assurance). When necessary, however, they can be applied more generally to the organization. For example, Process and Product Quality Assurance can be used with all other process areas to provide an objective review of the processes and work products described in them.

The SE/SW model includes five Support process areas:[9]

- Configuration Management (CM)
- Process and Product Quality Assurance (PPQA)
- Measurement and Analysis (MA)
- Decision Analysis and Resolution (DAR)
- Causal Analysis and Resolution (CAR)

The SE/SW/IPPD model includes one additional process area for the Support category:

- Organizational Environment for Integration (OEI)

---

9. The ordering of these process areas in the continuous representation of the CMMI-SE/SW model is as listed: CM, PPQA, MA, DAR, and CAR. In the CMMI-SE/SW/IPPD and CMMI-SE/SW/IPPD/SS versions the order is CM, PPQA, MA, DAR, OEI, and CAR.

This section describes the Support process areas in the SE/SW model. Section 7.5 provides a description of the OEI process area in the IPPD model extension.

7.4.1 Configuration Management

The purpose of Configuration Management is to establish and maintain the integrity of work products using configuration identification, configuration control, configuration status accounting, and configuration audits. CM (see Figure 7-21) has three specific goals that address establishing baselines, tracking and controlling changes, and establishing the integrity of baselines. It is assumed that Configuration Management can occur at multiple levels of granularity and formality. This process area is closely connected with the generic practice at CL 2 to manage configurations; it provides the process to be used when applying that generic practice.

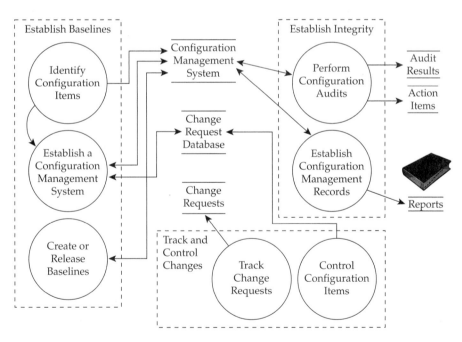

© 2002 by Carnegie Mellon University.

Figure 7-21: *Configuration Management context diagram*

The first goal—establishing baselines for work products—has three specific practices: identifying the items to be placed under configuration management, establishing a configuration management and change management system, and creating or releasing the baselines. Once baselines are established using a configuration management system, all changes are tracked and controlled in the second goal—track and control changes—with two specific practices. The first tracks the requests for changes, and the second tracks content changes to the configuration items. The third goal—establishing the integrity of the baselines—has two specific practices: one for keeping records on the configuration items, and another for performing configuration audits to ensure that the baselines are correct.

7.4.2 Process and Product Quality Assurance

The purpose of Process and Product Quality Assurance is to provide staff and management with objective insight into the processes and associated work products. PPQA (see Figure 7-22) has two specific

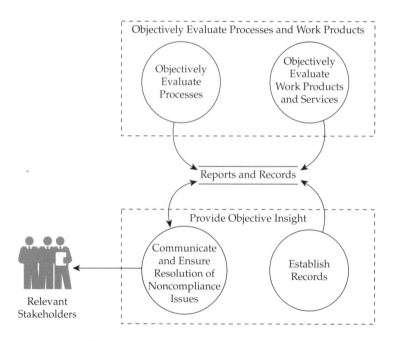

© 2000 by Carnegie Mellon University.

Figure 7-22: *Process and Product Quality Assurance context diagram*

goals: objectively evaluating adherence to process descriptions, standards, and procedures; and resolving noncompliance issues. To achieve objective evaluation, some organizations may strive for independent oversight of the processes and work products, perhaps via a quality assurance department. Other organizations may embed the quality assurance function within the process, placing greater emphasis on evaluation by peers. CMMI supports both options. This process area is closely connected with the generic practice at CL 2 to objectively evaluate adherence; it provides the process to be used when applying that generic practice.

The first goal—objectively evaluating adherence of the performed process and associated work products and services to applicable process descriptions, standards, and procedures—is addressed with two specific practices. One conducts an objective evaluation of the performed process, and the other performs an objective evaluation of designated work products. The second goal—resolving noncompliance issues—is also addressed by two specific practices. The first communicates noncompliance issues with relevant stakeholders and ensures their resolution by progressive escalation, and the second establishes and maintains records of quality assurance activities.

7.4.3 Measurement and Analysis

The purpose of Measurement and Analysis is to develop and sustain a measurement capability that is used to support management information needs. MA (see Figure 7-23) has two specific goals: one for aligning measurement activities with information needs, and one for providing measurement results that satisfy those needs. This process area is loosely connected with two generic practices at CL 2. That is, planning the process includes defining measurement objectives, and monitoring and controlling the process encompasses measuring performance against the plan.

The practices of the two MA goals provide an eight-step measurement process with four specific practices mapped to each of the two goals. For the first goal—align measurement and analysis activities—personnel define the objectives to meet the information needs, specify the measures that will be needed to meet the objectives, indicate how the data will be obtained and stored, and determine how the data will be analyzed and reported. For the second goal—provide measurement results—they collect the data, analyze and interpret the information

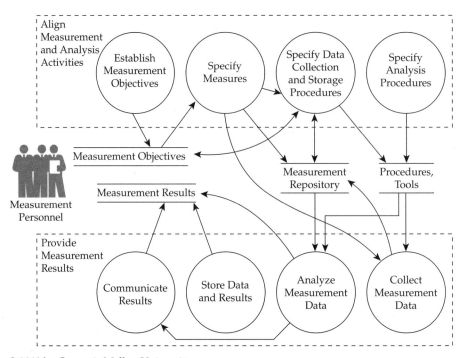

© 2002 by Carnegie Mellon University.

Figure 7-23: *Measurement and Analysis context diagram*

gathered, manage and store both the data and the analysis results, and communicate the results to the stakeholders.

7.4.4 Decision Analysis and Resolution

The purpose of Decision Analysis and Resolution is to analyze possible decisions using a formal evaluation process that evaluates identified alternatives against established criteria. DAR (see Figure 7-24) has one specific goal, related to evaluating alternatives using established criteria.

The practices of this process area identify a six-step process for making decisions in a structured manner:

1. Establish and maintain guidelines to determine which issues are subject to DAR.
2. Establish and maintain the criteria for evaluating alternatives, and the relative ranking of these criteria.

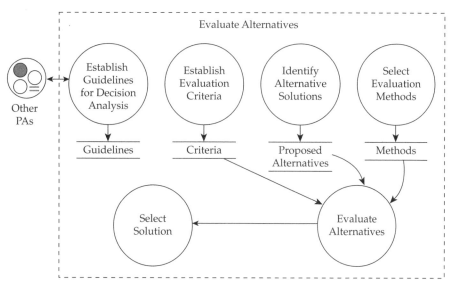

Evaluate Alternatives

© 2002 by Carnegie Mellon University.

Figure 7-24: *Decision Analysis and Resolution context diagram*

3. Identify alternative solutions to address issues.
4. Select the evaluation methods.
5. Evaluate alternative solutions using the established criteria and methods.
6. Select a solution, documenting its results and rationale.

Only the key issues for a project would warrant the structured decision-making process of DAR. But an organization can use DAR for any significant decision that needs to be made. Possible examples might include architectural or design alternatives, make–buy decisions, and tool selection. DAR should not be used for making relatively insignificant decisions, such as buying pencils or paper. In reality, some process is used even in low-level decisions; it just isn't required or expected by the CMMI models.

7.4.5 Causal Analysis and Resolution

The purpose of Causal Analysis and Resolution is to identify causes of defects and other problems and take action to prevent them from occurring in the future. CAR (see Figure 7-25) has two specific goals:

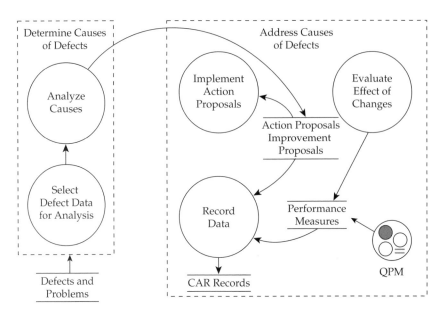

© 2002 by Carnegie Mellon University.

Figure 7-25: *Causal Analysis and Resolution context diagram*

one for determining the root causes of defects, and another for addressing these causes to prevent the future occurrence of those defects. This process area is closely related to the generic practice at capability level 5 that seeks to identify and correct the root causes of defects and other process-related problems; the processes of CAR should be used when applying that generic practice.

For the first goal—determining root causes—two specific practices exist: select the defects for analysis, and perform causal analysis and propose actions to address these problems. For the second goal—addressing the root causes of defects and other problems—three specific practices are provided: implement the action proposals, evaluate the effects of the changes on process performance, and record the data from the CAR activities for subsequent use by other projects in the organization.

7.5 Integrated Product and Process Development Process Areas

Integrated Product and Process Development (IPPD) represents a systematic approach to product development that achieves a timely collaboration of relevant stakeholders throughout the product life cycle so as to better satisfy customer needs. When an organization chooses to use IPPD in the CMMI model, two new process areas and two new specific goals in the Integrated Project Management process area are added to the model. Several new amplifications of other model elements and an additional front matter section are added as well. This section describes IPPD process areas.

7.5.1 Integrated Teaming

The purpose of Integrated Teaming is to form and sustain an integrated team for the development of work products. Integrated Teaming,[10] as shown in Figure 7-26, has two specific goals: establishing team composition so as to provide needed knowledge and skills, and governing the operation of the team.

The first goal—establishing team composition—has three specific practices. First, personnel identify and define the specific internal tasks needed to generate the team's expected output. Second, they identify the knowledge, skills, and functional expertise needed to perform those tasks. Third, the organization assigns the appropriate personnel to be team members, based on those employees having the required knowledge and skills.

The second goal—operating the integrated team according to established principles—has five specific practices. First, the integrated team establishes and maintains a shared vision that is aligned with its overarching or higher-level vision; a team with a shared vision is more likely to function with unity of purpose. Next, it establishes and maintains a team charter—a "contract" related to the expected work and the level of performance—based on the integrated team's shared vision and overall objectives. Then, it clearly defines each team member's

---

10. Although Integrated Teaming is categorized as a Project Management process area in the continuous representation, the authors decided to discuss it here in a separate IPPD section.

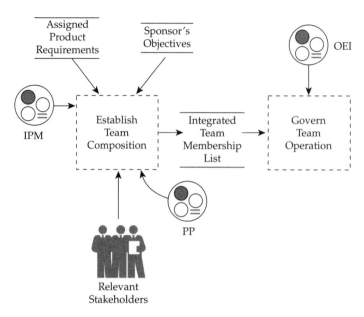

© 2002 by Carnegie Mellon University.

Figure 7-26: *Integrated Teaming context diagram*

roles and responsibilities based on the charter. The team then establishes operating procedures and, finally, collaborates with other teams as necessary.

7.5.2 Organizational Environment for Integration

The purpose of Organizational Environment for Integration is to provide an Integrated Product and Process Development infrastructure and manage people for integration. Organizational Environment for Integration,[11] as shown in Figure 7-27, has two specific goals: providing an IPPD infrastructure and managing people so as to nurture successful IPPD behavior.

For the first goal—providing an infrastructure that maximizes the productivity of people and effects the collaboration necessary for integration—three specific practices exist. First, the organization

---

11. Organizational Environment for Integration is considered as a Support process area in the continuous representation.

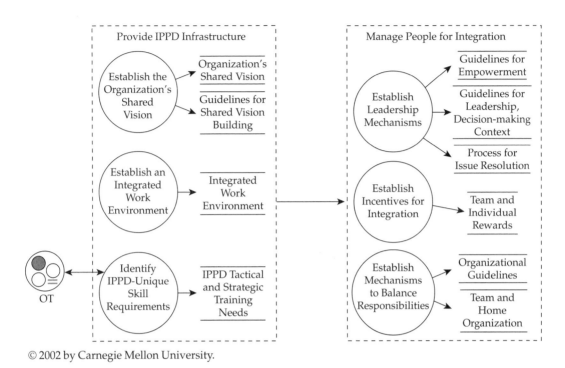

Figure 7-27: *Organizational Environment for Integration context diagram*

establishes a shared vision, including a mission, objectives, expected behavior, and values. Next, it creates an integrated work environment that supports IPPD by enabling collaboration and concurrent development. Finally, it identifies the unique skills needed to support the IPPD environment.

For the second goal—managing people so as to nurture the integrative and collaborative behaviors of an IPPD environment—three specific practices apply. First, the organization establishes leadership mechanisms to enable timely collaboration. Next, it specifies incentives for adopting and demonstrating integrative and collaborative behaviors at all levels of the organization. Finally, organizational guidelines are developed that seek to balance team and home organization responsibilities. The home organization includes the part of the organization to which personnel are assigned, their "homeroom," even when they function as members of integrated teams. It may also be called the "functional organization," "home base," "home office," or "direct organization." Whatever its title, the home organization typically is responsible for the career growth of the personnel assigned to it; for example, it may provide performance appraisals and training to maintain functional and discipline expertise.

7.6 Supplier Sourcing Process Areas

Supplier Sourcing is considered as a discipline in CMMI. The Integrated Supplier Management process area focuses on managing the acquisition of products and services, rather than developing them. Several "Supplier Sourcing amplifications" in other process areas describe how those practices should be interpreted when using them for acquisition projects or portions of a project that purchase (rather than make) product components. The user should constantly keep one question in mind: "How do I interpret these words in the context of Supplier Sourcing?"

7.6.1 Integrated Supplier Management

The purpose of Integrated Supplier Management is to proactively identify sources of products that may be used to satisfy the project's requirements and to manage selected suppliers while maintaining a cooperative project-supplier relationship. A close relationship exists between ISM and IPM, with both addressing integrated management. ISM has two goals that address analyzing sources of products and coordinating work with suppliers, as shown in Figure 7-28.

The first goal—analyze and select sources of products—has two practices. First the project analyzes and selects off-the-shelf products that may satisfy the requirements, analyzes and identifies sources of custom-made products, and then performs trade-off studies to determine the sources of products to be acquired. The informative material describes a more proactive approach than the one described in Supplier Agreement Management.

The second goal—coordinate work with suppliers—focuses on the supplier process and custom-made products throughout the agreement's period of performance. It is accomplished by monitoring and analyzing the supplier's engineering process and its results, and by making changes to the supplier agreement to accommodate the supplier-related risks.

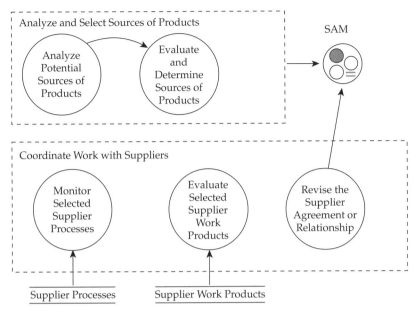

© 2002 by Carnegie Mellon University.

Figure 7-28: *Integrated Supplier Management context diagram*

7.7 Relationships within CMMI Components

The internal references in the CMMI models represent valuable information about how the processes work together to achieve improvement. Two major sources of relationships are found in the models: those among process areas and those between process areas and generic practices.

7.7.1 Relationships among Process Areas

Table 7-2 describes the key relationships among process areas by summarizing the references from the "Related Process Areas" section of each process area. The models discuss some key relationships between process areas but don't provide such a summary. Specific information about relationships between lower-level components, such as specific practices and subpractices, is also included in the models, but a summary at that level is beyond the scope of this book.

Table 7-2: *CMMI Related Process Areas*

Process Area	Related Process Areas
Organizational Process Focus	OPD
Organizational Process Definition	OPF
Organizational Training	OPD, PP, DAR
Organizational Process Performance	QPM, MA
Organizational Innovation and Deployment	OPF, OPD, OPP, OT, MA, IPM for IPPD, DAR
Project Planning	RD, REQM, RSKM, TS, MA
Project Monitoring and Control	PP, MA
Supplier Agreement Management	PMC, RD, REQM, TS
Integrated Project Management for IPPD	PP, PMC, VER, OPD, MA, IT, OEI
Risk Management	PP, PMC, DAR
Integrated Teaming	PP, OEI, IPM for IPPD
Integrated Supplier Management	SAM, PP, IPM for IPPD, RSKM, REQM, RD, TS
Quantitative Project Management	PMC, MA, OPP, OPD, IPM for IPPD, CAR, OID
Requirements Management	RD, TS, PP, CM, PMC, RSKM
Requirements Development	REQM, TS, PI, VER, VAL, RSKM, CM
Technical Solution	RD, VER, DAR, REQM, OID
Product Integration	RD, TS, VER, VAL, RSKM, DAR, CM, SAM
Verification	IPM for IPPD, RD, VAL, REQM

Process Area	Related Process Areas
Validation	RD, TS, VER
Configuration Management	PP, CAR, PMC
Process and Product Quality Assurance	PP, VER
Measurement and Analysis	PP, PMC, CM, RD, REQM, OPD, QPM
Decision Analysis and Resolution	PP, IPM for IPPD, RSKM
Organizational Environment for Integration	IPM for IPPD, OPD, OT
Causal Analysis and Resolution	QPM, OID, MA

We can make several observations after looking at Table 7-2. First, note the strong interrelationship within the Engineering process areas. Not surprisingly, Project Planning and Measurement and Analysis are key to successful implementation of a variety of process areas.

The references reveal the fundamental inter-relationships within the management processes through the number and type of cross-references within the Process Management category. Notice that the higher-capability-level process areas reference the lower-level process areas. Thus the higher-level process areas depend heavily on the lower-level process areas for implementation. The same type of relationship links Quantitative Project Management to the other Project Management process areas.

Probably the most telling observation is the lack of stand-alone process areas. This view of the model clearly indicates that an organization should pay close attention to its business objectives and ensure that its tailored model considers all aspects of the model at the appropriate time.

7.7.2 Relationships between Generic Practices and Process Areas

The references between the generic practices and process areas identify close relationships between those model components, as shown in Table 7-3. A close look at the generic practices reveals practices that are

Table 7-3: *Generic Practice References*

Generic Practice	Process Area
GP 2.6 Manage Configurations	CM
GP 2.7 Identify and Involve Relevant Stakeholders	PP
GP 2.8 Monitor and Control the Process	PMC, MA
GP 2.9 Objectively Evaluate Adherence	PPQA
GP 3.1 Establish a Defined Process	OPD
GP 3.2 Collect Improvement Information	OPD
GP 4.1 Establish Quality Objectives	QPM
GP 5.2 Correct Common Cause of Problems	CAR

almost identical to those specified in the process areas. Because the process areas provide the "detailed what to do" for implementing the generic practices, they may be thought of as "enabling" process areas. Notice, also, that each generic practice resides at the same capability level as the process area that enables it. This correspondence is not a random artifact, but was crafted in such a manner to provide the mechanism for staging.

The process area provides detailed guidance on how to implement the generic practice, which raises some interesting questions about capability and maturity levels. For example, could you be at CL 3 in Configuration Management if GP 2.6 were not met in other process areas? The answer is yes. The generic practices indicate a level of institutionalization separate from the capability level of the process areas. Another interesting question is, can you tailor an enabling process area?[12] Possibly, but it would go against the underlying theory of the models. Also, it would certainly make it more difficult to improve other processes by using the generic practices.

7.7.3 Relationships, Complexity, and Common Sense

Clearly, complex relationships exist among the elements of the CMMI models. Many of these stem from the theoretical bases of model-based

---

12. See the discussion of tailoring in Section 10.4.

process improvement, especially those that deal with organizational maturity. Others, like the relationships between the Engineering process areas and the relationships between the generic practice and enabling process areas, have roots in the source models and the work conducted in integrating the various representations.

Remember, however, that the models are merely guides and are intended to help—not mystify. When you encounter a seeming conundrum, you can either consult the process-improvement experts or simply make a reasonable decision that solves your immediate problem. Although some occasions will call for special expertise, usually a commonsense, "Gordian knot" approach will provide an answer that meets your needs.

Lewis and Clark Party at Three Forks
Detail from painting by E. S. Paxson,
Missoula County Courthouse, Missoula, Montana

© 2000–2001 *www.arttoday.com*

Part III

Using CMMI

On their historic journey of exploration, Meriwether Lewis and William Clark learned from the Nez Perce tribe and from Sacagawea that success in unknown territory often depends on having a knowledgeable guide. The CMMI, while not actually an untamed wilderness, does present a landscape where pitfalls and risks can confront the unwary user. Part III attempts to provide help in selecting the best routes based on your organization's particular process-improvement needs.

Part III Contents

Chapter 10. Appraisals with CMMI

In which the authors present the CMMI appraisal methods. A discussion of their use is provided as well as some advice on tailoring the models.

Chapter 8

Selecting the Appropriate Disciplines

Inclination snatches arguments to make indulgence seem judicious choice.
George Eliot, *Spanish Gypsy* (1868)

A little too late is much too late.
German proverb

The Capability Maturity Model Integration (CMMI) Product Suite offers a growing number of multi- and single-discipline models, all developed with integrated process improvement in mind. The best combination of disciplines for your organization will depend on its business, organization, environment, and process-improvement objectives. This chapter discusses ways to select the disciplines best suited to your situation. For Version 1.1 of the model there are four combinations of disciplines from which to choose, with an increasing scope of coverage.[1] The CMMI-SW

---

1. There were four combinations when we went to press with the Second Edition of this book, and we expect this to remain true until such time as model versions beyond 1.1 are developed. As always in such matters, consult the Software Engineering Institute's (SEI's) Web site or solicit information directly from the SEI.

model covers Software Engineering (SW); the CMMI-SE/SW model covers both Systems Engineering (SE) and Software Engineering; the CMMI-SE/SW/IPPD model adds in Integrated Product and Process Development (IPPD); and finally, the CMMI-SE/SW/IPPD/SS model provides additional emphasis on Supplier Sourcing (SS) and managing suppliers.

8.1 The Discipline Dilemma

The work of the CMMI Team resulted in a close integration of software engineering and systems engineering in the CMMI models. In one sense, a software-only or a systems engineering-only model is available with the integrated CMMI-SE/SW model by just ignoring the discipline amplifications that do not apply. However, because there were many users of the legacy CMM for Software who indicated an interest in having a software-only version of CMMI, CMMI-SW was published as a separate stand-alone version. While some may view CMMI-SW as better meeting their needs, in fact only a small amount of informative material was removed from CMMI-SE/SW to create CMMI-SW. For an organization whose primary focus is software, either CMMI-SW or CMMI-SE/SW will meet your needs equally well, and the choice has more to do with temperament than substance.[2]

An increase in coverage and substance does occur when it comes to the discipline of Integrated Product and Process Development, and also the discipline of Supplier Sourcing. For each of these there is an increase in the required and expected model material (the goals and practices), which may impact the scope of the process-improvement effort, the length of an appraisal, and the ratings that result from an appraisal. For each CMMI discipline that you add, your organization must meet and assess more process requirements. Hence more reflection is needed to make a decision whether or not to include these two additional disciplines.

---

2. Because usually there is a systems engineering aspect to most software development, the authors would recommend a preference for CMMI-SE/SW over the CMMI-SW version. If in the CMMI-SE/SW model you find an amplification for systems engineering that does not apply in your situation, it is easy just to ignore it.

As the CMMI Product Suite matures, other disciplines may be added to the official set or become available through other sources, such as after-market model developers or professional societies. When this proliferation occurs, the choice may become more complex.

8.2 Your Situation

You do not need a book written by "outsiders" to tell you about the situation that you confront in your own organization. We provide this section just as a reminder of some factors that are relevant to your selection of CMMI disciplines.

8.2.1 Your Core Business

Your organization's fundamental activities, business objectives, and organizational culture all influence the choice of the appropriate CMMI model. First, you should consider the disciplines used in producing the products or services that are central to your organization:

- Do you develop software?
- Do you establish requirements?
- Do you acquire or subcontract for key components?
- Do you integrate commercial materials or products created by others?
- Do you provide a service?
- Is some engineering specialty fundamental to your success?
- Are you constrained by security requirements?

All of these issues may have a bearing on which disciplines you choose. Ideally, you should choose the disciplines that are most critical to your business success. Of course, those may be difficult to define in a fast-changing business environment.

8.2.2 Your Organization

It is also crucial to understand how your organization affects the selection of disciplines. This consideration is especially important with the IPPD extensions, as they are based on the premise that you want to move toward an integrated or concurrent operation. You may want to consider the following questions:

- Do some groups want to independently improve and measure their process improvement?

- Does your organization support independent cost centers that may compete with each other?

- Are you moving toward an integrated way of doing business, perhaps by using enterprise tools?

You may find it helpful to align your process-improvement plans with any organizational changes that are concurrently under way. The IPPD extensions are particularly useful in change management.

8.2.3 Your Business Environment

The disciplines you choose should, of course, support your business environment. For example, if long-term projects and a stable workforce characterize your environment, your organization can generally support the efforts needed for multidiscipline process improvement over the spectrum of its business activities. On the other hand, if the organization faces a rapid development environment where projects are short, intense, and schedule-driven, it may need to focus on one specific discipline (or even just a few process areas) to realize a quick return on process-improvement investment.

Your customer base may also influence the choice of disciplines. Customers who have critical requirements for complex systems may force you to adopt certain disciplines to match their processes.

8.2.4 Your Process-Improvement Scope and Objectives

Disciplines provide the special subject matter for your process improvement. Consequently, you should understand the kind of processes you want to improve and the objectives for your process improvement before selecting a model. For example, the software and systems engineering disciplines describe the requirements for standard technical processes, so they can be used in a variety of engineering environments. On the other hand, the core CMMI Process Management and Project Management process areas and the corresponding generic practices provide a rich language and a consistent model to improve any process, regardless of its technical content.[3]

---

3. Many debates occurred regarding the application of CMMI outside the engineering world. It will be interesting to discover the extent to which interest in CMMI arises in nonengineering areas, such as human resources, medicine, and law.

If your organization's objectives are entirely related to internal process improvement, you have considerable leeway in selecting which disciplines to address. However, if the objective is to demonstrate to others the maturity of your organization's processes for specific disciplines (for example, by adding a level indication in your marketing material or when bidding on U.S. Department of Defense contracts), you must approach discipline selection in a stricter, more dogmatic manner.

8.3 CMMI-SE/SW/IPPD

Selecting the IPPD extension with the CMMI-SE/SW model provides two additional process areas (Integrated Teaming and Organizational Environment for Integration), plus one expanded process area (Integrated Project Management). The content of this material was described in Section 7.5. Note that all of these materials are staged at maturity level 3.

The following questions address some of the issues associated with IPPD:

- Do you use teams for any aspect of your projects?
- Does your organization need to know how to use teams effectively?
- Does your organization have difficulty in organizing and planning projects around teams?
- Does your organization have problems in communicating between disciplines or groups?
- Does your organization need to know how to promote integration by providing an environment that supports it?
- Do you want people to work together to get the maximum benefit of collaboration, even at a cost of some efficiency or schedule?
- Does your organization need to know how to nurture the integrative and collaborative behaviors of an IPPD environment?

Answering yes to any of these questions indicates that your organization could benefit from using the IPPD extension of the CMMI.

8.4 CMMI-SE/SW/IPPD/SS

Selecting the SS extension of the CMMI-SE/SW/IPPD model provides one additional process area (Integrated Supplier Management). The content of this material was described in Section 7.6. Note that this process area is an addition to the Project Management process category and is staged at maturity level 3.

The following questions address some of the issues associated with SS:

- In your projects, is the role of suppliers of sufficient importance to require a comprehensive, proactive effort to manage them?
- Do you keep a close watch on the availability of new products that will help you satisfy project requirements?
- Do you have multiple supplier sources for the products that you acquire?
- Is a cooperative relationship with your suppliers critical to your success?
- When a supplier delivers a product, do you need to thoroughly evaluate and test it before knowing that it will do the job?

Answering yes to any of these questions indicates that your organization could benefit from using the SS extension to the CMMI-SE/SW/IPPD model. You will have a keen interest in this model extension if you are a part of an acquisition-oriented organization or participate in a project where the acquisition of products and services from an external source is a central issue of concern.

8.5 Selecting the Appropriate Model

In deciding whether to use the IPPD extension or the SS extension, you will need to understand your organization's core business and to focus your process-improvement efforts where they will most dramatically affect your key operating parameters. Consider your business environment, and don't overtax personnel by attempting to improve too many areas at the same time. Make sure your efforts remain in sync with your customers' activities and requirements. Decide on your objectives, and then align the disciplines selected with your organization's business strategy.

Selecting the disciplines is an integral step in ensuring the success of your process-improvement initiatives. Another critical step is the selection of the type of model representation employed. Chapter 9 examines this decision in detail.

Chapter 9

Picking a Representation

You must choose . . . but choose wisely.
Spoken by the Grail Knight, *Indiana Jones and the Last Crusade* (1989)

We choose our joys and sorrows long before we experience them.
Kahlil Gibran, *Sand and Foam* (1926)

So far, you have selected (based on guidance from Chapter 8) a set of disciplines from the options provided in the Capability Maturity Model Integration (CMMI) Product Suite, a set that is appropriate for the scope of your planned process-improvement efforts. Your next important decision is to pick an architectural representation: continuous or staged. In Chapter 5, we described the distinguishing features of staged and continuous models, including some basic information about how CMMI provides these two alternative representations in its integrated suite of model products.

Each of the two architectural representations can provide a solid foundation for process improvement. For some people, however, the preference for one representation is deeply rooted and emotionally charged; they may simply mistrust the other representation. For other people, the preference is based on habit and grounded in the source model to which they are accustomed.

For most users, this preference will ideally be developed through a comprehensive understanding of the benefits (in their organization's specific environment) provided by each representation. Perhaps this choice merits the use of a structured decision-making process and the application of the CMMI process area for Decision Analysis and Resolution. While each organization must explore this issue for itself, this chapter highlights some important issues and considerations in making that decision.

This chapter is arranged so as to start you on the path to making the best decision for your organization. The first two sections address the representations individually and present (for undecided voters or independents) the salient arguments offered by the proponents of each representation. The third section brings these general considerations into the CMMI context.

9.1 Reasons for Liking Staged Models

The CMM for Software is a staged model that has been used successfully and with proven results for many years. This fact heads the list of reasons for using staged models; it is a powerful argument. Like Washington, D.C., insiders, staged model users can claim "Real Experience, Real Results." The path from an immature organization to a mature one has been demonstrated repeatedly with the CMM for Software, and it is marked by the following benefits:

- An ability to manage processes across the organization
- Good communication about process among employees
- Improved accuracy of project estimates
- Improved cost and quality control
- The use of measurable data to guide problem analysis and improvement efforts

These results are made possible and supported by a process infrastructure that provides discipline and motivation for both project and organizational process improvement.

For an organization that is just beginning its journey to greater process maturity, a staged model provides a well-defined and proven path. First, the organization's personnel work at process areas that facilitate improved project management (maturity level 2), then they provide organization-wide process definition (ML 3), and finally they use the standardized process definitions to support quantitative analysis for improving (ML 4) and optimizing (ML 5) process behavior. By building the staging of the process areas into its architecture, the model offers a clear path for improvement that can be followed without a lot of discussion and debate.

Consider the analogy of a child who is told to clean his room. There are toys everywhere with nary any floor to be seen. The child just looks at the problem. It seems so overwhelming that he doesn't know where to start. If he is told to pick up the blocks, however, he can sort through the mess and put all of the blocks away. Next, he can be told to pick up the balls, and so on, until the room is tidy. The approach taken by the staged model is similar, in that the model architects (rather than the model users) decide on the best order for process improvement.

Proven Path, Truth, and Untruth

To speak of a single path to process improvement with a staged model involves both truth and untruth.

The truth is that the maturity levels define plateau stages for process improvement, providing a common general structure for all model users and a predefined ordering of the process areas within a small, finite number of maturity levels. The single path is defined by first requiring the satisfaction of all goals at maturity level 2, and continuing stepwise (as appropriate) to the satisfaction of goals that reside at higher maturity levels.

The untruth is any suggestion that within this general structure, all organizations will do things in the same way. For example, the requirement to perform peer reviews on selected work products must be a part of achieving maturity level 3. The exact time when this issue is addressed prior to achieving ML 3 and the selection of products for peer review are both items that can vary greatly among organizations. Thus, when we speak of a single path to improvement with a staged model, understand that we intend to speak the truth, not the untruth.

Having a single system for defining process maturity facilitates making comparisons across organizations. The maturity-level numbers are broadly understood, so that (proponents would argue) there is a single meaning (more or less) regarding what it means to be a maturity level 2 organization, for example.[1]

For all of these reasons (and others), the CMM for Software—the premier staged model—has been used by organizations to achieve notable success in support of their efforts related to process improvement. An excellent source of information and data on the use of this model is the Software Engineering Information Repository (SEIR), which is housed at the Software Engineering Institute (SEI) of Carnegie Mellon University.[2]

9.2 Reasons for Liking Continuous Models

The concept of a continuous model for process improvement precedes the development of staged models. The writings of Philip Crosby, for example, define levels for improvement within individual areas.[3] In spite of this heritage, continuous process-improvement models have been used less often than staged models, and there has been no systematic data collection on the results of continuous model usage. Nonetheless, there is no shortage of proponents for the continuous approach, especially among systems engineers.

Proponents cite two fundamental reasons for using a continuous (as opposed to a staged) model: freedom and visibility. Unlike a staged model, which provides a single improvement path for all model users, a continuous model offers additional freedom for users, who can select

---

1. By having each process area reside at a specified maturity level and hence at a well-understood position in the path to organizational maturity, the model authors can create more uniform process areas. For example, in a staged model, a process area that is written for maturity level 2 would differ from a similar process area that is written for maturity level 3. When appraisals are conducted, the intended scope and application for the process area become very clear, as they are based on the staged level.

2. The Software Engineering Information Repository's Web address is http://seir.sei.cmu.edu/.

3. The five levels of Crosby's Quality Management Maturity Grid are Stage I—Uncertainty; Stage II—Awakening; Stage III—Enlightenment; Stage IV—Wisdom; and Stage V—Certainty. See Crosby, Philip B. *Quality Is Free: The Art of Making Quality Certain.* New York: McGraw-Hill, 1979.

the order for process-improvement activities based on organizational business objectives.[4] With a continuous model, individual organizations or organizational groups have the option of defining organizational maturity and an ordering for the process areas that (they may believe) are a better fit for their unique business environment. They may wish to achieve given capability levels for the process areas in an alternative order, rather than accepting the constraints of the "one size fits all" philosophy of the staged models.

As multiple capability levels are defined for each process area, an appraisal based on a continuous model may provide increased visibility into process-improvement strengths and weaknesses. The greater transparency comes from the way in which the results are reported, rather than the model content. Despite the unflattering portrayal of managers in the cartoon world of "Dilbert," those with more detailed process data can make more informed decisions. For example, a capability-level profile with a separate rating number for each individual process area could provide greater insight than a single maturity-level number.[5] Even a manager who initially may prefer the simplicity of a single number could, in time, develop greater appreciation for the capability profile that only a continuous representation provides. In the end, managers may want both.

By providing more detailed insight that is tailored to the individual business environment, an organization can benefit from:

- The complete application of all generic practices in each process area.
- A clearer focus on risks that are specific to individual process areas.

---

4. Just as a staged model allows for many choices and options, the wise use of a continuous model requires an understanding of the many inherent ordering relationships between various model elements. As with any freedom, the situation for the user of a continuous model is not "anything goes." In the CMMI continuous representation, for example, the organization needs to reach CL 1 in the Configuration Management process area before it applies the generic practice on configuration management, which resides at CL 2, to any process area. Even without a staging of process areas, CMMI continuous representations have many such ordering constraints. Chapter 7 highlighted some of these constraints.

5. While a staged model appraisal doesn't normally report a profile, it does provide organizational strengths and weaknesses on a process-area-by-process-area basis.

- A structure that is more immediately compatible with ISO/IEC 15504.

- A structure that more easily facilitates the addition of new process areas with minimal effects on the existing model structure.

For managers who have used and found benefit in a single maturity-level number, a continuous model can provide the same information. With any continuous model, a "staging" is possible. Fundamentally and simply, a staging comprises a set of rules of the following form: For an organization to be at maturity level x, it must achieve capability level y in process areas PA_1, PA_2, . . . PA_n.[6] To produce a single maturity-level number, the model need not have a staged architecture; it requires only an algorithm to produce the maturity rating based on a set of staging rules that define the maturity levels in terms of capability levels. As described in Section 5.3.3, CMMI includes an equivalent staging for users of the continuous representation.

As long as two organizations follow the same staging rules, their maturity-level ratings may be compared, just as is possible with a staged model. For organizations that want or need a predefined path for process improvement, a staging on a continuous model provides the same guidance as a staged model. If some groups support different staging schemes, however, then model users must choose a path for process improvement; they will not be given the path.

9.3 Reasons for Choosing a CMMI Representation

Based on the considerations cited in the preceding sections for liking either a staged or continuous architectural representation, a decision to favor one or the other would seem to involve almost philosophical musings. On the one hand, all other things being equal, having a single-number rating score and a single standard path for process improvement would seem to have many potential benefits. Many organizations would prefer to avoid the "anything goes" approach to process improvement that the continuous representation may seem (incorrectly) to engender. On the other hand, a rating profile may ultimately prove more useful than a single number.

---

6. A more complex rule is possible. For example, to be at maturity level x, you must reach capability level y in one set of process areas and capability level z in another set of process areas.

Furthermore, recognizing the realities of different business environments may lead to multiple approaches to process improvement, all of which are equally valid.[7] Most of us would likely prefer to receive the benefits available on both sides. That is, it would be nice to have a relatively small number of choices in process-improvement paths (one of which is the most common in any given business environment). Likewise, it would be nice to have clear recognition that one predefined path may not be appropriate for the entire world and all business environments. Finally, it would be nice to have a single-number rating for some contexts and a rating profile for other contexts.

CMMI holds out the promise of the benefits from both sides. A close examination reveals that the differences between the staged representation and the continuous representation are less pronounced in CMMI, and the choice of representation is less polarized than is the case with the legacy models that are either staged or continuous, but not both.[8]

In an effort to ensure that each representation would be just an alternative view of the same base model, the CMMI Team duplicated the required and expected material in both representations. Thus the process areas in both are the same. The goals (the required items) are the same, except for the fact that the generic goals residing at capability levels 1, 4, and 5 are not needed in the staged representation. The specific practices (the expected items from individual process areas) are the same, except for cases where an advanced practice supersedes a lower-level specific practice. The generic practices are the same for maturity level 2 and 3 generic goals. In the staged representation, process areas staged at maturity level 2 use the level 2 generic practices only, whereas all process areas staged at maturity level 3 or higher use the level 2 and 3 generic practices.

---

7. Within the Department of Defense environment, for example, personnel are not far removed from the debates that raged about the programming language Ada. While many claimed that having a single programming language within the Department offered strong potential benefits, others demurred, citing a need to recognize alternative valid approaches in different kinds of systems. For example, the software in a management information system and that in a real-time weapon system may be very different. Trade studies of widely varying system types relating to the best choice for a programming language would not rate any one language as always preferable. Sometimes the best place in standardization efforts is a middle ground, somewhere between one (at one extreme) and hundreds (at the other extreme); perhaps three, or seven, would keep everyone happy.

8. The IPD CMM (the Integrated Product Development model, which served as the third source model for the initial CMMI work) was a hybrid model, as is the FAA-iCMM (the Federal Aviation Administration's model).

Because the two representations are so closely aligned, and because both contain most of the good material from all of the source models, the reasons for preferring one over the other become more practical and less philosophical. Will your organization need less of a training effort with one representation than with the other due to legacy issues? Is the staging that is integral to the staged architecture and provided in the equivalent staging for the continuous architecture the better one for your business environment? Does management need the detail provided by a capability profile? Questions such as these may not have easy answers, but they can be investigated across all organizational components that seek to develop an integrated process-improvement strategy. [9]

Because the two architectural representations in CMMI are not dramatically different, in some ways you cannot make a bad choice; the fundamentals are the same. Perhaps, in time, the use of CMMI will show that two distinct representations are not necessary at all.

---

9. Currently the SEI Web site has a set of frequently asked questions (FAQs) relating to the model. One of those questions deals with how an organization might go about selecting a CMMI representation. For further information, go to http://www.sei.cmu.edu/cmmi/.

Chapter 10

Appraisals with CMMI

Not everything that can be counted counts, and
not everything that counts can be counted.
Albert Einstein (1879–1955)

Good, Fast, Cheap; Pick any two.
Sign in Print Shop

If you don't like something, change it. If you can't change it,
change your attitude. Don't complain.
Maya Angelou (1928–)

Just as three legacy source models provided the basis for the models contained in the Capability Maturity Model Integration (CMMI) Product Suite, two appraisal methods provided the primary basis for the initial CMMI appraisal method. The method used with the Systems Engineering Capability Model (SECM), EIA 731-1, was the SECM Appraisal Method, EIA 731-2.[1] The method used with the CMM for

---

1. *EIA Standard, Systems Engineering Capability.* EIA 731, Part 2: Appraisal Method. Arlington, VA: EIA, August 2002.

Software was the CMM-Based Appraisal for Internal Process Improvement (CBA IPI).[2] The initial CMMI appraisal method (SCAMPI)[3] has elements of these two legacy methods, but traces the majority of its features to the CBA IPI.

A complete discussion of process appraisal, its history, its role in the source models, and the many details about how it is addressed in CMMI, would warrant another book. The goal of this chapter is more modest: to briefly introduce the initial appraisal products in the CMMI Product Suite, as well as some of the primary concepts and issues regarding their use, to help orient the reader for further explorations in this area. Preparing for an appraisal may include considerations on tailoring the model, so we include a brief discussion of tailoring at the end of this chapter.

10.1 Appraisal Requirements for CMMI

One part of the CMMI Product Suite that deals with appraisals is the Appraisal Requirements for CMMI (ARC), version 1.1. This document comprises 42 "requirements" that provide a mixed set of requirements and design constraints on an appraisal method.[4] As such, it is perhaps of more interest to the designers of an appraisal method than to organizations seeking an appraisal to evaluate their capabilities. We discuss it here briefly to provide insight into the approach to appraisal taken to date by the CMMI Team, and to suggest promising future directions.

---

2. Donna K. Dunaway and Steve Masters. *CMM-Based Appraisal for Internal Process Improvement (CBA IPI): Method Description (CMU/SEI-1996-TR-007)*. Pittsburgh: Software Engineering Institute, Carnegie Mellon University, April 1996. There is also a guide for lead assessors on using the CBA IPI method.

3. Standard CMMI Appraisal Method for Process Improvement Version 1.1: Method Definition Document (CMU/SEI-2001-HB-001). *Pittsburgh: Software Engineering Institute, Carnegie Mellon University, December 2001. Other appraisal methods that were used as sources for SCAMPI include the Software Capability Evaluation (SCE) V3.0 Method Description, the Software Development Capability Evaluation (SDCE), and the FAA Appraisal Method (FAM).*

4. A method that satisfies all 42 requirements is considered to be a Class A method as defined in the ARC. Two other class types, B and C, are defined with lesser sets of requirements. The discussion here focuses on a "full" Class A method—the only type that offers the option of capability-level or maturity-level ratings.

The ARC includes seven categories of requirements:

1. Responsibilities. Lists responsibilities of the appraisal sponsor and the leader of the appraisal team.

2. Appraisal Method Documentation. Provides items of guidance that should be included in the documentation of a method. As examples, guidance should be provided for identifying the appraisal's purpose, model scope, organizational scope, team member and team leader qualifications, team size, team member and team leader roles, resource estimation, logistics, data collection, findings, data protection, nonattribution, and appraisal records.

3. Planning and Preparing for the Appraisal. Identifies a minimum set of appraisal preparation activities and the items needed in an appraisal plan.

4. Appraisal Data Collection. Requires the use of three methods for the collection of data: administering instruments (for example, questionnaires and surveys), conducting interviews, and reviewing documentation.

5. Data Consolidation and Validation. Specifies constraints on the way in which an appraisal method provides for the consolidation and validation of the data collected. The topics required include

    -   Team consensus leading to findings and ratings.
    -   A method for consolidating the data into accurate observations.
    -   A method for validating observations.
    -   A set of criteria for an observation to be "corroborated" (such as data from at least two different sources, from at least two different data-gathering sessions, with one data point reflecting work actually being done).
    -   Sufficiency of data to cover the scope of the appraisal (such as validated observations for each specific or generic practice, such that the extent of the implementation is understood and the observations are representative of the organizational unit and the relevant life-cycle phases).
    -   A mechanism to determine strengths and weaknesses relative to the CMMI model being used.
    -   Feedback of appraisal findings to the appraisal participants.

6. Rating. Provides more specific constraints on what is needed for a capability-level or maturity-level rating. The topics required include

the prerequisite of valid observations for each practice prior to the rating of goals, a judgment that goals are "satisfied" only when the associated practices are implemented (and the aggregate of weaknesses does not have a significant negative impact on goal achievement), and the satisfaction of all relevant goals as the basis for a capability-level or maturity-level rating.

7. Reporting Results. Requires documentation of the findings for the appraisal sponsor and a report made to the CMMI Steward (the Software Engineering Institute).

In three of these seven areas (data collection, data consolidation and validation, and rating), some of the ARC "requirements" seem to be method design constraints rather than true performance requirements. The performance requirements in this area would focus on issues such as accuracy, repeatability, stability, usefulness, and efficiency. The ARC authors placed design constraints in these areas for two reasons: to aid in meeting the challenge of specifying real performance requirements, and to ensure the accuracy and repeatability of the appraisal results and ratings. If we could deepen our understanding of what the performance requirements really should be and how to best measure results against those requirements, then perhaps the ARC might be recast to allow for more flexibility in developing methods that trade off differently between the various quality factors and efficiency.

The Authors' Perspective

The three authors of this book believe that user requirements for appraisal performance should be specified to address adequate reliability of results and cost control, in addition to the usefulness of appraisal results for process improvement. Then there would exist a basis to verify the extent to which a specific design for an appraisal method met those requirements. Currently, no ARC requirements address cost efficiency. While ratings to benchmark a process are emphasized, there is insufficient weight placed on the development of findings useful for process improvement.

Two distinct but not unrelated reasons for conducting an appraisal exist. One is to accurately diagnose internal process problems and areas for process improvement; the other is to provide a benchmark for process capability or process maturity relative to a larger community. These two purposes can pull in opposite directions. The identification of process-improvement opportunities requires exposing process weaknesses, whereas the effort made to achieve a benchmark score may encourage the hiding of process weaknesses and the "gaming" of numbers.

In the trade-offs between reliability, accuracy, repeatability, cost, and other factors, we believe that the ARC places too much emphasis on reliability and too little emphasis on cost. This choice is not unrelated to the issue on process improvement versus benchmark. For a benchmark, reliability is a central concern; for process improvement, a somewhat lesser level of reliability may be acceptable if cost is significantly less. The ARC requirements should not be written so that trying to focus on process improvement and reduction of cost means using a "less than full" (that is, less "good") method.

In the months and years ahead, the CMMI user community needs to collect data on various appraisal methods that make the cost and reliability trade-off in different ways. Eventually, we will have an empirical basis for knowing how much accuracy, reliability, and usefulness of findings is produced at what cost for a proposed appraisal method.

10.2 Standard CMMI Appraisal Method for Process Improvement

Another piece of the CMMI Product Suite that deals with appraisal is the Standard CMMI Appraisal Method for Process Improvement. The CMMI Appraisal Method Integrated Team, a part of the CMMI Team, developed SCAMPI V1.1 to meet the full set of ARC requirements. As published, the SCAMPI Method Definition Document (MDD) provides a thorough description of the SCAMPI method.

SCAMPI was designed with multiple uses in mind: internal process improvement, supplier selection, and process monitoring. Its creators wanted to address not only ARC compliance, but also these essential characteristics: accuracy, repeatability, cost and resource effectiveness, and meaningfulness of the appraisal results. In SCAMPI, any ratings that result from an appraisal should reflect the extent to which practices (which support the goals in a CMMI model) are planned and implemented in the organization. To determine this, SCAMPI relies on the collection by the appraisal team of objective evidence at the organization level and within projects. In line with the ARC requirement, multiple types of objective evidence are needed.

During a SCAMPI appraisal, the organization being appraised is encouraged to provide to the appraisal team evidence of its implemented processes, with clear mapping to the goals and practices of the model. This permits the appraisal team to be in a mode of "verification" rather than one of "discovery," which makes the appraisal activity more efficient and less error prone.

SCAMPI requires the use of three types of what it calls "Practice Implementation Indicators (PIIs)," which are the "footprints" of an activity or practice that provide the basis for verification by the appraisal team. These include (1) direct artifacts, which are the direct results of performing a practice (for example, the plan that results from the practice of establishing a plan); (2) indirect artifacts, which are a consequence of performing a practice, but not its purpose (for example, the minutes from a planning meeting); and (3) affirmations, which are oral or written statements confirming that a practice has been implemented (for example, an interview with the person who maintains the plan).

Whenever a SCAMPI appraisal team reaches conclusions about whether practices are implemented across an organizational unit, whether the model goals have been satisfied, and what capability levels or maturity level is appropriate, a consensus across the entire appraisal team is needed. Work that leads up to such conclusions may be assigned to smaller subteams to review and reach consensus.

Individual strengths and weaknesses that a SCAMPI appraisal team has identified are aggregated into preliminary findings, which are presented to the organizational unit for verification, prior to drafting the final findings (and ratings).

Because CMMI models are integrated across disciplines, an organization that wishes to obtain ratings (capability or maturity levels) has options that it should consider. Does it want a single rating across multiple disciplines, or does it want individual ratings (for example, one for software and one for systems engineering)? SCAMPI provides options for appraisals against multiple disciplines, with either separate or combined results.

Whether an appraisal meets the goals of an organization's appraisal sponsor depends in large part on how well the appraisal is planned. Some critical factors to consider during planning are clear identification of the sponsor and the organizational unit being appraised; a clear statement of appraisal purpose; the scope of the model being applied; the domains and projects included in the appraisal, with a clear statement of their key characteristics; and appraisal constraints (such as resources, schedule, logistics, risks, ownership of appraisal results, controls on information, and principles of nonattribution).

A SCAMPI appraisal is divided into three phases: (1) initial planning and preparation, (2) on-site appraisal, and (3) reporting of results. Each phase includes multiple steps. The first phase involves analyzing requirements, developing a plan, selecting and preparing the team, obtaining and analyzing the initial objective evidence, and preparing for the collection on-site of additional objective evidence. The second phase focuses on collecting and examining objective evidence, verifying and validating that evidence, making sure that it is adequately documented, and developing the appraisal results (findings and ratings). The third phase involves the presentation of the final findings to the sponsor, conducting any needed executive briefings, and appropriately packaging and archiving the appraisal assets, including submission of all the information needed by the CMMI Steward (the SEI).

Only a SCAMPI lead appraiser, who has been trained and authorized by the CMMI Steward, may lead a SCAMPI appraisal. To be a lead appraiser, an individual must have relevant discipline experience, knowledge of CMMI models, and training in appraisal techniques. Appraisal team members are also selected based on their knowledge, experience, and skills. There must be at least four members of a SCAMPI appraisal team, and a maximum of nine is recommended.

A considerable investment of resources is required for a full SCAMPI appraisal. Data on actual resources used to date is not easy to obtain. Clearly the time needed for the on-site appraisal includes that for the activities and efforts of a SCAMPI lead appraiser, the sponsor, the coordinator, each appraisal team member, and each appraisal participant. There are many variables in reaching an estimate, such as number of process areas, size of the team, number of disciplines to be investigated, and so on. This might end up being in the range of 100 to 200 days of effort. However, for a full appraisal this is not an accurate measure of the total effort required. In order for the team to operate in "verification" mode rather than in "discovery" mode, a much larger effort must precede the on-site visit to collect and organize all the individual pieces of evidence required by the team. The total cost could easily reach into the hundreds of thousands of dollars.

For organizations that seek to conform to ISO/IEC 15504, the emerging international standard on process appraisals, SCAMPI is designed for conformance.

In summary, SCAMPI is now a robust and well-defined appraisal method. To conclude our review, here are some of the key principles of any SCAMPI appraisal:

- Senior management sponsorship
- Focus on the organization's business goals
- Use of a documented appraisal method
- Use of a process reference model (such as a CMMI model)
- Confidentiality for interviewees
- Collaborative team approach
- Focus on follow-up actions for process improvement

10.3 Using Appraisals in Process Improvement

The ARC allows three classes of appraisals, as shown in Figure 10-1. The level of effort for each class varies based on the scope of the appraisal. In general, however, a Class C appraisal takes much less time than a Class B or A appraisal. The "quick look" approach is designed to provide guidance on process improvements that would not require a full appraisal. Such appraisals can be performed on small parts of an organization several times so as to prepare for a Class B appraisal.

The Class B appraisal provides a more in-depth look at the organization. In most cases, it does not go into as much depth or detail as a Class A appraisal. As a result, it can generally be completed within a

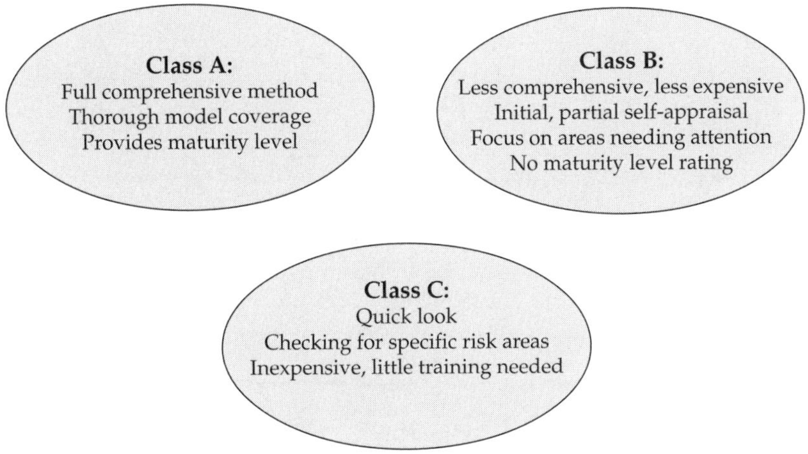

Class A:
Full comprehensive method
Thorough model coverage
Provides maturity level

Class B:
Less comprehensive, less expensive
Initial, partial self-appraisal
Focus on areas needing attention
No maturity level rating

Class C:
Quick look
Checking for specific risk areas
Inexpensive, little training needed

Figure 10-1: *ARC appraisal classes*

week. A Class B appraisal may be performed on limited parts of an organization in preparation for a Class A appraisal.[5]

Figure 10-2 depicts an example timeline for an organization. To start an improvement program that leads to a full SCAMPI appraisal, an organization could use several Class C appraisals leading up to a Class B appraisal. Process improvements are made based on the findings of the quick looks at parts of the organization. The lessons learned in this way can be used to provide broader organizational improvements.

As improvements indicate that the part of the organization is ready for the next step, a Class B appraisal can be performed, and its findings subsequently used to prepare for the full SCAMPI appraisal. To spot-check improvements, the organization may perform additional Class C appraisals. Other parts of the organization can use the same process and appraisal tools to prepare for the SCAMPI benchmark appraisal. The actual time needed to prepare for a SCAMPI appraisal will, of course, depend on several factors such as resources, budgets for

---

5. With letters available that commonly are used for grading, we are beginning to hear appraisal sponsors or members of appraisal teams (who are out of the official jargon loop) refer to "C+," "B-," "B+," and "A-" (or SCAMPI minus) appraisals. An example might be if you do a Class C appraisal but include a few interviews (even though interviews are not a part of a Class C appraisal), you might be inclined to refer to this as a C+ appraisal.

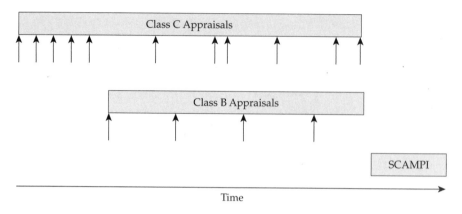

Figure 10-2: *Sample appraisal timeline*

process improvement, size of the organization, previous process improvement results, and management commitment.

Depending on the purpose of your appraisal, you will select a method from the appropriate method class. If you could use a Class C method to achieve your purpose, then the cost of performing the appraisal would be lower than that of using a Class B or A method. A different purpose might require the selection of an alternative appraisal method.

10.4 Making a CMMI Model Your Own (Tailoring)

If an organization were interested in using a CMMI model for process improvement, and at the same time was not interested in obtaining official ratings from an appraisal, it would have considerable leeway in focusing the appraisal on some parts of the model and not on others. The extent of the model scope, along with the number of disciplines covered and the number of projects to be investigated, all impact the resources required for an appraisal. To include more process areas means a greater effort and to include fewer process areas means a lesser effort.

Whether you have selected a continuous representation or a staged representation, if you are not going to produce ratings you may wish to tailor out some pieces of the model. For example, you may feel that the Supplier Agreement Management process area, which is staged at ML 2, could be ignored because agreements with suppliers are not a critical or problematic part of your business. In this case, you could identify the entire process area as out of scope. In other cases you might identify a part of a process area, such as a specific goal and its associated specific practices, as "not applicable."

An example of such a goal might be the first goal of the Requirements Development process area, which addresses the transformation of stakeholder needs into customer requirements. Perhaps in your business the customer requirements are just provided to you, and in your judgment they represent your starting point. Remember, however, that requirements can come from internal customers as well as external customers, so the transformation of internal customer needs into requirements may be critical to your business. For this reason, you should not rush to judgment when you suspect a goal is not applicable.

In another case, you might be inclined to declare one or more specific practices as "not applicable," even though the goal remains. As noted earlier, with any CMMI model a practice is an "expected" model element. Thus you may prefer to replace one or more practices with "alternative practices" that may represent a better path to achieving the goal for your organization.

Whenever you decide to customize or replace a model element that is required or expected (that is, a goal or a practice), a set of risks must be considered. First, from the perspective of process improvement, have you tailored an item that is really essential to developing an effective strategy for process improvement? Second, from the perspective of rating, have you modified an item that, when later you have an appraisal to obtain ratings, may undercut the accuracy, objectivity, or comparability of a rating number (either a capability-level rating or a maturity-level rating)?

While the first of these risks is no doubt the most important in terms of the long-term success of your process-improvement program, the second area—especially maturity-level ratings—tends to generate the most emotion. Indeed, a given appraisal method (for example, SCAMPI) will have rules for producing ratings that address what kind of tailoring of a CMMI model is or is not allowed.

A clear understanding of business objectives or goals is critical to developing effective processes. Similarly, an organization's business objectives should be considered when tailoring a CMMI model for internal use. The tailored model can then be used to guide process-improvement activities. An advantage to this approach is that the model should remain stable for several years while the processes undergo continuous improvement. The model also provides a good measure of process capability that is based on the organization's business objectives and goals.

Business models can also serve as a basis for tailoring the CMMI Product Suite. For example, they may help an organization determine the order in which process areas should be implemented. Such business models may help determine requirements for processes or the tailoring of the CMMI, as well.

Resources for process improvement can guide an organization during tailoring. They may be limited, which would indicate a need to customize the model in a series of smaller stages. Tailoring can aid in making the process-improvement activities match the resources that are available. Limited tailoring may be possible when adequate resources are available to support the broader process-improvement activities dictated by the CMMI model.

Tailoring of the model is discussed in the "Using CMMI Models" section of version 1.1. Tailoring of SCAMPI is addressed in the "Tailor Method" section of the MDD. The discussion of tailoring of the model describes ways to customize model components for both process improvement and benchmarking purposes. Tailoring allows you to select the process areas that align most closely with your business objectives, business model, and resources. However, when a maturity-level rating is desired, CMMI does not allow the tailoring out of required or expected model components during an appraisal. If it meets your purpose, however, tailoring at this level can reduce the cost of interim appraisals—that is, those leading up to a full SCAMPI appraisal.

Luckily, the appraisal tools can be tailored to meet almost any need that you might envision. For example, if your organization is not responsible for any of the standard process management processes, you might decide to ignore all practices in the Process Management category except those that deal with saving process-related assets in a library. If your organization is primarily responsible for project management, then you might concentrate your appraisal on the appropriate Project Management category process areas. The engineering department of your organization might select the Planning and Monitoring process areas along with the Engineering category process areas.

Finally, note that some organizations establish a standard process with traceability to models, such as CMMI, as well as other sources of process requirements (for example, standards and customers). This correspondence identifies where model components and process requirements are represented in the standard process. Should parts of the model be deemed not applicable to the organization, they may be eliminated from the process definition. Thus organizations assessing conformance to the standard process indirectly assess their work against the model and other requirement sources. Of course, tailored material may jeopardize the comparability of the appraisal results.

The Delphic Sybil
Michaelangelo Buonarotti
Cappella Sistina, Il Vaticano
Scala / Art Resource, NY

Part IV

The Future of CMMI

The historian Herodotus gave an account of King Croesus of Lydia (circa 546 BCE), who asked the Oracle at Delphi to consult the gods, look into the future, and determine whether he should invade Persian territory. The Oracle answered that, if he crossed a river, "Croesus will destroy a great empire." Croesus, thinking he would be victorious, invaded Persia. Unfortunately, it was his own empire that fell and subsequently was destroyed.

Prediction has always been risky. The evolution of process improvement to date has certainly been rapid and contentious. In Part IV, the authors don their mystical robes and stare deeply into their scrying crystals in an attempt to predict how CMMI may change in the future.

Part IV Contents

Chapter 11. Evolving CMMI

> *In which the authors wax philosophical about how CMMI may adapt and change as experience using it expands.*

Afterword

In which the authors conclude the work and challenge the readers.

The Maven

In which one of the authors, tongue firmly in cheek, offers a paean to process improvement experts everywhere.

Chapter 11

Evolving CMMI

The rung of a ladder was never meant to rest upon, but only to hold a man's foot long enough to enable him to put the other somewhat higher.
Thomas Henry Huxley, *Life and Letters of Thomas Huxley* (1825–1895)

Beware becoming change-averse change agents!
Barry Boehm, SEI Symposium 2000 Keynote Address

When we blindly adopt a religion, a political system, a literary dogma, we become automatons. We cease to grow.
Anaïs Nin, *The Diaries of Anaïs Nin* (1903–1977)

What lies ahead for Capability Maturity Model Integration (CMMI)? How will it evolve to meet the changing needs of its users? Will it widen its application? Can CMMI concepts be applied outside of the software and systems engineering disciplines? How might having only one architectural representation for the CMMI model affect process improvement and appraisals? Our discussion of (and musings on) such questions in this final chapter may be of greatest interest to those readers who are, in their heart of hearts, architects or system designers. Perhaps as you reflected on our description of the CMMI Product Suite in earlier chapters, you found yourself thinking: "Why did they do it that way?" or "I would have done it differently" or "What were they thinking?" If this description fits you, read on. In contrast, if your interest is focused (quite legitimately) on learning about and using the current

CMMI products, then you may prefer to make this chapter a "quick read" on your way to the Afterword, which contains our concluding remarks.

11.1 Support for CMMI Innovation

There are always creative people who see opportunities to apply existing tools in new ways. There are also times when the tool you have is simply inadequate for the job at hand and needs to be modified. Based on the needs of the wider population, there is a tremendous desire for CMMI to remain stable for several years. At the same time, CMMI must be able to adapt to a changing environment. The CMMI developers and the CMMI Steward have anticipated this need for change and have established several means for CMMI to be improved and adapted without overly frequent changes to the model itself.

First, the SEI has an Interpretive Guidance Project to broaden the adoption of CMMI. Created to help support new applications of CMMI, this project collects information from the user community and then determines where the development of additional interpretive guidance would be appropriate. An expert group has been formed to support this activity. More information is available at the SEI Web site.

Second, technical reports that describe how CMMI could be applied in a particular business or environment are available. Written by experienced practitioners and reviewed by the Steward for soundness, these publications can help organizations in deciding what parts of CMMI are most applicable to their situation and how to interpret some of the CMMI components. Technical notes, which are available on the SEI Web site, have been published (or are planned) to cover Product Lines, Operational Organizations, and Earned Value Management.

Another publication, called Method Implementation Guidance (MIG), interprets the SCAMPI Method Definition Document (MDD) for a specific type of appraisal environment. At the time of this writing, the only MIG available addresses government source selection and contract monitoring.

Third, discipline components or extensions can be developed. As discussed earlier, IPPD and Supplier Sourcing are the only discipline extensions currently approved as part of the version 1.1 CMMI Product Suite. However, there are several groups working on extensions for their specific areas. Of those, probably the most mature at this time is an effort to address safety and security practices in what is being called an "Integrity Assurance" extension. Based on +SAFE, an informal CMMI extension developed by the Australian Ministry of Defence (MOD), this work involves stakeholders from the U.S. government including DOD, NASA, FAA, and DOE; foreign governments including the Australian MOD and the United Kingdom MOD; and a number of aerospace and commercial firms. Currently, their work is scheduled to be released in 2004.

Even without official publications or additions, CMMI is being used in a number of ways not specifically associated with process improvement. Several acquisition organizations have used the model as a risk management tool by comparing the model components to statements of work, work breakdown structures, and other acquisition documents, in order to identify missing components and uncover high-risk areas. Other organizations have used CMMI to support competency modeling and skills development and appraisal. Steve Cross, the current director of the SEI, acknowledges this application of CMMI outside traditional process improvement when he describes CMMI as a "knowledge infrastructure" that "provides a common framework upon which to create, share, and use engineering knowledge."[1]

11.2 A Partially Staged CMMI Model

Many people, in discussing CMMI and its two architectural representations (continuous and staged), have expressed the viewpoint that in the future the CMMI models should move toward a single representation. After all, a close study of the two representations shows that while they have differences, they are much more alike than different. With two representations, an organization must endure confusion and (perhaps) wasted effort before deciding which one to use. Having two representations also affects the choice of appraisal method. The generic practices are handled differently depending on whether you are doing

---

1. Cross, S. "CMMI: A Knowledge Infrastructure," keynote at *2nd Annual CMMI Technology Conference & User Group,* November 12, 2002.

a staged or continuous appraisal.[2] Why not consolidate the two representations? We present one way that such a consolidation could occur.

The phrase "partially staged" refers to a model in which a subset of CMMI process areas (derived from the full set) is used to define a common understanding for stages and maturity levels (MLs). Currently, in the CMMI staged representations (and in the equivalent staging for the continuous representations), all process areas are staged at one of the maturity levels. In a partially staged model, some—but not all—of the process areas would be staged at a maturity level. Process areas that were not staged at a maturity level or used in their definition for a maturity-level rating would be available (either individually or collectively) for other types of rating, such as capability levels (CLs).

The path to creating a partially staged CMMI model would be strewn with many options and decisions, and here we speculate regarding only a small number of those possibilities. Our goal is not to provide a complete vision regarding what partial staging would mean to CMMI, but to stimulate exploration, discussion, and debate in this area.

The following principle would be important to observe in creating a partially staged model: If a process area could be tailored out in some organizations, then it would not be a part of the subset that defines the model staging. For example, the Supplier Agreement Management (SAM) process area may be identified in some process appraisals as "not applicable." Some organizations or projects may lack important supplier relationships that must be managed and hence have no supplier agreements to establish, maintain, or satisfy.

When SAM is applicable, it can be a significant process area that should not be ignored; managing suppliers can prove central to the success of a project, especially if the suppliers provide critical system components. As SAM does not have universal applicability, however, it should not be included in a calculation of organizational maturity. In general, process areas related to acquisition and the relationship between acquirers and suppliers would not be staged. They would not apply in every situation and would, therefore, be subject to "tailoring out."

Reporting the rating results from an appraisal with a partially staged model is not as simple as reporting with a fully staged model and its single-digit maturity level; likewise, it is not as complex as reporting

---

2. The Standard CMMI Appraisal Method for Process Improvement (SCAMPI) differs only in the final steps: determining the ratings for the maturity level or the capability profile.

with a continuous model and its capability profile, in which each process area is rated individually. To continue with the prior example, consider a CMMI staged representation for which all 25 process areas are staged as dictated in version 1.1, with the exception of SAM and ISM. In such a case, an organization could be rated at ML 3 based on everything but these two process areas, and its process for Supplier Management would be rated at a capability level (for example, CL 3) that merged the CL ratings from SAM and ISM. Then regardless of whether the organization had suppliers, you could have a comparable maturity-level rating across a larger set of organizations. Furthermore, you would have a vehicle for reporting an additional capability in the area of managing suppliers.[3]

In a partially staged CMMI model, what could be done with the process areas in the Engineering category? If you think of the CMMI model primarily as geared toward supporting process improvement for engineering development and maintenance, then the process areas (at least most of them) could be included in the partial staging. The Engineering process areas, however, comprise an inter-related group that could perhaps benefit from a rating other than a general process maturity rating.

Furthermore, if you think of CMMI models as having potential application in domains outside of engineering (for example, acquisition or human resources), then engineering development should not be an essential part of the maturity-level definitions. To accomplish this transformation, you could think about a collective Engineering capability rating outside of the basic maturity staging. While the maturity staging would remain focused on process management (in the context of projects, and making use of support processes), a collective "engineering capability rating" could be defined to include most of the material in the Engineering process areas.[4]

---

3. The CMMI Team had no shortage of discussion and debate regarding the key process area from the CMM for Software version 2(c) related to product lines. Some team members who strongly opposed its inclusion as a process area in CMMI were nevertheless among the strongest advocates of product-line development. They simply did not believe that a product-line approach had sufficiently universal application to warrant inclusion in a fully staged model. If partial staging had been an option, the contents of this process area would likely have appeared in CMMI, but not as a part of the maturity staging.

4. If some items had less than universal applicability (for example, Validation or the goal in Requirements Development on transforming stakeholder needs into customer requirements), then they could be omitted from the Engineering capability rating. In this way, the rating would have more general applicability across a wider range of organizations.

If the process areas in the Engineering category were not staged, how would the organization report the results of an appraisal? As an example, an organization might have achieved ML 2 in basic Process Management (with Project Management and Support), an Engineering CL 3, a Validation CL 3, and a Supplier Management CL 2. This result becomes even more complicated than a single maturity-level number, but perhaps would not be all that bad, really. Such an understandable (and small) collection of ratings paints a picture of overall capability and maturity in an organization—one that is much easier to comprehend than a 22-, 24-, or 25-number capability profile—and simultaneously reveals more than the single maturity-level number.

Sample Requirements for CMMI Partial Staging

Following is a candidate list of requirements or principles that might be followed on the path to creating a single, partially staged CMMI representation:

1. There is just one integrated CMMI model.
2. There is just one architectural representation of this model.
3. The CMMI model includes all process areas that are available in all possible discipline combinations.
4. A discipline combination (for example, CMMI-SW, CMMI-SE/SW, CMMI-SE/SW/IPPD, or CMMI-SE/SW/IPPD/SS) provides a view of the single integrated model.
5. A discipline view may encompass a set of process areas that is a subset of all the process areas in the base CMMI model.
6. CMMI process areas are constructed to avoid duplication of the required or expected material in two or more process areas.
7. Only one version of any CMMI process area exists at any given time.
8. Every process area in the CMMI model has capability levels that define an improvement path within that individual area. The process areas that are included in a discipline view are available for rating, either individually or collectively, with capability levels.
9. One partial staging for the one integrated CMMI model exists, and it defines organizational maturity levels.

10. The set of process areas that define the organizational maturity levels constitutes "the core CMMI process areas."

11. Those who do not wish to adopt the single definition of CMMI organizational maturity levels, for whatever reason, may rely on capability-level ratings (singly or in groups) that are available in each CMMI process area. They may not redefine the meaning of the maturity-level ratings based on an alternative partial staging.

12. Generally speaking, the scope of the core CMMI process areas includes the categories of Process Management processes, Project Management processes, and Support processes.

13. Generally speaking, the scope of the core CMMI process areas does not include the categories of Engineering processes or Acquisition processes.

14. Generally speaking, the scope of the core CMMI process areas includes only those process areas (within the categories of Process Management processes, Project Management processes, and Support processes) that have universal applicability. That is, a wide spectrum of organizations should not have good grounds for wanting to eliminate any process area or goal from the core CMMI process areas as not applicable to them.

15. Every discipline view encompasses the core CMMI process areas, and a label such as "a CMMI maturity level 2 organization" has only one meaning based on that core set.

16. A discipline view may identify some of the noncore process areas as "essential" for that view and other noncore process areas as "optional."

17. A discipline view may identify collections of noncore process areas that are subject to a collective capability level rating; for example, Engineering capability, Integrated Product and Process Development (IPPD) capability, or Acquisition capability. That is, an organization may be at maturity level i, with an Engineering capability of j or an Acquisition capability of k.

18. References between process areas do not change with discipline views. An amplification-like entry after a reference may indicate that the CMMI process area cited is not included in the particular discipline view.

11.3 A Universal CMMI Model

While the "partially staged" model represents a step in the downsizing of the CMMI core components, other ideas have been raised that move farther along that continuum. Several members of the CMMI Team have long advocated a simpler, more streamlined approach to CMMI. Dubbed the "Universal CMMI" (U-CMMI), the idea is to produce a model consisting of only generic practices and the process areas that "enable" or support them.[5] Written in a conceptual, extensible manner, those components, accompanied by a template for defining organization-specific target processes, would define a model that could apply to any process—engineering or otherwise. Capability levels would be process capability levels and would be measured by the implementation of generic practices. Maturity levels would be based on the staging of the enabling process areas in the same way as the equivalent staging described earlier.

As an example, suppose that a printing company wanted to apply the U-CMMI to its processes. It would first need to establish its "core discipline" processes—perhaps layout, printing, finishing, and delivery— according to the template provided with the U-CMMI. Once these processes were defined, the company could begin improvement with the level 2 generic practices and their enabling process areas.

Although the universal model would be similar to the existing CMMI models, its lack of an engineering orientation would provide two broad benefits. First, it could act as a process-improvement model for a much wider range of enterprises, such as banking, consulting services, light industry, government, and retail. Second, it could provide a layman's view of process improvement that could be taught in undergraduate management and business curricula. Additionally, because of its reduced structure, applying U-CMMI to additional disciplines would not require the complex support infrastructure or large development teams needed by existing models.

This approach may have some drawbacks, however. It is not clear that the language in the model could be suitably simplified so as to apply universally. Some question might arise as to the comparability of level

---

5. For example, a process area for configuration management that supports the Configuration Management generic practice at CL 2.

ratings, given the variation in the organization-specific processes. Of course, training and appraisal materials would be needed that were as simple and clear as the model language, as well as trainers and appraisers needed to support its use.

The automated framework of CMMI could support the production of such a model, but it is still too early to predict whether the will to simplify could ever extend this far.

11.4 CMMI as an Enterprise Process-Improvement Framework

There has been a great deal of discussion about the possibility and desirability of process-improvement models that could reach out to all of the processes within a large, complex enterprise. A recent workshop, sponsored by the U.S. Office of the Under Secretary of Defense for Acquisition, Technology, and Logistics and the U.S. Federal Aviation Administration, gathered a group of experts to address process improvement from an enterprise perspective. While there was much discussion and learned argument, there was very little consensus on what such a model might look like. However, some specific requirements were highlighted. Such a model would:

- Tie process improvement directly to business results.
- Be flexible enough to adapt to changing business goals.
- Be scalable. It should be as easy for a 10-person group to use as for a 1,500-person group.
- Emphasize measuring process improvement (goals and changes) and performance, not a particular "maturity" (level x). The framework must have the ability to show short-term as well as long-term benefit (i.e., less than one year).
- Help develop a roadmap to achieve business objectives.
- Address *all* enterprise processes, as well as provide for integration of functional areas.
- Be accepted by the government and international communities as *the* framework.
- Be supported by infrastructure-training, ownership, and so on.
- Cost less than today's frameworks.

- Trace to existing standards where appropriate.
- Be flexible and provide guidance on which elements to use and when.
- Be cost-effective to implement.
- Help the enterprise focus on the interfaces within their system.
- Be specific with regard to appropriate variations for different users.
- Be supported by an appraisal method.
- Be transparent to the interviewee during an appraisal.[6]

Certainly the CMMI Product Suite could provide the foundation for such a model. However, the need to address such wide-ranging processes as financial practice (funding, labor distribution, budgeting), human resources (hiring, benefits, succession planning), marketing (customer research advertising, product lines), manufacturing (yield, suppliers, efficiency), and administration (facilities management, information technology) makes it easy to see a CMMI framework growing to 40 or more process areas. This would raise many questions. Would it make sense to have a single maturity-level rating covering all these areas together? "No" seems the likely answer. Are there areas in an enterprise where process improvement that is not model-based would make more sense? "Yes" may be the likely answer.

One possibility raised at the conference was the idea of a hierarchical framework of process-improvement methods, models, and requirements. In this concept, CMMI framework-based process models would tier from the enterprise down through executive and business-unit management to functional business process practitioners. Each tier would focus primarily on the work performed within its particular scope, but would interface with the tiers above and below it.

Maturity and capability scales might vary from tier to tier, and might be combined in various ways to meet specific enterprise needs. An enterprise-wide process asset library and knowledge base would support the multitiered models. The higher-level tiers would certainly have unique goals and critical success factors. They might also have some common and unique process areas and generic practices. The functional level might use CMMI instantiations with a standard set of Process and Project Management process areas, the standard CMMI

---

6. Software Productivity Consortium. "The October 2002 Enterprise Process Improvement Frameworks Workshop" (SPC-2003034-N, Version 01.01.00), April 2003.

generic practices, plus a set of function-specific process areas. There could be a reduced set of common generic practices that provided a unified process focus and maintained the shared vision across the enterprise. The IPPD extension could play an integrating role as well.

This is not an easy modification from the existing CMMI framework. Research and development would have to be conducted to identify the new mechanisms for integrating the models, both vertically and horizontally. Cross-functional and cross-tier processes would need to be in the framework, perhaps with different goals depending on the tier. The applicability of process improvement at the executive level is not clear, but its application at the enterprise level seems obvious. Integrating other models such as ISO 9000 or Malcolm Baldrige at the enterprise levels may prove challenging.

We believe the decision to develop this or some other extension to the CMMI concept for enterprise improvement is up to the market—if there is a user need, a model should be developed to meet it. CMMI offers a great deal of flexibility, proven methodology, and an active community of practice that will be hard to ignore if and when the challenge to create an enterprise improvement model is taken up.

11.5 Collection of Issues for Beyond Version 1.1

The public review period for CMMI version 0.2 in 1999 resulted in about 2,500 change requests to the model and the "books" that represent the model. Of these requests, approximately 400 were classified as "minor" and 500 were considered "global" (affecting several process areas or other elements). The remaining change requests were classified as being "local" to the individual model elements. For several of the change requests in the global and local categories, the CMMI Team lacked sufficient time to deal with them properly. Instead, they were placed on a list of potentially good ideas warranting more exploration.

The use of version 1.0 resulted in many more change requests to the model components. The CMMI Team used the same process to deal with the large number of changes requested, and as happened prior to version 1.0's release, version 1.1 does not address all of the potentially good ideas from the reviewers. In this section, we discuss a few of the other major open issues—that is, issues deferred for consideration to after version 1.1.

11.5.1 Advanced Practices

The implementation of advanced practices remains an issue. Version 1.1 allows advanced practices in the Engineering category but not in the other process area categories. For the future, we would expect that as the model is used, one of two things would occur. First, process improvement in the Engineering process areas might be aided by the presence of advanced practices, prompting users of this model to seek the expansion of this concept across the entire model.

Second, the value that advanced practices may have for process improvement might be viewed as insufficient to justify the architectural complexity they introduce, prompting model users to ask for their elimination across the entire model. The decision within the CMMI Team to put them into the initial model releases in a limited way was intended to lay the foundation for feedback either in favor of or opposed to advanced practices, as the team could not reach a consensus view. This disagreement was a part of the debate between proponents of staged versus continuous architectures.

11.5.2 Generic Attributes

EIA 731 contains generic attributes, an aspect of process improvement that is not included in any other source model. Generic attributes address the effectiveness of the process and the value of the work products produced by it. Proponents of generic attributes on the CMMI Team generated a proposal for CMMI generic attributes by making changes to improve the objectivity of the generic attributes in EIA 731. In the end, however, that proposal was not adopted.

Generic attributes add a significant aspect to process improvement that is not addressed by the capability dimension or the process dimension: How effective are the processes in your environment, and do they produce work products that the stakeholders find valuable? Some organizations have developed the ability to evaluate this process-improvement dimension by adopting the Lean initiative. For CMMI, the question remains: Would the inclusion of generic attributes in a CMMI appraisal be of sufficient value, given the issue of their objectivity?

11.5.3 Relationship to Other Process Areas

CMMI version 1.1 includes a section in each process area titled "Related Process Areas," which contains (not surprisingly) references to other process areas. A recommendation was made and accepted by the CMMI Team (but not implemented in version 1.1) to change the title of this section to "Relationships with Other Process Areas," and to make its content more meaningful.[7]

The needs related to this issue are as follows:

- Model users need to understand the high-level (key) relationships between process areas.
- Those who develop CMMI training materials need a mechanism to generate a high-level diagram to show relationships between process areas.
- Model users need to understand the difference between references at different levels (components) of the model.

The following guidelines were defined to restrict the use of the initial reference section in each process area to key process area interfaces:

- Change the title of "Related Process Areas" to "Relationships with Other Process Areas."
- Use the "Reference" architectural component but change the structure of the reference, in this section only, to an active statement of the relationship with other process areas.
- Allow one to three sentences for each relationship description.
- Include only the key relationships (that is, what the user needs to see at a high level).
- Retain the normal references in the model from other components.
- Generate a view in the Product Suite Repository that shows these relationships.

The CMMI Product Team has recommended such a change for each process area as a part of the next release of CMMI.

---

7. An earlier version of CMMI (predating version 1.0) used two levels of reference: the currently used "informative" reference and a stronger reference. The stronger reference invoked another process area, stating "Use the x process areas to achieve y." The application of the "Use" reference was not consistent across the model, confused model users, and raised issues in the area of appraisal. It was not clear exactly what was implied by the stronger relationship between process areas. Given the many calls to reduce the model's complexity and of the time to adequately study the issue, the stronger reference was eliminated in version 1.0. Whether anyone will make the case to revive multiple forms of reference in CMMI remains to be seen.

Example Update to Relationships Section

The following example is a proposed update to the Technical Solution process area:

Relationship with Other Process Areas

The Requirements Development process area provides product-component requirements to this process area so that alternative solutions can be developed.

The Requirements Development process area receives technical solutions, selected from the alternatives, to refine the product-component requirements.

The Work Product Verification process area verifies that the product components meet their requirements. As verification issues are identified, the design may need to change. This is an iterative process and occurs throughout the development of the product.

The Decision Analysis and Resolution process area provides structured decision-making practices that are used in selecting a technical solution from the alternative solutions.

The Product Integration process area receives the product components following their implementation.

The Product Integration process area provides integration test deficiencies to this process area for corrective action.

The Validation process area provides validation deficiencies to this process area for corrective action.

The Supplier Agreement Management process area handles the acquisition of all product components once the purchase decision is made in this process area.

11.6 A Final Note on CMMI Evolution

The ideas presented in this chapter are no more than seeds of possibilities. How CMMI actually evolves should be driven by you—the user community. At the end of the day, if CMMI isn't useful to organizations like yours, it won't be applied and will stagnate, wither, and disappear into the graveyard of lost management tools *du jour.* On the other hand, if CMMI remains responsive to your needs by changing to better serve organizations like yours, it will be a vital and beneficial tool for a long period of time.

For this to happen, though, requires that you, the user community, actively participate in CMMI evolution. There are a number of ways available, each requiring the expenditure of different levels of time and effort.

1. Attend conferences, workshops, and courses to learn more about CMMI and to provide feedback to the sponsors.
2. Join organizations that are sponsors and actively lobby for your positions on CMMI issues.
3. Participate in a CMMI working group like the interpretive guidance project or a model extension development team.
4. Have your organization (or your industry association) join the CMMI Steering Group.

We believe that the more users are involved, each bringing their diverse needs and viewpoints, the better CMMI will be. And the better CMMI is, the easier it will be for integrated process improvement to benefit hundreds of organizations throughout the world. It really is up to you.

Afterword

There is, and always will be, tension between the desire to improve, change, and grow, and the desire for stability and an avoidance of moving targets. This choice should not apply to Capability Maturity Model Integration (CMMI), however; both change and stability are fundamental to process improvement. The CMMI models must have sufficient stability so that an investment in process improvement is not undercut by radical and pervasive changes to the models. At the same time, the CMMI models must change to incorporate new knowledge, proven experience, and the continuous creativity of those who practice and preach process improvement.

As we said at the beginning of this book, the task of producing integrated models was a largely unprecedented task. The likelihood that the CMMI Team got everything "right," even after more than three years of diligent work, is not high. Furthermore, as every proponent of process improvement knows, change focused on making improvements never ends. Surely this axiom applies to process-improvement models just as much as it does to engineering development processes.

Of course, the determination of whether a given change proposed is too radical or pervasive lies somewhat in the eye of the beholder. For some, moving to a single representation would be a significant change with significant impact. For others, who are perhaps struck by the degree of commonality between the existing two CMMI representational architectures, it seems a logical step that would not undermine process improvement for anyone. By discussing such possible evolutionary paths for CMMI, we do not intend to diminish the stability or the acceptance of the model. It is our view that making a good thing better would only improve its acceptance in the community.

Throughout this book, we have tried to distill our experiences in responding to the need for integrated process improvement and participating in a major initiative aimed at developing innovative products. Some readers may have the chance to enjoy a similar opportunity, and we wish you well. For the rest of you, we hope that you can understand the hard work, difficult decisions, intellectual fireworks, and friendships that are an integral part of any such endeavor. We also hope that we have provided an accessible view into the results of the CMMI project so that you can make more informed decisions about applying this model in your organization. As CMMI evolves, whether along the paths that we have suggested or some other course, we will continue to update this information through the Addison-Wesley Web site.

Chapter 1 began with a quote from W. Edwards Deming, which proves as useful at this juncture as it did for our opening act: "It is not necessary to change. Survival is not mandatory." As you have survived your reading of this book, please let us know whether it has helped you on your path to integrated process improvement. Like engineering development processes and process-improvement models, books about these topics can be improved. We look forward to hearing from you and using your suggestions in future editions.

The Maven

by Richard Turner *(with abject apologies to Edgar Allan Poe)*

The following poem is dedicated to past, present, and future process improvement practitioners—internal champions, consultants, lead appraisers, team members—who have labored to reach out to middle managers and executives and share the light. We hope that CMMI will expand the ranks of these often overlooked, but important, change agents, and through them help a host of organizations improve their capabilities and reach their business goals.

Of course, the characters represented in the poem are fictional, and any resemblance to any person, living or dead, is not intended and is purely coincidental.

Once upon a late night dreary, a CEO sat tired and bleary,
Pondering his business, weighing why poor products left its floor.
While he nodded, nearly napping, suddenly there came a tapping,
As of someone harshly rapping, rapping at his office door.
"Tis the janitor," he muttered, "tapping at my office door—
Only this, and nothing more."

Silently he sat, not moving, hoping to maintain his musing,
Certain that the interloper would retreat and knock no more.
But with new insistence tapping, still the visitor kept rapping,
Louder, louder came the tapping, till it seemed it shook the door,
"Right, alright, hang on, I heard you," and he opened wide the door;
A woman there, just five-foot four.

Pushing by him, smiling, sitting, as if she'd but left her knitting,
She said, "I can help you with the business problems you deplore.
I can solve your cost prediction, defect rate, and staff retention,
If you'll simply pay attention to my tried and tested lore."
Then, with smile and hand extended, "by the way, my name's Lenore.
Glad to meet you."—nothing more.

Flabbergasted at her playing, but intrigued with all her saying,
The CEO considered, weighing. Was she what he'd waited for?
"Tell me how to start improving," he requested, hope renewing,
"What's the first thing to be doing? Please continue, wise Lenore."
"Settle down and I'll inform you of the key you're looking for—
CMMI is at the core.

"First you need to take the measure of your processes to make sure
That you have the fundamentals covered—let me underscore—
Not an easy undertaking. Yet you can be sure you're making
Progress, even while you're staking out your current process score.
If you find you've implemented all these basics heretofore,
You're level 1—but there's much more.

"Managing your work is vital, planning, monitoring, et al.
Making sure you've documented how the job's done on the floor.
Ensure the things your people need are there to help them to succeed,
Like skills, authority to lead, and resources—but don't ignore
Control of versions, and compliance, stakeholders outside your door.
That's level 2—though quite a chore.

"Once local chaos is behind you, it's time to focus on the wide view.
Standard process assets give you baselined measures as you explore
New ways to do the process better. And it leaves your staff unfettered.
Since they always know the letter of the process, they're prepared for
Flexible deployment when some broader need comes to the fore.
That's level 3—but more's in store.

"You can now make each decision with a quantified precision
That is based on the provision of data you've not had before.
You can know as it begins, before a project augurs in,
And you can move to find wherein the problem lies and not ignore
The very things that may have caused your product problems heretofore.
And this, my friend, is level 4."

"Eureka!" cried the glad exec, "You've saved me—I could hug your neck!"
"Please don't," she said, "for we're not done yet. See, there still is something more.
It's not enough to simply measure, though it yields insightful treasure,
You must not fall into leisure—not adapt to what's in store.
You must optimize your process, continuously, more and more.
At level 5, your business soars."

With this, the wise and welcome maven, disappeared into the raven
Darkness of the office suite—a memory of imparted lore.
The CEO, try as he would, could not believe advice so good
Had started with a rap on wood, a tapping at his office door.
Swearing to himself to follow all the sage words of Lenore—
"CMMI Forevermore!"

Appendix A

Summary of CMMI-SE/SW/IPPD/SS Models

Summary of Continuous Representation

Process Management

ORGANIZATIONAL PROCESS FOCUS

Plan and implement organizational process improvement based on a thorough understanding of the current strengths and weaknesses of the organization's processes and process assets.

Strengths, weaknesses, and improvement opportunities for the organization's processes are identified periodically and as needed. SG 1

Establish and maintain the description of the process needs and objectives for the organization. SP 1.1-1

Appraise the processes of the organization periodically and as needed to maintain an understanding of their strengths and weaknesses. SP 1.2-1

Identify improvements to the organization's processes and process assets. SP 1.3-1

Improvements are planned and implemented, organizational process assets are deployed, and process-related experiences are incorporated into the organizational process assets. SG 2

Establish and maintain process action plans to address improvements to the organization's processes and process assets. SP 2.1-1

Implement process action plans across the organization. SP 2.2-1

Deploy organizational process assets across the organization. SP 2.3-1

Incorporate process-related work products, measures, and improvement information derived from planning and performing the process into the organizational process assets. SP 2.4-1

ORGANIZATIONAL PROCESS DEFINITION

Establish and maintain a usable set of organizational process assets.

A set of organizational process assets is established and maintained. SG 1

Establish and maintain the organization's set of standard processes. SP 1.1-1

Establish and maintain descriptions of the life-cycle models approved for use in the organization. SP 1.2-1

Establish and maintain the tailoring criteria and guidelines for the organization's set of standard processes. SP 1.3-1

Establish and maintain the organization's measurement repository. SP 1.4-1

Establish and maintain the organization's process asset library. SP 1.5-1

ORGANIZATIONAL TRAINING

Develop the skills and knowledge of people so they can perform their roles effectively and efficiently.

A training capability that supports the organization's management and technical roles is established and maintained. SG 1

Establish and maintain the strategic training needs of the organization. SP 1.1-1

Determine which training needs are the responsibility of the organization and which will be left to the individual project or support group. SP 1.2-1

Establish and maintain an organizational training tactical plan. SP 1.3-1

Establish and maintain training capability to address organizational training needs. SP 1.4-1

Training necessary for individuals to perform their roles effectively is provided. SG 2

Deliver the training following the organizational training tactical plan. SP 2.1-1

Establish and maintain records of the organizational training. SP 2.2-1

Assess the effectiveness of the organization's training program. SP 2.3-1

ORGANIZATIONAL PROCESS PERFORMANCE

Establish and maintain a quantitative understanding of the performance of the organization's set of standard processes in support of quality and process-performance objectives, and provide the process performance data, baselines, and models to quantitatively manage the organization's projects.

Baselines and models that characterize the expected process performance of the organization's set of standard processes are established and maintained. SG 1

Select the processes or process elements in the organization's set of standard processes that are to be included in the organization's process performance analyses. SP 1.1-1

Establish and maintain definitions of the measures that are to be included in the organization's process performance analyses. SP 1.2-1

Establish and maintain quantitative objectives for quality and process performance for the organization. SP 1.3-1

Establish and maintain the organization's process performance baselines. SP 1.4-1

Establish and maintain the process performance models for the organization's set of standard processes. SP 1.5-1

ORGANIZATIONAL INNOVATION AND DEPLOYMENT

Select and deploy incremental and innovative improvements that measurably improve the organization's processes and technologies. The improvements support the organization's quality and process performance objectives as derived from the organization's business objectives.

Process and technology improvements that contribute to meeting quality and process-performance objectives are selected. SG 1

Collect and analyze process- and technology-improvement proposals. SP 1.1-1

Identify and analyze innovative improvements that could increase the organization's quality and process performance. SP 1.2-1

Pilot process and technology improvements to select which ones to implement. SP 1.3-1

Select process- and technology-improvement proposals for deployment across the organization. SP 1.4-1

Measurable improvements to the organization's processes and technologies are continually and systematically deployed. SG 2

Establish and maintain the plans for deploying the selected process and technology improvements. SP 2.1-1

Manage the deployment of the selected process and technology improvements. SP 2.2-1

Measure the effects of the deployed process and technology improvements. SP 2.3-1

Project Management

PROJECT PLANNING

Establish and maintain plans that define project activities.

Estimates of project planning parameters are established and maintained. SG 1

Establish a top-level work breakdown structure (WBS) to estimate the scope of the project. SP 1.1-1

Establish and maintain estimates of the attributes of the work products and tasks. SP 1.2-1

Define the project life-cycle phases upon which to scope the planning effort. SP 1.3-1

Estimate the project effort and cost for the work products and tasks based on estimation rationale. SP 1.4-1

A project plan is established and maintained as the basis for managing the project. SG 2

Establish and maintain the project's budget and schedule. SP 2.1-1

Identify and analyze project risks. SP 2.2-1

Plan for the management of project data. SP 2.3-1

Plan for necessary resources to perform the project. SP 2.4-1

Plan for knowledge and skills needed to perform the project. SP 2.5-1

Plan the involvement of identified stakeholders. SP 2.6-1

Establish and maintain the overall project plan content. SP 2.7-1

Commitments to the project plan are established and maintained. SG 3

Review all plans that affect the project to understand project commitments. SP 3.1-1

Reconcile the project plan to reflect available and estimated resources. SP 3.2-1

Obtain commitment from relevant stakeholders responsible for performing and supporting plan execution. SP 3.3-1

Project Monitoring and Control

Provide an understanding of the project's progress so that appropriate corrective actions can be taken when the project's performance deviates significantly from the plan.

Actual performance and progress of the project are monitored against the project plan. SG 1

Monitor the actual values of the project planning parameters against the project plan. SP 1.1-1

Monitor commitments against those identified in the project plan. SP 1.2-1

Monitor risks against those identified in the project plan. SP 1.3-1

Monitor the management of project data against the project plan. SP 1.4-1

Monitor stakeholder involvement against the project plan. SP 1.5-1

Periodically review the project's progress, performance, and issues. SP 1.6-1

Review the accomplishments and results of the project at selected project milestones. SP 1.7-1

Corrective actions are managed to closure when the project's performance or results deviate significantly from the plan. SG 2

Collect and analyze the issues and determine the corrective actions necessary to address the issues. SP 2.1-1

Take corrective action on identified issues. SP 2.2-1

Manage corrective actions to closure. SP 2.3-1

SUPPLIER AGREEMENT MANAGEMENT

Manage the acquisition of products from suppliers for which there exists a formal agreement.

Agreements with the suppliers are established and maintained. SG 1

Determine the type of acquisition for each product or product component to be acquired. SP 1.1-1

Select suppliers based on an evaluation of their ability to meet the specified requirements and established criteria. SP 1.2-1

Establish and maintain formal agreements with the supplier. SP 1.3-1

Agreements with the suppliers are satisfied by both the project and the supplier. SG 2

Review candidate COTS products to ensure that they satisfy the specified requirements that are covered under a supplier agreement. SP 2.1-1

Perform activities with the supplier as specified in the supplier agreement. SP 2.2-1

Ensure that the supplier agreement is satisfied before accepting the acquired product. SP 2.3-1

Transition the acquired products from the supplier to the project. SP 2.4-1

INTEGRATED PROJECT MANAGEMENT (IPPD)

Establish and manage the project and the involvement of the relevant stakeholders according to an integrated and defined process that is tailored from the organization's set of standard processes. Establish a shared vision for the project and a team structure for integrated teams that will carry out the objectives of the project.

The project is conducted using a defined process that is tailored from the organization's set of standard processes. SG 1

Establish and maintain the project's defined process. SP 1.1-1

Use the organizational process assets and measurement repository for estimating and planning the project's activities. SP 1.2-1

Integrate the project plan and the other plans that affect the project to describe the project's defined process. SP 1.3-1

Manage the project using the project plan, the other plans that affect the project, and the project's defined process. SP 1.4-1

Contribute work products, measures, and documented experiences to the organizational process assets. SP 1.5-1

Coordination and collaboration of the project with relevant stakeholders is conducted. SG 2

Manage the involvement of the relevant stakeholders in the project. SP 2.1-1

Participate with relevant stakeholders to identify, negotiate, and track critical dependencies. SP 2.2-1

Resolve issues with relevant stakeholders. SP 2.3-1

The project is conducted using the project's shared vision. SG 3

Identify expectations, constraints, interfaces, and operational conditions applicable to the project's shared vision. SP 3.1-1

Establish and maintain a shared vision for the project. SP 3.2-1

The integrated teams needed to execute the project are identified, defined, structured, and tasked. SG 4

Determine the integrated team structure that will best meet the project objectives and constraints. SP 4.1-1

Develop a preliminary distribution of requirements, responsibilities, authorities, tasks, and interfaces to teams in the selected integrated team structure. SP 4.2-1

Establish and maintain teams in the integrated team structure. SP 4.3-1

RISK MANAGEMENT

Identify potential problems before they occur, so that risk-handling activities may be planned and invoked as needed across the life of the product or project to mitigate adverse impacts on achieving objectives.

Preparation for risk management is conducted. SG 1

> Determine risk sources and categories. SP 1.1-1
>
> Define the parameters used to analyze and categorize risks, and the parameters used to control the risk management effort. SP 1.2-1
>
> Establish and maintain the strategy to be used for risk management. SP 1.3-1

Risks are identified and analyzed to determine their relative importance. SG 2

> Identify and document the risks. SP 2.1-1
>
> Evaluate and categorize each identified risk using the defined risk categories and parameters, and determine its relative priority. SP 2.2-1

Risks are handled and mitigated, where appropriate, to reduce adverse impacts on achieving objectives. SG 3

> Develop a risk mitigation plan for the most important risks to the project, as defined by the risk management strategy. SP 3.1-1
>
> Monitor the status of each risk periodically and implement the risk mitigation plan as appropriate. SP 3.2-1

INTEGRATED TEAMING

Form and sustain an integrated team for the development of work products.

A team composition that provides the knowledge and skills required to deliver the team's product is established and maintained. SG 1

> Identify and define the team's specific internal tasks to generate the team's expected output. SP 1.1-1
>
> Identify the knowledge, skills, and functional expertise needed to perform team tasks. SP 1.2-1
>
> Assign the appropriate personnel to be team members based on required knowledge and skills. SP 1.3-1

Operation of the integrated team is governed according to established principles. SG 2

Establish and maintain a shared vision for the integrated team that is aligned with any overarching or higher-level vision. SP 2.1-1

Establish and maintain a team charter based on the integrated team's shared vision and overall team objectives. SP 2.2-1

Clearly define and maintain each team member's roles and responsibilities. SP 2.3-1

Establish and maintain integrated team operating procedures. SP 2.4-1

Establish and maintain collaboration among interfacing teams. SP 2.5-1

Integrated Supplier Management

Proactively identify sources of products that may be used to satisfy the project's requirements and manage selected suppliers while maintaining a cooperative project-supplier relationship.

Potential sources of products that best fit the needs of the project are identified, analyzed, and selected. SG 1

Identify and analyze potential sources of products that may be used to satisfy the project's requirements. SP 1.1-1

Use a formal evaluation process to determine which sources of custom-made and off-the-shelf products to use. SP 1.2-1

Work is coordinated with suppliers to ensure the supplier agreement is executed appropriately. SG 2

Monitor and analyze selected processes used by the supplier. SP 2.1-1

For custom-made products, evaluate selected supplier work products. SP 2.2-1

Revise the supplier agreement or relationship, as appropriate, to reflect changes in conditions. SP 2.3-1

Quantitative Project Management

Quantitatively manage the project's defined process to achieve the project's established quality and process-performance objectives.

The project is quantitatively managed using quality and process-performance objectives. SG 1

Establish and maintain the project's quality and process-performance objectives. SP 1.1-1

Select the subprocesses that compose the project's defined process based on historical stability and capability data. SP 1.2-1

Select the subprocesses of the project's defined process that will be statistically managed. SP 1.3-1

Monitor the project to determine whether the project's objectives for quality and process performance will be satisfied, and identify corrective action as appropriate. SP 1.4-1

The performance of selected subprocesses within the project's defined process is statistically managed. SG 2

Select the measures and analytic techniques to be used in statistically managing the selected subprocesses. SP 2.1-1

Establish and maintain an understanding of the variation of the selected subprocesses using the selected measures and analytic techniques. SP 2.2-1

Monitor the performance of the selected subprocesses to determine their capability to satisfy their quality and process-performance objectives, and identify corrective action as necessary. SP 2.3-1

Record statistical and quality management data in the organization's measurement repository. SP 2.4-1

Engineering

REQUIREMENTS MANAGEMENT

Manage the requirements of the project's products and product components and identify inconsistencies between those requirements and the project's plans and work products.

Requirements are managed and inconsistencies with project plans and work products are identified. SG 1

Develop an understanding with the requirements providers on the meaning of the requirements. SP 1.1-1

Obtain commitment to the requirements from the project participants. SP 1.2-2

Manage changes to the requirements as they evolve during the project. SP 1.3-1

Maintain bidirectional traceability among the requirements and the project plans and work products. SP 1.4-2

Identify inconsistencies between the project plans and work products and the requirements. SP 1.5-1

REQUIREMENTS DEVELOPMENT

Produce and analyze customer, product, and product-component requirements.

Stakeholder needs, expectations, constraints, and interfaces are collected and translated into customer requirements. SG 1

Identify and collect stakeholder needs, expectations, constraints, and interfaces for all phases of the product life cycle. SP 1.1-1

Elicit stakeholder needs, expectations, constraints, and interfaces for all phases of the product life cycle. SP 1.1-2

Transform stakeholder needs, expectations, constraints, and interfaces into customer requirements. SP 1.2-1

Customer requirements are refined and elaborated to develop product and product-component requirements. SG 2

Establish and maintain product and product-component requirements, which are based on the customer requirements. SP 2.1-1

Allocate the requirements for each product component. SP 2.2-1

Identify interface requirements. SP 2.3-1

The requirements are analyzed and validated, and a definition of required functionality is developed. SG 3

Establish and maintain operational concepts and associated scenarios. SP 3.1-1

Establish and maintain a definition of required functionality. SP 3.2-1

Analyze requirements to ensure that they are necessary and sufficient. SP 3.3-1

Analyze requirements to balance stakeholder needs and constraints. SP 3.4-3

Validate requirements to ensure the resulting product will perform appropriately in its intended-use environment. SP 3.5-1

Validate requirements to ensure the resulting product will perform as intended in the user's environment using multiple techniques as appropriate. SP 3.5-2

TECHNICAL SOLUTION

Design, develop, and implement solutions to requirements. Solutions, designs, and implementations encompass products, product components, and product-related life-cycle processes either singly or in combinations as appropriate.

Product or product-component solutions are selected from alternative solutions. SG 1

Develop alternative solutions and selection criteria. SP 1.1-1

Develop detailed alternative solutions and selection criteria. SP 1.1-2

Evolve the operational concept, scenarios, and environments to describe the conditions, operating modes, and operating states specific to each product component. SP 1.2-2

Select the product-component solutions that best satisfy the criteria established. SP 1.3-1

Product or product-component designs are developed. SG 2

Develop a design for the product or product component. SP 2.1-1

Establish and maintain a technical data package. SP 2.2-3

Establish and maintain the solution for product-component interfaces. SP 2.3-1

Design comprehensive product-component interfaces in terms of established and maintained criteria. SP 2.3-3

Evaluate whether the product components should be developed, purchased, or reused based on established criteria. SP 2.4-3

Product components, and associated support documentation, are implemented from their designs. SG 3

Implement the designs of the product components. SP 3.1-1

Develop and maintain the end-use documentation. SP 3.2-1

PRODUCT INTEGRATION

Assemble the product from the product components, ensure that the product, as integrated, functions properly, and deliver the product.

Preparation for product integration is conducted. SG 1

Determine the product-component integration sequence. SP 1.1-1

Establish and maintain the environment needed to support the integration of the product components. SP 1.2-2

Establish and maintain procedures and criteria for integration of the product components. SP 1.3-3

The product-component interfaces, both internal and external, are compatible. SG 2

Review interface descriptions for coverage and completeness. SP 2.1-1

Manage internal and external interface definitions, designs, and changes for products and product components. SP 2.2-1

Verified product components are assembled and the integrated, verified, and validated product is delivered. SG 3

Confirm, prior to assembly, that each product component required to assemble the product has been properly identified, functions according to its description, and that the product-component interfaces comply with the interface descriptions. SP 3.1-1

Assemble product components according to the product integration sequence and available procedures. SP 3.2-1

Evaluate assembled product components for interface compatibility. SP 3.3-1

Package the assembled product or product component and deliver it to the appropriate customer. SP 3.4-1

VERIFICATION

Ensure that selected work products meet their specified requirements.

Preparation for verification is conducted. SG 1

Select the work products to be verified and the verification methods that will be used for each. SP 1.1-1

Establish and maintain the environment needed to support verification. SP 1.2-2

Establish and maintain verification procedures and criteria for the selected work products. SP 1.3-3

Peer reviews are performed on selected work products. SG 2

Prepare for peer reviews of selected work products. SP 2.1-1

Conduct peer reviews on selected work products and identify issues resulting from the peer review. SP 2.2-1

Analyze data about preparation, conduct, and results of the peer reviews. SP 2.3-2

Selected work products are verified against their specified requirements. SG 3

Perform verification on the selected work products. SP 3.1-1

Analyze the results of all verification activities and identify corrective action. SP 3.2-2

VALIDATION

Demonstrate that a product or product component fulfills its intended use when placed in its intended environment.

Preparation for validation is conducted. SG 1

Select products and product components to be validated and the validation methods that will be used for each. SP 1.1-1

Establish and maintain the environment needed to support validation. SP 1.2-2

Establish and maintain procedures and criteria for validation. SP 1.3-3

The product or product components are validated to ensure that they are suitable for use in their intended operating environment. SG 2

Perform validation on the selected products and product components. SP 2.1-1

Analyze the results of the validation activities and identify issues. SP 2.2-1

Support

CONFIGURATION MANAGEMENT

Establish and maintain the integrity of work products using configuration identification, configuration control, configuration status accounting, and configuration audits.

Baselines of identified work products are established. SG 1

Identify the configuration items, components, and related work products that will be placed under configuration management. SP 1.1-1

Establish and maintain a configuration management and change management system for controlling work products. SP 1.2-1

Create or release baselines for internal use and for delivery to the customer. SP 1.3-1

Changes to the work products under configuration management are tracked and controlled. SG 2

Track change requests for the configuration items. SP 2.1-1

Control changes to the configuration items. SP 2.2-1

Integrity of baselines is established and maintained. SG 3

Establish and maintain records describing configuration items. SP 3.1-1

Perform configuration audits to maintain integrity of the configuration baselines. SP 3.2-1

PROCESS AND PRODUCT QUALITY ASSURANCE

Provide staff and management with objective insight into processes and associated work products.

Adherence of the performed process and associated work products and services to applicable process descriptions, standards and procedures is objectively evaluated. SG 1

Objectively evaluate the designated performed processes against the applicable process descriptions, standards, and procedures. SP 1.1-1

Objectively evaluate the designated work products and services against the applicable process descriptions, standards, and procedures. SP 1.2-1

Noncompliance issues are objectively tracked and communicated, and resolution is ensured. SG 2

Communicate quality issues and ensure resolution of noncompliance issues with the staff and managers. SP 2.1-1

Establish and maintain records of the quality assurance activities. SP 2.2-1

MEASUREMENT AND ANALYSIS

Develop and sustain a measurement capability that is used to support management information needs.

Measurement objectives and activities are aligned with identified information needs and objectives. SG 1

Establish and maintain measurement objectives that are derived from identified information needs and objectives. SP 1.1-1

Specify measures to address the measurement objectives. SP 1.2-1

Specify how measurement data will be obtained and stored. SP 1.3-1

Specify how measurement data will be analyzed and reported. SP 1.4-1

Measurement results that address identified information needs and objectives are provided. SG 2

Obtain specified measurement data. SP 2.1-1

Analyze and interpret measurement data. SP 2.2-1

Manage and store measurement data, measurement specifications, and analysis results. SP 2.3-1

Report results of measurement and analysis activities to all relevant stakeholders. SP 2.4-1

DECISION ANALYSIS AND RESOLUTION

Analyze possible decisions using a formal evaluation process that evaluates identified alternatives against established criteria.

Decisions are based on an evaluation of alternatives using established criteria. SG 1

Establish and maintain guidelines to determine which issues are subject to a formal evaluation process. SP 1.1-1

Establish and maintain the criteria for evaluating alternatives, and the relative ranking of these criteria. SP 1.2-1

Identify alternative solutions to address issues. SP 1.3-1

Select the evaluation methods. SP 1.4-1

Evaluate alternative solutions using the established criteria and methods. SP 1.5-1

Select solutions from the alternatives based on the evaluation criteria. SP 1.6-1

Organizational Environment for Integration

Provide an IPPD infrastructure and manage people for integration.

An infrastructure that maximizes the productivity of people and affects the collaboration necessary for integration is provided. SG 1

Establish and maintain a shared vision for the organization. SP 1.1-1

Establish and maintain an integrated work environment that supports IPPD by enabling collaboration and concurrent development. SP 1.2-1

Identify the unique skills needed to support the IPPD environment. SP 1.3-1

People are managed to nurture the integrative and collaborative behaviors of an IPPD environment. SG 2

Establish and maintain leadership mechanisms to enable timely collaboration. SP 2.1-1

Establish and maintain incentives for adopting and demonstrating integrative and collaborative behaviors at all levels of the organization. SP 2.2-1

Establish and maintain organizational guidelines to balance team and home organization responsibilities. SP 2.3-1

Causal Analysis and Resolution

Identify causes of defects and other problems and take action to prevent them from occurring in the future.

Root causes of defects and other problems are systematically determined. SG 1

Select the defects and other problems for analysis. SP 1.1-1

Perform causal analysis of selected defects and other problems and propose actions to address them. SP 1.2-1

Root causes of defects and other problems are systematically addressed to prevent their future occurrence. SG 2

Implement the selected action proposals that were developed in causal analysis. SP 2.1-1

Evaluate the effect of changes on process performance. SP 2.2-1

Record causal analysis and resolution data for use across the project and organization. SP 2.3-1

Generic Goals and Generic Practices

The process supports and enables achievement of the specific goals of the process area by transforming identifiable input work products to produce identifiable output work products. GG 1

Perform the base practices of the process area to develop work products and provide services to achieve the specific goals of the process area. GP 1.1

The process is institutionalized as a managed process. GG 2

Establish and maintain an organizational policy for planning and performing the process. GP 2.1

Establish and maintain the plan for performing the process. GP 2.2

Provide adequate resources for performing the process, developing the work products, and providing the services of the process. GP 2.3

Assign responsibility and authority for performing the process, developing the work products, and providing the services of the process. GP 2.4

Train the people performing or supporting the process as needed. GP 2.5

Place designated work products of the process under appropriate levels of configuration management. GP 2.6

Identify and involve the relevant stakeholders as planned. GP 2.7

Monitor and control the process against the plan for performing the process and take appropriate corrective action. GP 2.8

Objectively evaluate adherence of the process against its process description, standards, and procedures, and address noncompliance. GP 2.9

Review the activities, status, and results of the process with higher-level management and resolve issues. GP 2.10

The process is institutionalized as a defined process. GG 3

Establish and maintain the description of a defined process. GP 3.1

Collect work products, measures, measurement results, and improvement information derived from planning and performing the process to support the future use and improvement of the organization's processes and process assets. GP 3.2

The process is institutionalized as a quantitatively managed process. GG 4

Establish and maintain quantitative objectives for the process that address quality and process performance based on customer needs and business objectives. GP 4.1

Stabilize the performance of one or more subprocesses to determine the ability of the process to achieve the established quantitative quality and process-performance objectives. GP 4.2

The process is institutionalized as an optimizing process. GG 5

Ensure continuous improvement of the process in fulfilling the relevant business objectives of the organization. GP 5.1

Identify and correct the root causes of defects and other problems in the process. GP 5.2

Summary of CMMI-SE/SW/ IPPD/SS Models

Summary of Staged Representation

Note: **Specific practices that are included in the staged model for information only are not included in the following summaries.**

Maturity Level: 2

REQUIREMENTS MANAGEMENT

Manage the requirements of the project's products and product components and identify inconsistencies between those requirements and the project's plans and work products.

Requirements are managed and inconsistencies with project plans and work products are identified. SG 1

Develop an understanding with the requirements providers on the meaning of the requirements. SP 1.1

Obtain commitment to the requirements from the project participants. SP 1.2

Manage changes to the requirements as they evolve during the project. SP 1.3

Maintain bidirectional traceability among the requirements and the project plans and work products. SP 1.4

Identify inconsistencies between the project plans and work products and the requirements. SP 1.5

The process is institutionalized as a managed process. GG 2

Commitment to Perform

Establish and maintain an organizational policy for planning and performing the requirements management process. GP 2.1 (CO 1)

Ability to Perform

Establish and maintain the plan for performing the requirements management process. GP 2.2 (AB 1)

Provide adequate resources for performing the requirements management process, developing the work products, and providing the services of the process. GP 2.3 (AB 2)

Assign responsibility and authority for performing the process, developing the work products, and providing the services of the requirements management process. GP 2.4 (AB 3)

Train the people performing or supporting the requirements management process as needed. GP 2.5 (AB 4)

Directing Implementation

Place designated work products of the requirements management process under appropriate levels of configuration management. GP 2.6 (DI 1)

Identify and involve the relevant stakeholders of the requirements management process as planned. GP 2.7 (DI 2)

Monitor and control the requirements management process against the plan for performing the process and take appropriate corrective action. GP 2.8 (DI 3)

Verifying Implementation

Objectively evaluate adherence of the requirements management process against its process description, standards, and procedures and address noncompliance. GP 2.9 (VE 1)

Review the activities, status, and results of the requirements management process with higher-level management and resolve issues. GP 2.10 (VE 2)

PROJECT PLANNING

Establish and maintain plans that define project activities.

Estimates of project planning parameters are established and maintained. SG 1

Establish a top-level work breakdown structure (WBS) to estimate the scope of the project. SP 1.1

Establish and maintain estimates of the attributes of the work products and tasks. SP 1.2

Define the project life-cycle phases upon which to scope the planning effort. SP 1.3

Estimate the project effort and cost for the work products and tasks based on estimation rationale. SP 1.4

A project plan is established and maintained as the basis for managing the project. SG 2

Establish and maintain the project's budget and schedule. SP 2.1

Identify and analyze project risks. SP 2.2

Plan for the management of project data. SP 2.3

Plan for necessary resources to perform the project. SP 2.4

Plan for knowledge and skills needed to perform the project. SP 2.5

Plan the involvement of identified stakeholders. SP 2.6

Establish and maintain the overall project plan content. SP 2.7

Commitments to the project plan are established and maintained. SG 3

Review all plans that affect the project to understand project commitments. SP 3.1

Reconcile the project plan to reflect available and estimated resources. SP 3.2

Obtain commitment from relevant stakeholders responsible for performing and supporting plan execution. SP 3.3

The process is institutionalized as a managed process. GG 2

Commitment to Perform

Establish and maintain an organizational policy for planning and performing the project planning process. GP 2.1 (CO 1)

Ability to Perform

Establish and maintain the plan for performing the project planning process. GP 2.2 (AB 1)

Provide adequate resources for performing the project planning process, developing the work products, and providing the services of the process. GP 2.3 (AB 2)

Assign responsibility and authority for performing the process, developing the work products, and providing the services of the project planning process. GP 2.4 (AB 3)

Train the people performing or supporting the project planning process as needed. GP 2.5 (AB 4)

Directing Implementation

Place designated work products of the project planning process under appropriate levels of configuration management. GP 2.6 (DI 1)

Identify and involve the relevant stakeholders of the project planning process as planned. GP 2.7 (DI 2)

Monitor and control the project planning process against the plan for performing the process and take appropriate corrective action. GP 2.8 (DI 3)

Verifying Implementation

Objectively evaluate adherence of the project planning process against its process description, standards, and procedures and address noncompliance. GP 2.9 (VE 1)

Review the activities, status, and results of the project planning process with higher-level management and resolve issues. GP 2.10 (VE 2)

PROJECT MONITORING AND CONTROL

Provide an understanding of the project's progress so that appropriate corrective actions can be taken when the project's performance deviates significantly from the plan.

Actual performance and progress of the project are monitored against the project plan. SG 1

Monitor the actual values of the project planning parameters against the project plan. SP 1.1

Monitor commitments against those identified in the project plan. SP 1.2

Monitor risks against those identified in the project plan. SP 1.3

Monitor the management of project data against the project plan. SP 1.4

Monitor stakeholder involvement against the project plan. SP 1.5

Periodically review the project's progress, performance, and issues. SP 1.6

Review the accomplishments and results of the project at selected project milestones. SP 1.7

Corrective actions are managed to closure when the project's performance or results deviate significantly from the plan. SG 2

Collect and analyze the issues and determine the corrective actions necessary to address the issues. SP 2.1

Take corrective action on identified issues. SP 2.2

Manage corrective actions to closure. SP 2.3

The process is institutionalized as a managed process. GG 2

Commitment to Perform

Establish and maintain an organizational policy for planning and performing the project monitoring and control process. GP 2.1 (CO 1)

Ability to Perform

Establish and maintain the plan for performing the project monitoring and control process. GP 2.2 (AB 1)

Provide adequate resources for performing the project monitoring and control process, developing the work products, and providing the services of the process. GP 2.3 (AB 2)

Assign responsibility and authority for performing the process, developing the work products, and providing the services of the project monitoring and control process. GP 2.4 (AB 3)

Train the people performing or supporting the project monitoring and control process as needed. GP 2.5 (AB 4)

Directing Implementation

Place designated work products of the project monitoring and control process under appropriate levels of configuration management. GP 2.6 (DI 1)

Identify and involve the relevant stakeholders of the project monitoring and control process as planned. GP 2.7 (DI 2)

Monitor and control the project monitoring and control process against the plan for performing the process and take appropriate corrective action. GP 2.8 (DI 3)

Verifying Implementation

Objectively evaluate adherence of the project monitoring and control process against its process description, standards, and procedures and address noncompliance. GP 2.9 (VE 1)

Review the activities, status, and results of the project monitoring and control process with higher-level management and resolve issues. GP 2.10 (VE 2)

Supplier Agreement Management

Manage the acquisition of products from suppliers for which there exists a formal agreement.

Agreements with the suppliers are established and maintained. SG 1

Determine the type of acquisition for each product or product component to be acquired. SP 1.1

Select suppliers based on an evaluation of their ability to meet the specified requirements and established criteria. SP 1.2

Establish and maintain formal agreements with the supplier. SP 1.3

Agreements with the suppliers are satisfied by both the project and the supplier. SG 2

Review candidate COTS products to ensure that they satisfy the specified requirements that are covered under a supplier agreement. SP 2.1

Perform activities with the supplier as specified in the supplier agreement. SP 2.2

Ensure that the supplier agreement is satisfied before accepting the acquired product. SP 2.3

Transition the acquired products from the supplier to the project. SP 2.4

The process is institutionalized as a managed process. GG 2

Commitment to Perform

Establish and maintain an organizational policy for planning and performing the supplier agreement management process. GP 2.1 (CO 1)

Ability to Perform

Establish and maintain the plan for performing the supplier agreement management process. GP 2.2 (AB 1)

Provide adequate resources for performing the supplier agreement management process, developing the work products, and providing the services of the process. GP 2.3 (AB 2)

Assign responsibility and authority for performing the process, developing the work products, and providing the services of the supplier agreement management process. GP 2.4 (AB 3)

Train the people performing or supporting the supplier agreement management process as needed. GP 2.5 (AB 4)

Directing Implementation

Place designated work products of the supplier agreement management process under appropriate levels of configuration management. GP 2.6 (DI 1)

Identify and involve the relevant stakeholders of the supplier agreement management process as planned. GP 2.7 (DI 2)

Monitor and control the supplier agreement management process against the plan for performing the process and take appropriate corrective action. GP 2.8 (DI 3)

Verifying Implementation

Objectively evaluate adherence of the supplier agreement management process against its process description, standards, and procedures and address noncompliance. GP 2.9 (VE 1)

Review the activities, status, and results of the supplier agreement management process with higher-level management and resolve issues. GP 2.10 (VE 2)

MEASUREMENT AND ANALYSIS

Develop and sustain a measurement capability that is used to support management information needs.

Measurement objectives and activities are aligned with identified information needs and objectives. SG 1

Establish and maintain measurement objectives that are derived from identified information needs and objectives. SP 1.1

Specify measures to address the measurement objectives. SP 1.2

Specify how measurement data will be obtained and stored. SP 1.3

Specify how measurement data will be analyzed and reported. SP 1.4

Measurement results that address identified information needs and objectives are provided. SG 2

Obtain specified measurement data. SP 2.1

Analyze and interpret measurement data. SP 2.2

Manage and store measurement data, measurement specifications, and analysis results. SP 2.3

Report results of measurement and analysis activities to all relevant stakeholders. SP 2.4

The process is institutionalized as a managed process. GG 2

Commitment to Perform

Establish and maintain an organizational policy for planning and performing the measurement and analysis process. GP 2.1 (CO 1)

Ability to Perform

Establish and maintain the plan for performing the measurement and analysis process. GP 2.2 (AB 1)

Provide adequate resources for performing the measurement and analysis process, developing the work products, and providing the services of the process. GP 2.3 (AB 2)

Assign responsibility and authority for performing the process, developing the work products, and providing the services of the measurement and analysis process. GP 2.4 (AB 3)

Train the people performing or supporting the measurement and analysis process as needed. GP 2.5 (AB 4)

Directing Implementation

Place designated work products of the measurement and analysis process under appropriate levels of configuration management. GP 2.6 (DI 1)

Identify and involve the relevant stakeholders of the measurement and analysis process as planned. GP 2.7 (DI 2)

Monitor and control the measurement and analysis process against the plan for performing the process and take appropriate corrective action. GP 2.8 (DI 3)

Verifying Implementation

Objectively evaluate adherence of the measurement and analysis process against its process description, standards, and procedures and address noncompliance. GP 2.9 (VE 1)

Review the activities, status, and results of the measurement and analysis process with higher-level management and resolve issues. GP 2.10 (VE 2)

PROCESS AND PRODUCT QUALITY ASSURANCE

Provide staff and management with objective insight into processes and associated work products.

Adherence of the performed process and associated work products and services to applicable process descriptions, standards, and procedures is objectively evaluated. SG 1

Objectively evaluate the designated performed processes against the applicable process descriptions, standards, and procedures. SP 1.1

Objectively evaluate the designated work products and services against the applicable process descriptions, standards, and procedures. SP 1.2

Noncompliance issues are objectively tracked and communicated, and resolution is ensured. SG 2

Communicate quality issues and ensure resolution of noncompliance issues with the staff and managers. SP 2.1

Establish and maintain records of the quality assurance activities. SP 2.2

The process is institutionalized as a managed process. GG 2

Commitment to Perform

Establish and maintain an organizational policy for planning and performing the process and product quality assurance process. GP 2.1 (CO 1)

Ability to Perform

Establish and maintain the plan for performing the process and product quality assurance process. GP 2.2 (AB 1)

Provide adequate resources for performing the process and product quality assurance process, developing the work products, and providing the services of the process. GP 2.3 (AB 2)

Assign responsibility and authority for performing the process, developing the work products, and providing the services of the process and product quality assurance process. GP 2.4 (AB 3)

Train the people performing or supporting the process and product quality assurance process as needed. GP 2.5 (AB 4)

Directing Implementation

Place designated work products of the process and product quality assurance process under appropriate levels of configuration management. GP 2.6 (DI 1)

Identify and involve the relevant stakeholders of the process and product quality assurance process as planned. GP 2.7 (DI 2)

Monitor and control the process and product quality assurance process against the plan for performing the process and take appropriate corrective action. GP 2.8 (DI 3)

Verifying Implementation

Objectively evaluate adherence of the process and product quality assurance process against its process description, standards, and procedures and address noncompliance. GP 2.9 (VE 1)

Review the activities, status, and results of the process and product quality assurance process with higher-level management and resolve issues. GP 2.10 (VE 2)

Configuration Management

Establish and maintain the integrity of work products using configuration identification, configuration control, configuration status accounting, and configuration audits.

Baselines of identified work products are established. SG 1

Identify the configuration items, components, and related work products that will be placed under configuration management. SP 1.1

Establish and maintain a configuration management and change management system for controlling work products. SP 1.2

Create or release baselines for internal use and for delivery to the customer. SP 1.3

Changes to the work products under configuration management are tracked and controlled. SG 2

Track change requests for the configuration items. SP 2.1

Control changes to the configuration items. SP 2.2

Integrity of baselines is established and maintained. SG 3

Establish and maintain records describing configuration items. SP 3.1

Perform configuration audits to maintain integrity of the configuration baselines. SP 3.2

The process is institutionalized as a managed process. GG 2

Commitment to Perform

Establish and maintain an organizational policy for planning and performing the configuration management process. GP 2.1 (CO 1)

Ability to Perform

Establish and maintain the plan for performing the configuration management process. GP 2.2 (AB 1)

Provide adequate resources for performing the configuration management process, developing the work products, and providing the services of the process. GP 2.3 (AB 2)

Assign responsibility and authority for performing the process, developing the work products, and providing the services of the configuration management process. GP 2.4 (AB 3)

Train the people performing or supporting the configuration management process as needed. GP 2.5 (AB 4)

Directing Implementation

Place designated work products of the configuration management process under appropriate levels of configuration management. GP 2.6 (DI 1)

Identify and involve the relevant stakeholders of the configuration management process as planned. GP 2.7 (DI 2)

Monitor and control the configuration management process against the plan for performing the process and take appropriate corrective action. GP 2.8 (DI 3)

Verifying Implementation

Objectively evaluate adherence of the configuration management process against its process description, standards, and procedures and address noncompliance. GP 2.9 (VE 1)

Review the activities, status, and results of the configuration management process with higher-level management and resolve issues. GP 2.10 (VE 2)

Maturity Level: 3

REQUIREMENTS DEVELOPMENT
Produce and analyze customer, product, and product-component requirements.

Stakeholder needs, expectations, constraints, and interfaces are collected and translated into customer requirements. SG 1

Elicit stakeholder needs, expectations, constraints, and interfaces for all phases of the product life cycle. SP 1.1

Transform stakeholder needs, expectations, constraints, and interfaces into customer requirements. SP 1.2

Customer requirements are refined and elaborated to develop product and product-component requirements. SG 2

Establish and maintain product and product-component requirements, which are based on the customer requirements. SP 2.1

Allocate the requirements for each product component. SP 2.2

Identify interface requirements. SP 2.3

The requirements are analyzed and validated, and a definition of required functionality is developed. SG 3

Establish and maintain operational concepts and associated scenarios. SP 3.1

Establish and maintain a definition of required functionality. SP 3.2

Analyze requirements to ensure that they are necessary and sufficient. SP 3.3

Analyze requirements to balance stakeholder needs and constraints. SP 3.4

Validate requirements to ensure the resulting product will perform as intended in the user's environment using multiple techniques as appropriate. SP 3.5

The process is institutionalized as a defined process. GG 3

Commitment to Perform

Establish and maintain an organizational policy for planning and performing the requirements development process. GP 2.1 (CO 1)

Ability to Perform

Establish and maintain the description of a defined requirements development process. GP 3.1 (AB 1)

Establish and maintain the plan for performing the requirements development process. GP 2.2 (AB 2)

Provide adequate resources for performing the requirements development process, developing the work products, and providing the services of the process. GP 2.3 (AB 3)

Assign responsibility and authority for performing the process, developing the work products, and providing the services of the requirements development process. GP 2.4 (AB 4)

Train the people performing or supporting the requirements development process as needed. GP 2.5 (AB 5)

Directing Implementation

Place designated work products of the requirements development process under appropriate levels of configuration management. GP 2.6 (DI 1)

Identify and involve the relevant stakeholders of the requirements development process as planned. GP 2.7 (DI 2)

Monitor and control the requirements development process against the plan for performing the process and take appropriate corrective action. GP 2.8 (DI 3)

Collect work products, measures, measurement results, and improvement information derived from planning and performing the requirements development process to support the future use and improvement of the organization's processes and process assets. GP 3.2 (DI 4)

Verifying Implementation

Objectively evaluate adherence of the requirements development process against its process description, standards, and procedures and address noncompliance. GP 2.9 (VE 1)

Review the activities, status, and results of the requirements development process with higher-level management and resolve issues. GP 2.10 (VE 2)

Technical Solution

Design, develop, and implement solutions to requirements. Solutions, designs, and implementations encompass products, product components, and product-related life-cycle processes either singly or in combinations as appropriate.

Product or product-component solutions are selected from alternative solutions. SG 1

Develop detailed alternative solutions and selection criteria. SP 1.1

Evolve the operational concept, scenarios, and environments to describe the conditions, operating modes, and operating states specific to each product component. SP 1.2

Select the product-component solutions that best satisfy the criteria established. SP 1.3

Product or product-component designs are developed. SG 2

Develop a design for the product or product component. SP 2.1

Establish and maintain a technical data package. SP 2.2

Design comprehensive product-component interfaces in terms of established and maintained criteria. SP 2.3

Evaluate whether the product components should be developed, purchased, or reused based on established criteria. SP 2.4

Product components, and associated support documentation, are implemented from their designs. SG 3

Implement the designs of the product components. SP 3.1

Develop and maintain the end-use documentation. SP 3.2

The process is institutionalized as a defined process. GG 3

Commitment to Perform

Establish and maintain an organizational policy for planning and performing the technical solution process. GP 2.1 (CO 1)

Ability to Perform

Establish and maintain the description of a defined technical solution process. GP 3.1 (AB 1)

Establish and maintain the plan for performing the technical solution process. GP 2.2 (AB 2)

Provide adequate resources for performing the technical solution process, developing the work products, and providing the services of the process. GP 2.3 (AB 3)

Assign responsibility and authority for performing the process, developing the work products, and providing the services of the technical solution process. GP 2.4 (AB 4)

Train the people performing or supporting the technical solution process as needed. GP 2.5 (AB 5)

Directing Implementation

Place designated work products of the technical solution process under appropriate levels of configuration management. GP 2.6 (DI 1)

Identify and involve the relevant stakeholders of the technical solution process as planned. GP 2.7 (DI 2)

Monitor and control the technical solution process against the plan for performing the process and take appropriate corrective action. GP 2.8 (DI 3)

Collect work products, measures, measurement results, and improvement information derived from planning and performing the technical solution process to support the future use and improvement of the organization's processes and process assets. GP 3.2 (DI 4)

Verifying Implementation

Objectively evaluate adherence of the technical solution process against its process description, standards, and procedures and address noncompliance. GP 2.9 (VE 1)

Review the activities, status, and results of the technical solution process with higher-level management and resolve issues. GP 2.10 (VE 2)

PRODUCT INTEGRATION

Assemble the product from the product components, ensure that the product, as integrated, functions properly, and deliver the product.

Preparation for product integration is conducted. SG 1

Determine the product-component integration sequence. SP 1.1

Establish and maintain the environment needed to support the integration of the product components. SP 1.2

Establish and maintain procedures and criteria for integration of the product components. SP 1.3

The product-component interfaces, both internal and external, are compatible. SG 2

Review interface descriptions for coverage and completeness. SP 2.1

Manage internal and external interface definitions, designs, and changes for products and product components. SP 2.2

Verified product components are assembled and the integrated, verified, and validated product is delivered. SG 3

Confirm, prior to assembly, that each product component required to assemble the product has been properly identified, functions according to its description, and that the product-component interfaces comply with the interface descriptions. SP 3.1

Assemble product components according to the product integration sequence and available procedures. SP 3.2

Evaluate assembled product components for interface compatibility. SP 3.3

Package the assembled product or product component and deliver it to the appropriate customer. SP 3.4

The process is institutionalized as a defined process. GG 3

Commitment to Perform

Establish and maintain an organizational policy for planning and performing the product integration process. GP 2.1 (CO 1)

Ability to Perform

Establish and maintain the description of a defined product integration process. GP 3.1 (AB 1)

Establish and maintain the plan for performing the product integration process. GP 2.2 (AB 2)

Provide adequate resources for performing the product integration process, developing the work products, and providing the services of the process. GP 2.3 (AB 3)

Assign responsibility and authority for performing the process, developing the work products, and providing the services of the product integration process. GP 2.4 (AB 4)

Train the people performing or supporting the product integration process as needed. GP 2.5 (AB 5)

Directing Implementation

Place designated work products of the product integration process under appropriate levels of configuration management. GP 2.6 (DI 1)

Identify and involve the relevant stakeholders of the product integration process as planned. GP 2.7 (DI 2)

Monitor and control the product integration process against the plan for performing the process and take appropriate corrective action. GP 2.8 (DI 3)

Collect work products, measures, measurement results, and improvement information derived from planning and performing the product integration process to support the future use and improvement of the organization's processes and process assets. GP 3.2 (DI 4)

Verifying Implementation

Objectively evaluate adherence of the product integration process against its process description, standards, and procedures and address noncompliance. GP 2.9 (VE 1)

Review the activities, status, and results of the product integration process with higher-level management and resolve issues. GP 2.10 (VE 2)

VERIFICATION

Ensure that selected work products meet their specified requirements.

Preparation for verification is conducted. SG 1

Select the work products to be verified and the verification methods that will be used for each. SP 1.1

Establish and maintain the environment needed to support verification. SP 1.2

Establish and maintain verification procedures and criteria for the selected work products. SP 1.3

Peer reviews are performed on selected work products. SG 2

Prepare for peer reviews of selected work products. SP 2.1

Conduct peer reviews on selected work products and identify issues resulting from the peer review. SP 2.2

Analyze data about preparation, conduct, and results of the peer reviews. SP 2.3

Selected work products are verified against their specified requirements. SG 3

Perform verification on the selected work products. SP 3.1

Analyze the results of all verification activities and identify corrective action. SP 3.2

The process is institutionalized as a defined process. GG 3

Commitment to Perform

Establish and maintain an organizational policy for planning and performing the verification process. GP 2.1 (CO 1)

Ability to Perform

Establish and maintain the description of a defined verification process. GP 3.1 (AB 1)

Establish and maintain the plan for performing the verification process. GP 2.2 (AB 2)

Provide adequate resources for performing the verification process, developing the work products, and providing the services of the process. GP 2.3 (AB 3)

Assign responsibility and authority for performing the process, developing the work products, and providing the services of the verification process. GP 2.4 (AB 4)

Train the people performing or supporting the verification process as needed. GP 2.5 (AB 5)

Directing Implementation

Place designated work products of the verification process under appropriate levels of configuration management. GP 2.6 (DI 1)

Identify and involve the relevant stakeholders of the verification process as planned. GP 2.7 (DI 2)

Monitor and control the verification process against the plan for performing the process and take appropriate corrective action. GP 2.8 (DI 3)

Collect work products, measures, measurement results, and improvement information derived from planning and performing the verification process to support the future use and improvement of the organization's processes and process assets. GP 3.2 (DI 4)

Verifying Implementation

Objectively evaluate adherence of the verification process against its process description, standards, and procedures and address noncompliance. GP 2.9 (VE 1)

Review the activities, status, and results of the verification process with higher-level management and resolve issues. GP 2.10 (VE 2)

VALIDATION

Demonstrate that a product or product component fulfills its intended use when placed in its intended environment.

Preparation for validation is conducted. SG 1

Select products and product components to be validated and the validation methods that will be used for each. SP 1.1

Establish and maintain the environment needed to support validation. SP 1.2

Establish and maintain procedures and criteria for validation. SP 1.3

The product or product components are validated to ensure that they are suitable for use in their intended operating environment. SG 2

Perform validation on the selected products and product components. SP 2.1

Analyze the results of the validation activities and identify issues. SP 2.2

The process is institutionalized as a defined process. GG 3

Commitment to Perform

Establish and maintain an organizational policy for planning and performing the validation process. GP 2.1 (CO 1)

Ability to Perform

Establish and maintain the description of a defined validation process. GP 3.1 (AB 1)

Establish and maintain the plan for performing the validation process. GP 2.2 (AB 2)

Provide adequate resources for performing the validation process, developing the work products, and providing the services of the process. GP 2.3 (AB 3)

Assign responsibility and authority for performing the process, developing the work products, and providing the services of the validation process. GP 2.4 (AB 4)

Train the people performing or supporting the validation process as needed. GP 2.5 (AB 5)

Directing Implementation

Place designated work products of the validation process under appropriate levels of configuration management. GP 2.6 (DI 1)

Identify and involve the relevant stakeholders of the validation process as planned. GP 2.7 (DI 2)

Monitor and control the validation process against the plan for performing the process and take appropriate corrective action. GP 2.8 (DI 3)

Collect work products, measures, measurement results, and improvement information derived from planning and performing the validation process to support the future use and improvement of the organization's processes and process assets. GP 3.2 (DI 4)

Verifying Implementation

Objectively evaluate adherence of the validation process against its process description, standards, and procedures and address noncompliance. GP 2.9 (VE 1)

Review the activities, status, and results of the validation process with higher-level management and resolve issues. GP 2.10 (VE 2)

ORGANIZATIONAL PROCESS FOCUS

Plan and implement organizational process improvement based on a thorough understanding of the current strengths and weaknesses of the organization's processes and process assets.

Strengths, weaknesses, and improvement opportunities for the organization's processes are identified periodically and as needed. SG 1

> Establish and maintain the description of the process needs and objectives for the organization. SP 1.1
>
> Appraise the processes of the organization periodically and as needed to maintain an understanding of their strengths and weaknesses. SP 1.2
>
> Identify improvements to the organization's processes and process assets. SP 1.3

Improvements are planned and implemented, organizational process assets are deployed, and process-related experiences are incorporated into the organizational process assets. SG 2

> Establish and maintain process action plans to address improvements to the organization's processes and process assets. SP 2.1
>
> Implement process action plans across the organization. SP 2.2
>
> Deploy organizational process assets across the organization. SP 2.3
>
> Incorporate process-related work products, measures, and improvement information derived from planning and performing the process into the organizational process assets. SP 2.4

The process is institutionalized as a defined process. GG 3

Commitment to Perform

> Establish and maintain an organizational policy for planning and performing the organizational process focus process. GP 2.1 (CO 1)

Ability to Perform

> Establish and maintain the description of a defined organizational process focus process. GP 3.1 (AB 1)
>
> Establish and maintain the plan for performing the organizational process focus process. GP 2.2 (AB 2)

Provide adequate resources for performing the organizational process focus process, developing the work products, and providing the services of the process. GP 2.3 (AB 3)

Assign responsibility and authority for performing the process, developing the work products, and providing the services of the organizational process focus process. GP 2.4 (AB 4)

Train the people performing or supporting the organizational process focus process as needed. GP 2.5 (AB 5)

Directing Implementation

Place designated work products of the organizational process focus process under appropriate levels of configuration management. GP 2.6 (DI 1)

Identify and involve the relevant stakeholders of the organizational process focus process as planned. GP 2.7 (DI 2)

Monitor and control the organizational process focus process against the plan for performing the process and take appropriate corrective action. GP 2.8 (DI 3)

Collect work products, measures, measurement results, and improvement information derived from planning and performing the organizational process focus process to support the future use and improvement of the organization's processes and process assets. GP 3.2 (DI 4)

Verifying Implementation

Objectively evaluate adherence of the organizational process focus process against its process description, standards, and procedures and address noncompliance. GP 2.9 (VE 1)

Review the activities, status, and results of the organizational process focus process with higher-level management and resolve issues. GP 2.10 (VE 2)

ORGANIZATIONAL PROCESS DEFINITION

Establish and maintain a usable set of organizational process assets.

A set of organizational process assets is established and maintained. SG 1

Establish and maintain the organization's set of standard processes. SP 1.1

Establish and maintain descriptions of the life-cycle models approved for use in the organization. SP 1.2

Establish and maintain the tailoring criteria and guidelines for the organization's set of standard processes. SP 1.3

Establish and maintain the organization's measurement repository. SP 1.4

Establish and maintain the organization's process asset library. SP 1.5

The process is institutionalized as a defined process. GG 3

Commitment to Perform

Establish and maintain an organizational policy for planning and performing the organizational process definition process. GP 2.1 (CO 1)

Ability to Perform

Establish and maintain the description of a defined organizational process definition process. GP 3.1 (AB 1)

Establish and maintain the plan for performing the organizational process definition process. GP 2.2 (AB 2)

Provide adequate resources for performing the organizational process definition process, developing the work products, and providing the services of the process. GP 2.3 (AB 3)

Assign responsibility and authority for performing the process, developing the work products, and providing the services of the organizational process definition process. GP 2.4 (AB 4)

Train the people performing or supporting the organizational process definition process as needed. GP 2.5 (AB 5)

Directing Implementation

Place designated work products of the organizational process definition process under appropriate levels of configuration management. GP 2.6 (DI 1)

Identify and involve the relevant stakeholders of the organizational process definition process as planned. GP 2.7 (DI 2)

Monitor and control the organizational process definition process against the plan for performing the process and take appropriate corrective action. GP 2.8 (DI 3)

Collect work products, measures, measurement results, and improvement information derived from planning and performing the organizational process definition process to support the future use and improvement of the organization's processes and process assets. GP 3.2 (DI 4)

Verifying Implementation

Objectively evaluate adherence of the organizational process definition process against its process description, standards, and procedures and address noncompliance. GP 2.9 (VE 1)

Review the activities, status, and results of the organizational process definition process with higher-level management and resolve issues. GP 2.10 (VE 2)

ORGANIZATIONAL TRAINING

Develop the skills and knowledge of people so they can perform their roles effectively and efficiently.

A training capability that supports the organization's management and technical roles is established and maintained. SG 1

Establish and maintain the strategic training needs of the organization. SP 1.1

Determine which training needs are the responsibility of the organization and which will be left to the individual project or support group. SP 1.2

Establish and maintain an organizational training tactical plan. SP 1.3

Establish and maintain training capability to address organizational training needs. SP 1.4

Training necessary for individuals to perform their roles effectively is provided. SG 2

Deliver the training following the organizational training tactical plan. SP 2.1

Establish and maintain records of the organizational training. SP 2.2

Assess the effectiveness of the organization's training program. SP 2.3

The process is institutionalized as a defined process. GG 3

Commitment to Perform

Establish and maintain an organizational policy for planning and performing the organizational training process. GP 2.1 (CO 1)

Ability to Perform

Establish and maintain the description of a defined organizational training process. GP 3.1 (AB 1)

Establish and maintain the plan for performing the organizational training process. GP 2.2 (AB 2)

Provide adequate resources for performing the organizational training process, developing the work products, and providing the services of the process. GP 2.3 (AB 3)

Assign responsibility and authority for performing the process, developing the work products, and providing the services of the organizational training process. GP 2.4 (AB 4)

Train the people performing or supporting the organizational training process as needed. GP 2.5 (AB 5)

Directing Implementation

Place designated work products of the organizational training process under appropriate levels of configuration management. GP 2.6 (DI 1)

Identify and involve the relevant stakeholders of the organizational training process as planned. GP 2.7 (DI 2)

Monitor and control the organizational training process against the plan for performing the process and take appropriate corrective action. GP 2.8 (DI 3)

Collect work products, measures, measurement results, and improvement information derived from planning and performing the organizational training process to support the future use and improvement of the organization's processes and process assets. GP 3.2 (DI 4)

Verifying Implementation

Objectively evaluate adherence of the organizational training process against its process description, standards, and procedures and address noncompliance. GP 2.9 (VE 1)

Review the activities, status, and results of the organizational training process with higher-level management and resolve issues. GP 2.10 (VE 2)

Integrated Project Management (IPPD)

Establish and manage the project and the involvement of the relevant stakeholders according to an integrated and defined process that is tailored from the organization's set of standard processes. Establish a shared vision for the project and a team structure for integrated teams that will carry out the objectives of the project.

The project is conducted using a defined process that is tailored from the organization's set of standard processes. SG 1

Establish and maintain the project's defined process. SP 1.1

Use the organizational process assets and measurement repository for estimating and planning the project's activities. SP 1.2

Integrate the project plan and the other plans that affect the project to describe the project's defined process. SP 1.3

Manage the project using the project plan, the other plans that affect the project, and the project's defined process. SP 1.4

Contribute work products, measures, and documented experiences to the organizational process assets. SP 1.5

Coordination and collaboration of the project with relevant stakeholders is conducted. SG 2

Manage the involvement of the relevant stakeholders in the project. SP 2.1

Participate with relevant stakeholders to identify, negotiate, and track critical dependencies. SP 2.2

Resolve issues with relevant stakeholders. SP 2.3

The project is conducted using the project's shared vision. SG 3

Identify expectations, constraints, interfaces, and operational conditions applicable to the project's shared vision. SP 3.1

Establish and maintain a shared vision for the project. SP 3.2

The integrated teams needed to execute the project are identified, defined, structured, and tasked. SG 4

Determine the integrated team structure that will best meet the project objectives and constraints. SP 4.1

Develop a preliminary distribution of requirements, responsibilities, authorities, tasks, and interfaces to teams in the selected integrated team structure. SP 4.2

Establish and maintain teams in the integrated team structure. SP 4.3

The process is institutionalized as a defined process. GG 3

Commitment to Perform

Establish and maintain an organizational policy for planning and performing the integrated project management process. GP 2.1 (CO 1)

Ability to Perform

Establish and maintain the description of a defined integrated project management process. GP 3.1 (AB 1)

Establish and maintain the plan for performing the integrated project management process. GP 2.2 (AB 2)

Provide adequate resources for performing the integrated project management process, developing the work products, and providing the services of the process. GP 2.3 (AB 3)

Assign responsibility and authority for performing the process, developing the work products, and providing the services of the integrated project management process. GP 2.4 (AB 4)

Train the people performing or supporting the integrated project management process as needed. GP 2.5 (AB 5)

Directing Implementation

Place designated work products of the integrated project management process under appropriate levels of configuration management. GP 2.6 (DI 1)

Identify and involve the relevant stakeholders of the integrated project management process as planned. GP 2.7 (DI 2)

Monitor and control the integrated project management process against the plan for performing the process and take appropriate corrective action. GP 2.8 (DI 3)

Collect work products, measures, measurement results, and improvement information derived from planning and performing the integrated project management process to support the future use and improvement of the organization's processes and process assets. GP 3.2 (DI 4)

Verifying Implementation

Objectively evaluate adherence of the integrated project management process against its process description, standards, and procedures and address noncompliance. GP 2.9 (VE 1)

Review the activities, status, and results of the integrated project management process with higher-level management and resolve issues. GP 2.10 (VE 2)

RISK MANAGEMENT

Identify potential problems before they occur, so that risk-handling activities may be planned and invoked as needed across the life of the product or project to mitigate adverse impacts on achieving objectives.

Preparation for risk management is conducted. SG 1

Determine risk sources and categories. SP 1.1

Define the parameters used to analyze and categorize risks, and the parameters used to control the risk management effort. SP 1.2

Establish and maintain the strategy to be used for risk management. SP 1.3

Risks are identified and analyzed to determine their relative importance. SG 2

Identify and document the risks. SP 2.1

Evaluate and categorize each identified risk using the defined risk categories and parameters, and determine its relative priority. SP 2.2

Risks are handled and mitigated, where appropriate, to reduce adverse impacts on achieving objectives. SG 3

Develop a risk mitigation plan for the most important risks to the project, as defined by the risk management strategy. SP 3.1

Monitor the status of each risk periodically and implement the risk mitigation plan as appropriate. SP 3.2

The process is institutionalized as a defined process. GG 3

Commitment to Perform

Establish and maintain an organizational policy for planning and performing the risk management process. GP 2.1 (CO 1)

Ability to Perform

Establish and maintain the description of a defined risk management process. GP 3.1 (AB 1)

Establish and maintain the plan for performing the risk management process. GP 2.2 (AB 2)

Provide adequate resources for performing the risk management process, developing the work products, and providing the services of the process. GP 2.3 (AB 3)

Assign responsibility and authority for performing the process, developing the work products, and providing the services of the risk management process. GP 2.4 (AB 4)

Train the people performing or supporting the risk management process as needed. GP 2.5 (AB 5)

Directing Implementation

Place designated work products of the risk management process under appropriate levels of configuration management. GP 2.6 (DI 1)

Identify and involve the relevant stakeholders of the risk management process as planned. GP 2.7 (DI 2)

Monitor and control the risk management process against the plan for performing the process and take appropriate corrective action. GP 2.8 (DI 3)

Collect work products, measures, measurement results, and improvement information derived from planning and performing the risk management process to support the future use and improvement of the organization's processes and process assets. GP 3.2 (DI 4)

Verifying Implementation

Objectively evaluate adherence of the risk management process against its process description, standards, and procedures and address noncompliance. GP 2.9 (VE 1)

Review the activities, status, and results of the risk management process with higher-level management and resolve issues. GP 2.10 (VE 2)

Integrated Teaming

Form and sustain an integrated team for the development of work products.

A team composition that provides the knowledge and skills required to deliver the team's product is established and maintained. SG 1

Identify and define the team's specific internal tasks to generate the team's expected output. SP 1.1

Identify the knowledge, skills, and functional expertise needed to perform team tasks. SP 1.2

Assign the appropriate personnel to be team members based on required knowledge and skills. SP 1.3

Operation of the integrated team is governed according to established principles. SG 2

Establish and maintain a shared vision for the integrated team that is aligned with any overarching or higher-level vision. SP 2.1

Establish and maintain a team charter based on the integrated team's shared vision and overall team objectives. SP 2.2

Clearly define and maintain each team member's roles and responsibilities. SP 2.3

Establish and maintain integrated team operating procedures. SP 2.4

Establish and maintain collaboration among interfacing teams. SP 2.5

The process is institutionalized as a defined process. GG 3

Commitment to Perform

Establish and maintain an organizational policy for planning and performing the integrated teaming process. GP 2.1 (CO 1)

Ability to Perform

Establish and maintain the description of a defined integrated teaming process. GP 3.1 (AB 1)

Establish and maintain the plan for performing the integrated teaming process. GP 2.2 (AB 2)

Provide adequate resources for performing the integrated teaming process, developing the work products, and providing the services of the process. GP 2.3 (AB 3)

Assign responsibility and authority for performing the process, developing the work products, and providing the services of the integrated teaming process. GP 2.4 (AB 4)

Train the people performing or supporting the integrated teaming process as needed. GP 2.5 (AB 5)

Directing Implementation

Place designated work products of the integrated teaming process under appropriate levels of configuration management. GP 2.6 (DI 1)

Identify and involve the relevant stakeholders of the integrated teaming process as planned. GP 2.7 (DI 2)

Monitor and control the integrated teaming process against the plan for performing the process and take appropriate corrective action. GP 2.8 (DI 3)

Collect work products, measures, measurement results, and improvement information derived from planning and performing the integrated teaming process to support the future use and improvement of the organization's processes and process assets. GP 3.2 (DI 4)

Verifying Implementation

Objectively evaluate adherence of the integrated teaming process against its process description, standards, and procedures and address noncompliance. GP 2.9 (VE 1)

Review the activities, status, and results of the integrated teaming process with higher-level management and resolve issues. GP 2.10 (VE 2)

INTEGRATED SUPPLIER MANAGEMENT

Proactively identify sources of products that may be used to satisfy the project's requirements and manage selected suppliers while maintaining a cooperative project-supplier relationship.

Potential sources of products that best fit the needs of the project are identified, analyzed, and selected. SG 1

Identify and analyze potential sources of products that may be used to satisfy the project's requirements. SP 1.1-1

Use a formal evaluation process to determine which sources of custom-made and off-the-shelf products to use. SP 1.2-1

Work is coordinated with suppliers to ensure the supplier agreement is executed appropriately. SG 2

Monitor and analyze selected processes used by the supplier. SP 2.1-1

For custom-made products, evaluate selected supplier work products. SP 2.2-1

Revise the supplier agreement or relationship, as appropriate, to reflect changes in conditions. SP 2.3-1

The process is institutionalized as a defined process. GG 3

Commitment to Perform

Establish and maintain an organizational policy for planning and performing the integrated supplier management process. GP 2.1 (CO 1)

Ability to Perform

Establish and maintain the description of a defined integrated supplier management process. GP 3.1 (AB 1)

Establish and maintain the plan for performing the integrated supplier management process. GP 2.2 (AB 2)

Provide adequate resources for performing the integrated supplier management process, developing the work products, and providing the services of the process. GP 2.3 (AB 3)

Assign responsibility and authority for performing the process, developing the work products, and providing the services of the integrated supplier management process. GP 2.4 (AB 4)

Train the people performing or supporting the integrated supplier management process as needed. GP 2.5 (AB 5)

Directing Implementation

Place designated work products of the integrated supplier management process under appropriate levels of configuration management. GP2.6 (DI 1)

Identify and involve the relevant stakeholders of the integrated supplier management process as planned. GP 2.7 (DI 2)

Monitor and control the integrated supplier management process against the plan for performing the process and take appropriate corrective action. GP 2.8 (DI 3)

Collect work products, measures, measurement results, and improvement information derived from planning and performing the integrated supplier management process to support the future use and improvement of the organization's processes and process assets. GP 3.2 (DI 4)

Verifying Implementation

Objectively evaluate adherence of the integrated supplier management process against its process description, standards, and procedures and address noncompliance. GP 2.9 (VE 1)

Review the activities, status, and results of the integrated supplier management process with higher-level management and resolve issues. GP 2.10 (VE 2)

DECISION ANALYSIS AND RESOLUTION

Analyze possible decisions using a formal evaluation process that evaluates identified alternatives against established criteria.

Decisions are based on an evaluation of alternatives using established criteria. SG 1

Establish and maintain guidelines to determine which issues are subject to a formal evaluation process. SP 1.1

Establish and maintain the criteria for evaluating alternatives, and the relative ranking of these criteria. SP 1.2

Identify alternative solutions to address issues. SP 1.3

Select the evaluation methods. SP 1.4

Evaluate alternative solutions using the established criteria and methods. SP 1.5

Select solutions from the alternatives based on the evaluation criteria. SP 1.6

The process is institutionalized as a defined process. GG 3

Commitment to Perform

Establish and maintain an organizational policy for planning and performing the decision analysis and resolution process. GP 2.1 (CO 1)

Ability to Perform

Establish and maintain the description of a defined decision analysis and resolution process. GP 3.1 (AB 1)

Establish and maintain the plan for performing the decision analysis and resolution process. GP 2.2 (AB 2)

Provide adequate resources for performing the decision analysis and resolution process, developing the work products, and providing the services of the process. GP 2.3 (AB 3)

Assign responsibility and authority for performing the process, developing the work products, and providing the services of the decision analysis and resolution process. GP 2.4 (AB 4)

Train the people performing or supporting the decision analysis and resolution process as needed. GP 2.5 (AB 5)

Directing Implementation

Place designated work products of the decision analysis and resolution process under appropriate levels of configuration management. GP 2.6 (DI 1)

Identify and involve the relevant stakeholders of the decision analysis and resolution process as planned. GP 2.7 (DI 2)

Monitor and control the decision analysis and resolution process against the plan for performing the process and take appropriate corrective action. GP 2.8 (DI 3)

Collect work products, measures, measurement results, and improvement information derived from planning and performing the decision analysis and resolution process to support the future use and improvement of the organization's processes and process assets. GP 3.2 (DI 4)

Verifying Implementation

Objectively evaluate adherence of the decision analysis and resolution process against its process description, standards, and procedures and address noncompliance. GP 2.9 (VE 1)

Review the activities, status, and results of the decision analysis and resolution process with higher-level management and resolve issues. GP 2.10 (VE 2)

ORGANIZATIONAL ENVIRONMENT FOR INTEGRATION

Provide an IPPD infrastructure and manage people for integration.

An infrastructure that maximizes the productivity of people and affects the collaboration necessary for integration is provided. SG 1

Establish and maintain a shared vision for the organization. SP 1.1

Establish and maintain an integrated work environment that supports IPPD by enabling collaboration and concurrent development. SP 1.2

Identify the unique skills needed to support the IPPD environment. SP 1.3

People are managed to nurture the integrative and collaborative behaviors of an IPPD environment. SG 2

Establish and maintain leadership mechanisms to enable timely collaboration. SP 2.1

Establish and maintain incentives for adopting and demonstrating integrative and collaborative behaviors at all levels of the organization. SP 2.2

Establish and maintain organizational guidelines to balance team and home organization responsibilities. SP 2.3

The process is institutionalized as a defined process. GG 3

Commitment to Perform

Establish and maintain an organizational policy for planning and performing the organizational environment for integration process. GP 2.1 (CO 1)

Ability to Perform

Establish and maintain the description of a defined organizational environment for integration process. GP 3.1 (AB 1)

Establish and maintain the plan for performing the organizational environment for integration process. GP 2.2 (AB 2)

Provide adequate resources for performing the organizational environment for integration process, developing the work products, and providing the services of the process. GP 2.3 (AB 3)

Assign responsibility and authority for performing the process, developing the work products, and providing the services of the organizational environment for integration process. GP 2.4 (AB 4)

Train the people performing or supporting the organizational environment for integration process as needed. GP 2.5 (AB 5)

Directing Implementation

Place designated work products of the organizational environment for integration process under appropriate levels of configuration management. GP 2.6 (DI 1)

Identify and involve the relevant stakeholders of the organizational environment for integration process as planned. GP 2.7 (DI 2)

Monitor and control the organizational environment for integration process against the plan for performing the process and take appropriate corrective action. GP 2.8 (DI 3)

Collect work products, measures, measurement results, and improvement information derived from planning and performing the organizational environment for integration process to support the future use and improvement of the organization's processes and process assets. GP 3.2 (DI 4)

Verifying Implementation

Objectively evaluate adherence of the organizational environment for integration process against its process description, standards, and procedures and address noncompliance. GP 2.9 (VE 1)

Review the activities, status, and results of the organizational environment for integration process with higher-level management and resolve issues. GP 2.10 (VE 2)

Maturity Level: 4

ORGANIZATIONAL PROCESS PERFORMANCE

Establish and maintain a quantitative understanding of the performance of the organization's set of standard processes in support of quality and process-performance objectives, and provide the process performance data, baselines, and models to quantitatively manage the organization's projects.

Baselines and models that characterize the expected process performance of the organization's set of standard processes are established and maintained. SG 1

Select the processes or process elements in the organization's set of standard processes that are to be included in the organization's process performance analyses. SP 1.1

Establish and maintain definitions of the measures that are to be included in the organization's process performance analyses. SP 1.2

Establish and maintain quantitative objectives for quality and process performance for the organization. SP 1.3

Establish and maintain the organization's process performance baselines. SP 1.4

Establish and maintain the process performance models for the organization's set of standard processes. SP 1.5

The process is institutionalized as a defined process. GG 3

Commitment to Perform

Establish and maintain an organizational policy for planning and performing the organizational process performance process. GP 2.1 (CO 1)

Ability to Perform

Establish and maintain the description of a defined organizational process performance process. GP 3.1 (AB 1)

Establish and maintain the plan for performing the organizational process performance process. GP 2.2 (AB 2)

Provide adequate resources for performing the organizational process performance process, developing the work products, and providing the services of the process. GP 2.3 (AB 3)

Assign responsibility and authority for performing the process, developing the work products, and providing the services of the organizational process performance process. GP 2.4 (AB 4)

Train the people performing or supporting the organizational process performance process as needed. GP 2.5 (AB 5)

Directing Implementation

Place designated work products of the organizational process performance process under appropriate levels of configuration management. GP 2.6 (DI 1)

Identify and involve the relevant stakeholders of the organizational process performance process as planned. GP 2.7 (DI 2)

Monitor and control the organizational process performance process against the plan for performing the process and take appropriate corrective action. GP 2.8 (DI 3)

Collect work products, measures, measurement results, and improvement information derived from planning and performing the organizational process performance process to support the future use and improvement of the organization's processes and process assets. GP 3.2 (DI 4)

Verifying Implementation

Objectively evaluate adherence of the organizational process performance process against its process description, standards, and procedures and address noncompliance. GP 2.9 (VE 1)

Review the activities, status, and results of the organizational process performance process with higher-level management and resolve issues. GP 2.10 (VE 2)

QUANTITATIVE PROJECT MANAGEMENT

Quantitatively manage the project's defined process to achieve the project's established quality and process-performance objectives.

The project is quantitatively managed using quality and process-performance objectives. SG 1

Establish and maintain the project's quality and process-performance objectives. SP 1.1

Select the subprocesses that compose the project's defined process based on historical stability and capability data. SP 1.2

Select the subprocesses of the project's defined process that will be statistically managed SP 1.3

Monitor the project to determine whether the project's objectives for quality and process performance will be satisfied, and identify corrective action as appropriate. SP 1.4

The performance of selected subprocesses within the project's defined process is statistically managed. SG 2

Select the measures and analytic techniques to be used in statistically managing the selected subprocesses. SP 2.1

Establish and maintain an understanding of the variation of the selected subprocesses using the selected measures and analytic techniques. SP 2.2

Monitor the performance of the selected subprocesses to determine their capability to satisfy their quality and process-performance objectives, and identify corrective action as necessary. SP 2.3

Record statistical and quality management data in the organization's measurement repository. SP 2.4

The process is institutionalized as a defined process. GG 3

Commitment to Perform

Establish and maintain an organizational policy for planning and performing the quantitative project management process. GP 2.1 (CO 1)

Ability to Perform

Establish and maintain the description of a defined quantitative project management process. GP 3.1 (AB 1)

Establish and maintain the plan for performing the quantitative project management process. GP 2.2 (AB 2)

Provide adequate resources for performing the quantitative project management process, developing the work products, and providing the services of the process. GP 2.3 (AB 3)

Assign responsibility and authority for performing the process, developing the work products, and providing the services of the quantitative project management process. GP 2.4 (AB 4)

Train the people performing or supporting the quantitative project management process as needed. GP 2.5 (AB 5)

Directing Implementation

Place designated work products of the quantitative project management process under appropriate levels of configuration management. GP 2.6 (DI 1)

Identify and involve the relevant stakeholders of the quantitative project management process as planned. GP 2.7 (DI 2)

Monitor and control the quantitative project management process against the plan for performing the process and take appropriate corrective action. GP 2.8 (DI 3)

Collect work products, measures, measurement results, and improvement information derived from planning and performing the quantitative project management process to support the future use and improvement of the organization's processes and process assets. GP 3.2 (DI 4)

Verifying Implementation

Objectively evaluate adherence of the quantitative project management process against its process description, standards, and procedures and address noncompliance. GP 2.9 (VE 1)

Review the activities, status, and results of the quantitative project management process with higher-level management and resolve issues. GP 2.10 (VE 2)

Maturity Level: 5

ORGANIZATIONAL INNOVATION AND DEPLOYMENT

Select and deploy incremental and innovative improvements that measurably improve the organization's processes and technologies. The improvements support the organization's quality and process-performance objectives as derived from the organization's business objectives.

Process and technology improvements that contribute to meeting quality and process-performance objectives are selected. SG 1

Collect and analyze process- and technology-improvement proposals. SP 1.1

Identify and analyze innovative improvements that could increase the organization's quality and process performance. SP 1.2

Pilot process and technology improvements to select which ones to implement. SP 1.3

Select process- and technology-improvement proposals for deployment across the organization. SP 1.4

Measurable improvements to the organization's processes and technologies are continually and systematically deployed. SG 2

Establish and maintain the plans for deploying the selected process and technology improvements. SP 2.1

Manage the deployment of the selected process and technology improvements. SP 2.2

Measure the effects of the deployed process and technology improvements. SP 2.3

The process is institutionalized as a defined process. GG 3

Commitment to Perform

Establish and maintain an organizational policy for planning and performing the organizational innovation and deployment process. GP 2.1 (CO 1)

Ability to Perform

Establish and maintain the description of a defined organizational innovation and deployment process. GP 3.1 (AB 1)

Establish and maintain the plan for performing the organizational innovation and deployment process. GP 2.2 (AB 2)

Provide adequate resources for performing the organizational innovation and deployment process, developing the work products, and providing the services of the process. GP 2.3 (AB 3)

Assign responsibility and authority for performing the process, developing the work products, and providing the services of the organizational innovation and deployment process. GP 2.4 (AB 4)

Train the people performing or supporting the organizational innovation and deployment process as needed. GP 2.5 (AB 5)

Directing Implementation

Place designated work products of the organizational innovation and deployment process under appropriate levels of configuration management. GP 2.6 (DI 1)

Identify and involve the relevant stakeholders of the organizational innovation and deployment process as planned. GP 2.7 (DI 2)

Monitor and control the organizational innovation and deployment process against the plan for performing the process and take appropriate corrective action. GP 2.8 (DI 3)

Collect work products, measures, measurement results, and improvement information derived from planning and performing the organizational innovation and deployment process to support the future use and improvement of the organization's processes and process assets. GP 3.2 (DI 4)

Verifying Implementation

Objectively evaluate adherence of the organizational innovation and deployment process against its process description, standards, and procedures and address noncompliance. GP 2.9 (VE 1)

Review the activities, status, and results of the organizational innovation and deployment process with higher-level management and resolve issues. GP 2.10 (VE 2)

CAUSAL ANALYSIS AND RESOLUTION

Identify causes of defects and other problems and take action to prevent them from occurring in the future.

Root causes of defects and other problems are systematically determined. SG 1

Select the defects and other problems for analysis. SP 1.1

Perform causal analysis of selected defects and other problems and propose actions to address them. SP 1.2

Root causes of defects and other problems are systematically addressed to prevent their future occurrence. SG 2

Implement the selected action proposals that were developed in causal analysis. SP 2.1

Evaluate the effect of changes on process performance. SP 2.2

Record causal analysis and resolution data for use across the project and organization. SP 2.3

The process is institutionalized as a defined process. GG 3

Commitment to Perform

Establish and maintain an organizational policy for planning and performing the causal analysis and resolution process. GP 2.1 (CO 1)

Ability to Perform

Establish and maintain the description of a defined causal analysis and resolution process. GP 3.1 (AB 1)

Establish and maintain the plan for performing the causal analysis and resolution process. GP 2.2 (AB 2)

Provide adequate resources for performing the causal analysis and resolution process, developing the work products, and providing the services of the process. GP 2.3 (AB 3)

Assign responsibility and authority for performing the process, developing the work products, and providing the services of the causal analysis and resolution process. GP 2.4 (AB 4)

Train the people performing or supporting the causal analysis and resolution process as needed. GP 2.5 (AB 5)

Directing Implementation

Place designated work products of the causal analysis and resolution process under appropriate levels of configuration management. GP 2.6 (DI 1)

Identify and involve the relevant stakeholders of the causal analysis and resolution process as planned. GP 2.7 (DI 2)

Monitor and control the causal analysis and resolution process against the plan for performing the process and take appropriate corrective action. GP 2.8 (DI 3)

Collect work products, measures, measurement results, and improvement information derived from planning and performing the causal analysis and resolution process to support the future use and improvement of the organization's processes and process assets. GP 3.2 (DI 4)

Verifying Implementation

Objectively evaluate adherence of the causal analysis and resolution process against its process description, standards, and procedures and address noncompliance. GP 2.9 (VE 1)

Review the activities, status, and results of the causal analysis and resolution process with higher-level management and resolve issues. GP 2.10 (VE 2)

Appendix C

References

Bate, Roger, et al. *Systems Engineering Capability Maturity Model, Version 1.1.* Pittsburgh: Enterprise Process Improvement Collaboration and Software Engineering Institute, Carnegie Mellon University, November 1995.

Britcher, Robert. *The Limits of Software.* Reading, MA: Addison-Wesley, 1999.

Butler, K., and W. Lipke. "Software Process Achievement at Tinker Air Force Base, Oklahoma," CMU/SEI-2000-TR-014, Pittsburgh: Software Engineering Institute, Carnegie Mellon University, September 2000.

Carr, M., and W. N. Crowder. "Continuous Appraisal Method (CAM): A New Paradigm for Benchmarking Process Maturity." *Proceedings of the Tenth Annual International Symposium of the International Council on Systems Engineering (INCOSE),* Minneapolis, July 2000.

Carter, L., et al. "The Road to CMMI: Results of the First Technology Transition Workshop," CMU/SEI-2002-TR-007, Pittsburgh: Software Engineering Institute, Carnegie Mellon University, February 2002.

Chrissis, M., M. Konrad, and S. Shrum. *CMMI: Guidelines for Process Integration and Product Improvement.* Boston: Addison-Wesley, 2003.

Clouse, Aaron, and R. Shaw. "An Integrated Product Development Process Case Study." *Proceedings of the Sixth Annual International Symposium of the International Council on Systems Engineering (INCOSE),* Boston, July 7–11, 1996, vol. I, pp. 541–546.

CMMI Product Development Team. *Standard CMMI Assessment Method for Process Improvement: Method Description (SCAMPI), Version 1.0 (CMU/SEI-2000-TR-009).*

CMMI Product Development Team. *Assessment Requirements for CMMI (ARC), Version 1.0 (CMU/SEI-2000-TR-011)*, August 2000.

CMMI Product Team, *CMMI version 1.1, CMMI-SE/SW/IPPD/SS, V1.1 (CMU/SEI-2002-TR-011 and ESC-TR-2002-011), Improving processes for better products,* Pittsburgh: Software Engineering Institute, Carnegie Mellon University, March 2002

Crosby, P. B. *Quality Is Free: The Art of Making Quality Certain.* New York: McGraw-Hill, 1979.

Cross, S. "CMMI: A Knowledge Infrastructure," keynote, 2nd Annual CMMI Technology Conference & User Group, November 12, 2002.

Curtis, Bill, William E. Hefley, and Sally Miller. *People Capability Maturity Model (CMU/SEI-95-MM-002).* Pittsburgh: Software Engineering Institute, Carnegie Mellon University, September 1995.

Deming, W. Edwards. *Out of the Crisis.* Cambridge, MA: MIT Center for Advanced Engineering, 1986.

Department of Defense. *DOD Directive 5000.1: Defense Acquisition.* Washington, DC: Department of Defense, 1991.

Department of Defense. *DOD Regulation 5000.2: Mandatory Procedures for Major Defense Acquisition Programs and Major Automated Information Systems.* Washington, DC: Department of Defense, 1996.

Department of Defense. *DOD Guide to Integrated Product and Process Development (Version 1.0).* Washington, DC: Office of the Under Secretary of Defense (Acquisition and Technology), February 5, 1996. http://www.acq.osd.mil/te/survey/table_of_contents.html.

Department of Defense. *Defense Acquisition Deskbook, Version 3.2.* http://web2.deskbook.osd.mil/default.asp. (This Web site is continually updated.)

Dunaway, D., and S. Masters. *CMM-Based Appraisal for Internal Process Improvement (CBA IPI): Method Description (CMU/SEI-96-TR-007, CMU/SEI-2001-TR-033).* Pittsburgh: Software Engineering Institute, Carnegie Mellon University, November 2001.

EIA Standard, Systems Engineering Capability. EIA 731, Part 2: Appraisal Method, (EIA 731-2-2002). Arlington, VA: EIA, August 2002.

EIA Interim Standard, Systems Engineering Capability. EIA/IS 731 (Part 1: Model, EIA/IS 731-1, V 1.0; Part 2: Appraisal Method, EIA/IS 731-2, V 1.0). Arlington, VA: EIA, 1999.

Eisner, H. *Essentials of Project and Systems Engineering Management.* New York: Wiley Interscience, 1997.

Federal Aviation Administration—Integrated Capability Maturity Model, Version 1.0. November 1997. http://www.faa.gov/aio/iCMM/FAA.htm.

Ferguson, Jack, Jack Cooper, Michael Falat, Matthew Fisher, Anthony Guido, Jack Marciniak, J. Matejceck, and R. Webster. *Software Acquisition Capability Maturity Model Version 1.01 (CMU/SEI-96-TR-020).* Pittsburgh: Software Engineering Institute, Carnegie Mellon University, December 1996.

Freeman, D., M. Hinkey, and J. Martak. *Integrated Engineering Process Covering All Engineering Disciplines,* SEPG99.

Goldenson, D., and J. Herbsleb. *After the Appraisal: A Systematic Survey of Process Improvement, Its Benefits, and Factors That Influence Success (CMU/SEI-95-TR-009).* Pittsburgh: Software Engineering Institute, Carnegie Mellon University, 1995.

Hayes, W., and D. Zubrow. *Moving On Up: Data and Experience Doing CMM-Based Process Improvement (CMU/SEI-95-TR-008).* Pittsburgh: Software Engineering Institute, Carnegie Mellon University, 1995.

Herbsleb, James, David Zubrow, Dennis Goldenson, Will Hayes, and Mark Paulk. "Software Quality and the Capability Maturity Model." *Communications of the ACM,* 40, June 1977, 30–40.

Humphrey, Watts S. *Winning with Software.* Boston: Addison-Wesley, 2002.

Humphrey, Watts S. *Managing the Software Process.* Reading, MA: Addison-Wesley, 1989.

Ibrahim, Linda. "Using an Integrated Capability Maturity Model—The FAA Experience." *Proceedings of the Tenth Annual International Symposium of the International Council on Systems Engineering (INCOSE).* Minneapolis, July 2000, pp. 643–648.

Ibrahim, Rosalind, and I. Hirmanpour. *The Subject Matter of Process Improvement: A Topic and Reference Source for Software Engineering Educators and Trainers (CMU/SEI-95-TR-003)*. Pittsburgh: Software Engineering Institute, Carnegie Mellon University, May 1995.

IEEE Standard Glossary of Software Engineering Terminology (IEEE Standard 610.12-1990). New York: Institute of Electrical and Electronics Engineers, 1990.

INCOSE. *Systems Engineering Capability Assessment Model, Version 1.50.* International Council on Systems Engineering, June 1996.

International Organization for Standardization. *ISO 9000: International Standard.* New York: International Organization for Standardization, 1987.

International Organization for Standardization and International Electrotechnical Commission. *Information Technology: Software Life Cycle Processes (ISO 12207)*. Geneva, Switzerland: International Organization for Standardization/International Electrotechnical Commission, 1995.

Juran, J. M. *Juran on Planning for Quality.* New York: MacMillan, 1988.

Masters, S., and C. Bothwell. *CMM Appraisal Framework (CMU/SEI-95-TR-001)*. Pittsburgh: Software Engineering Institute, Carnegie Mellon University, February 1995.

Paulk, Mark. *Software Capability Maturity Model (SW-CMM) Case Study Bibliography* (online). 1998. http://www.sei.cmu.edu/activities/cmm/docs/roi.html.

Paulk, Mark. "The Evolution of the SEI's Capability Maturity Model for Software." *Software Process—Improvement and Practice,* 1995, pp. 3–15.

Paulk, Mark, and M. Chrissis. "The 2001 High Maturity Workshop" *(CMU/SEI-2001-SR-014).* Pittsburgh: Software Engineering Institute, Carnegie Mellon University, January 2002.

Paulk, Mark, et al. *The Capability Maturity Model: Guidelines for Improving the Software Process.* Reading, MA: Addison-Wesley, 1995.

Paulk, Mark, et al. *Capability Maturity Model for Software, Version 1.1 (CMU/SEI-93-TR-24;* also *ESC-TR-93-177).* Pittsburgh: Software Engineering Institute, Carnegie Mellon University, February 1993.

Radice, R. A., J. T. Harding, P. E. Munnis, and R. W. Phillips. "A Programming Process Study." *IBM Systems Journal,* 2/3, 1999.

Radice, R. A., and R. W. Phillips. *Software Engineering, an Industrial Approach, Vol. 1.* Englewood Cliffs, NJ: Prentice Hall, 1988.

Software Engineering Institute. *CMMI A—Specification, Version 1.3.* July 15, 1998. http://www.sei. cmu.edu/cmm/cmmi/cmmi.spec.html.

Software Productivity Consortium. "The October 2002 Enterprise Process Improvement Frameworks Workshop" (SPC-2003034-N, Version 01.01.00), April 2003.

Software Program Managers Network. *Program Managers Guide to Software Acquisition Best Practices, Version 2.* April 1997. http://www.pmn. com/products_guidebooks.html.

Standard CMMI Appraisal Method for Process Improvement Version 1.1: Method Definition Document (CMU/SEI-2001-HB-001). Pittsburgh: Software Engineering Institute, Carnegie Mellon University, December 2001.

Womack, James P., and Daniel Jones. *Lean Thinking.* New York: Simon and Schuster, 1996.

Appendix D

Resources

This appendix lists some other places where readers can look for information and support. While certainly not complete, this list should provide a springboard for further research. If you know of other resources that you would like to share, please contact us at cmmi-distilled@awl.com. We will be maintaining an updated list of resources and contacts at www.awl.com/cseng/titles/0-201-73500-8.

Electronic Industries Alliance

The Electronic Industries Alliance (EIA) is a partnership of electronic and high-tech associations and companies committed to shared knowledge and shared influence. The EIA includes the Consumer Electronics Association (CEA); Electronic Components, Assemblies, Equipment, and Supplies Association (ECA); Electronic Industries Foundation (EIF); Government Electronics and Information Technology Association (GEIA); JEDEC—Solid State Technology Association; and Telecommunications Industry Association (TIA). Accredited by the American National Standards Institute (ANSI), the EIA provides a forum for industry to develop standards and publications in the major technical areas of electronic components, consumer electronics, electronic information, and telecommunications.

In addition, the EIA publishes standards and technical publications to serve the public interest by minimizing misunderstandings between manufacturers and purchasers, facilitating interchangeability and improvement of products, and assisting purchasers in quickly selecting and obtaining the proper product for a particular need. The EIA Interim Standard, Systems Engineering Capability, EIA/IS 731, was one of the three source models for CMMI. More on the EIA may be found at www.eia.org.

European Software Process Improvement Foundation

The European Software Process Improvement Foundation (ESPI) promotes good software practice in Europe through the adoption of software process improvement. It provides information and training to assist those starting out on the process-improvement journey, and it facilitates the exchange of knowledge and experience between practicing organizations. ESPI and the Software Engineering Institute (SEI) cosponsor the European Software Engineering Process Group (E-SEPG) Conference every spring. ESPI's Web site is www.espi.co.uk/.

Federal Aviation Administration

The Federal Aviation Administration (FAA) has been involved with integrated process improvement since 1995 and released the first integrated CMM, the FAA-iCMM, in 1997. Version 2.0 of the model was released in 2002. The agency has provided a steering group member and a developer to the CMMI project, and it has publicly expressed a desire to migrate from the FAA-iCMM to the CMMI at an appropriate time in the near future. For information on the FAA-iCMM and the FAA's experience with integrated process improvement, visit its Web site at www.faa.gov/aio/ProcessEngr/iCMM/index.htm.

Institute of Electrical and Electronic Engineers

The Institute of Electrical and Electronic Engineers (IEEE) is a nonprofit, technical professional association with more than 350,000 members in 150 countries. Thanks to the expertise of its members, the IEEE is a leading authority in technical areas ranging from computer engineering, biomedical technology, and telecommunications to electric power, aerospace, and consumer electronics, among others. Through its technical publishing, conferences, and consensus-based standards activities, the IEEE:

- Produces 30 percent of the world's published literature on electrical engineering, computers, and control technology.
- Holds more than 300 major conferences annually.
- Has more than 800 active standards and 700 standards under development.

Of particular interest to CMMI users are the IEEE Computer Society (www.computer.org/) and the IEEE Engineering Management Society (www.ewh.ieee.org/soc/ems/). The IEEE can support your integrated process-improvement activities through conferences, collections of best practices, standards, cutting-edge engineering articles, and networking with its international members. You can reach the IEEE at www.ieee.org.

International Council on Systems Engineering

The International Council on Systems Engineering (INCOSE) is an international nonprofit organization formed to develop, nurture, and enhance the systems engineering approach to multidisciplinary system product development. It was established in 1990 and has grown to serve a membership of more than 3,900 systems engineering professionals. INCOSE was the primary force behind the development of EIA 731, and it has provided systems engineering expertise throughout the CMMI project.

INCOSE offers several categories of systems engineering resources to its members and the public:

- The INCOSE hotlist: links to items of interest to systems engineers on the Internet
- The INCOSE Web site library index
- INCOSE's Yellow Pages: vendors of interest to systems engineers
- List of INCOSE publications
- Standards references: a detailed standards reference
- Technical Committee, Working Groups, and Interest Groups: resources such as the Capability Assessment Working Group

See INCOSE's Web site at www.incose.org.

National Defense Industrial Association

As the "Voice of the Industrial Base," the National Defense Industrial Association (NDIA) educates and provides a link for its members to defense officials and leaders of industry. Located in Arlington, Virginia, it stands in a key position to share issues and influence defense policies related to acquisition and procurement. The NDIA, a nonpartisan, nonprofit international association founded in 1997, leads the way in communicating industrial perspectives to Congress, the Pentagon, and the American people.

The NDIA provides steering committee support and product development team members to CMMI through representatives of its member companies. More about the NDIA and its activities may be found at its Web site at *www.ndia.org*.

Practical Software and Systems Measurement

The Practical Software and Systems Measurement (PSM) project is sponsored by the Department of Defense and the U.S. Army. Its goal is to provide project managers with the objective information needed to successfully meet the cost, schedule, and technical objectives of programs. The measurement methodologies developed by PSM have wide applicability across disciplines and support the measurement aspects of the CMMI products. PSM activities and capabilities are described at the Web site at www.psmsc.com.

Software Engineering Institute at Carnegie Mellon University

The Software Engineering Institute at Carnegie Mellon University is a federally funded research and development center (FFRDC) and the world leader in software process-improvement technology. Established in 1984, the SEI has as its long-range goal making the acquisition, development, and sustainment of software-intensive systems predictably better, faster, and cheaper for the U.S. Department of Defense. For the SEI, the hallmark of the engineering discipline is predictability:

predictable cost, predictable schedule, predictable quality, and predictable functionality. The Institute is committed to the evolution of software engineering away from an ad hoc, labor-intensive, heroic activity. It seeks to facilitate the development of a managed, technology-supported engineering discipline, focused on technical and management practices that yield high-quality systems delivered on time and within expected cost every time. In short, it seeks predictable acquisition, development, and evolution of systems that depend on software.

To this end, the SEI provides a variety of resources for improving management practices. At the center of this effort is its role as the Steward for the CMMI Product Suite, and its efforts in developing, expanding, or maintaining other Capability Maturity Models (CMMs). The SEI has developed CMMs for software, people, and software acquisition, and it has assisted in the development of CMMs for systems engineering and integrated product development. The SEI's goals in developing CMMs include the following:

- Addressing software and disciplines that affect software.
- Providing integrated process-improvement reference models.
- Building broad community consensus.
- Harmonizing with standards.
- Enabling efficient improvement across disciplines.

Currently, the highest priority of the management practices work at the SEI is CMM Integration. For information on CMMI and the many other resources available to support process improvement, see the SEI's Web site at www.sei.cmu.edu.

Software Engineers Association of Japan

Software Engineers Association of Japan (SEA Japan) was established in December 1985 to create a vehicle for technical exchange between software engineers in a wide variety of fields. Its goal is to provide a mechanism for technology transfer that does not naturally exist within Japanese society. SEA Japan's major activities include publication of a monthly newsletter (*SEAMAIL*); support of local chapters and special-interest groups; and seminars, workshops, and symposia, held in cooperation with related academic/professional societies in and outside Japan.

At present, SEA Japan has approximately 500 individual members and more than 20 institutional members. Seven local chapters and a number of special-interest groups, including one on software process, are currently in operation. SEA Japan can be found on the Web at www.iijnet.or.jp/sea/index-e.html.

Software Productivity Consortium

The Software Productivity Consortium (SPC) is a nonprofit partnership of industry, government, and academia. For its more than 90 member companies, SPC provides technologies and expertise needed to improve the quality, reliability, and time-to-market performance of systems and software. The Consortium's technical program serves to integrate the essential process-based activities of integrated systems and software development. The SPC offers courses in a variety of improvement models and methods, including CMM for Software and CMMI, measurement and software engineering techniques, and integrated system and software process development. The Consortium provides appraisal and consulting services, and it publishes a quarterly newsletter and other technical articles concerning systems engineering, software engineering, system and software integration, and process improvement. For more information, see www.software.org.

Software Technology Support Center

The U.S. Air Force Software Technology Support Center (STSC) at Hill Air Force Base in Ogden, Utah, was established to help Air Force organizations identify, evaluate, and adopt technologies that improve software product quality, production efficiency, and predictability. Using the term *technology* in its broadest sense to include processes, methods, techniques, and tools that enhance human capability, the STSC focuses on field-proven technologies that will benefit the DOD mission. Along with its support and consulting roles, STSC publishes *CrossTalk, The Journal of Defense Software Engineering* and maintains an extensive Web site at www.stsc.hill.af.mil. It also cohosts the annual Defense Software Technology Conference in Salt Lake City. A strong proponent of CMMI, the STSC has been a leader in piloting CMMI training and assessment activities and so can provide a wealth of practical experience for help in using CMMI.

SEI Figure Credit List

Figure 7-2 © 2002 by Carnegie Mellon University. Introduction to CMMI-Continuous Module 8-062602, page 25

Figure 7-3 © 2002 by Carnegie Mellon University. Introduction to CMMI-Continuous Module 8-062602, page 16

Figure 7-4 © 2002 by Carnegie Mellon University. Introduction to CMMI-Continuous Module 9-062602, page 17

Figure 7-5 © 2002 by Carnegie Mellon University. Introduction to CMMI-Continuous Module 9-062602, page 58

Figure 7-6 © 2002 by Carnegie Mellon University. Introduction to CMMI-Continuous Module 8-062602, page 45

Figure 7-8 © 2002 by Carnegie Mellon University. Introduction to CMMI-Continuous Module 5-062602, page 17

Figure 7-9 © 2002 by Carnegie Mellon University . Introduction to CMMI-Continuous Module 5-062602, page 31

Figure 7-10 © 2002 by Carnegie Mellon University. Introduction to CMMI-Continuous Module 8-062602, page 37

Figure 7-11 © 2002 by Carnegie Mellon University. Introduction to CMMI-Continuous Module 10-062602, page 24

Figure 7-12 © 2002 by Carnegie Mellon University. Introduction to CMMI-Continuous Module 9-062602, page 25

Figure 7-13 © 2002 by Carnegie Mellon University. Introduction to CMMI-Continuous Module 5-062602, page 38

Figure 7-14 © 2002 by Carnegie Mellon University. Introduction to CMMI-Continuous Module 5-062602, page 45

Figure 7-15 © 2002 by Carnegie Mellon University. Introduction to CMMI-Continuous Module 7-062602, page 9

Figure 7-16 © 2002 by Carnegie Mellon University. Introduction to CMMI-Continuous Module 7-062602, page 21

Figure 7-17 © 2002 by Carnegie Mellon University. Introduction to CMMI-Continuous Module 7-062602, page 34

Figure 7-18 © 2002 by Carnegie Mellon University. Introduction to CMMI-Continuous Module 7-062602, page 47

Figure 7-19 © 2002 by Carnegie Mellon University. Introduction to CMMI-Continuous Module 7-062602, page 61

Figure 7-20 © 2002 by Carnegie Mellon University. Introduction to CMMI-Continuous Module 7-062602, page 74

Figure 7-21 © 2002 by Carnegie Mellon University. Introduction to CMMI-Continuous Module 6-062602, page 12

Figure 7-22 © 2002 by Carnegie Mellon University. Introduction to CMMI-Continuous Module 6-062602, page 21

Figure 7-23 © 2002 by Carnegie Mellon University. Introduction to CMMI-Continuous Module 6-062602, page 28

Figure 7-24 © 2002 by Carnegie Mellon University. Introduction to CMMI-Continuous Module 6-062602, page 36

Figure 7-25 © 2002 by Carnegie Mellon University. Introduction to CMMI-Continuous Module 9-062602, page 51

Figure 7-26 © 2002 by Carnegie Mellon University. Introduction to CMMI-Continuous Module 10-062602, page 31

Figure 7-27 © 2002 by Carnegie Mellon University. Introduction to CMMI-Continuous Module 10-062602, page 15

Figure 7-28 © 2002 by Carnegie Mellon University. Introduction to CMMI-Continuous Module 5-062602, page 52

Index

A

The SEI Series in Software Engineering

ISBN 0-321-18613-3

ISBN 0-321-11886-3

ISBN 0-201-73723-X

ISBN 0-321-15495-9

ISBN 0-201-54664-7

ISBN 0-321-15496-7

ISBN 0-201-70372-6

ISBN 0-201-70482-X

ISBN 0-201-70332-7

ISBN 0-201-60445-0

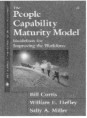

ISBN 0-201-60444-2

ISBN 0-201-52577-1

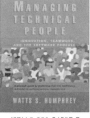

ISBN 0-201-25592-8

ISBN 0-201-54597-7

ISBN 0-201-54809-7

ISBN 0-201-18095-2

ISBN 0-201-54610-8

ISBN 0-201-47719-X

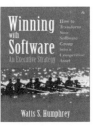

ISBN 0-201-77639-1

ISBN 0-201-61626-2

ISBN 0-201-70454-4

ISBN 0-201-73409-5

ISBN 0-201-85480-5

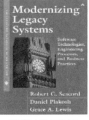

ISBN 0-321-11884-7

ISBN 0-201-70064-6

ISBN 0-201-17782-X

Please see our web site at www.awprofessional.com for more information on these titles.

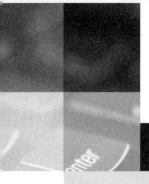